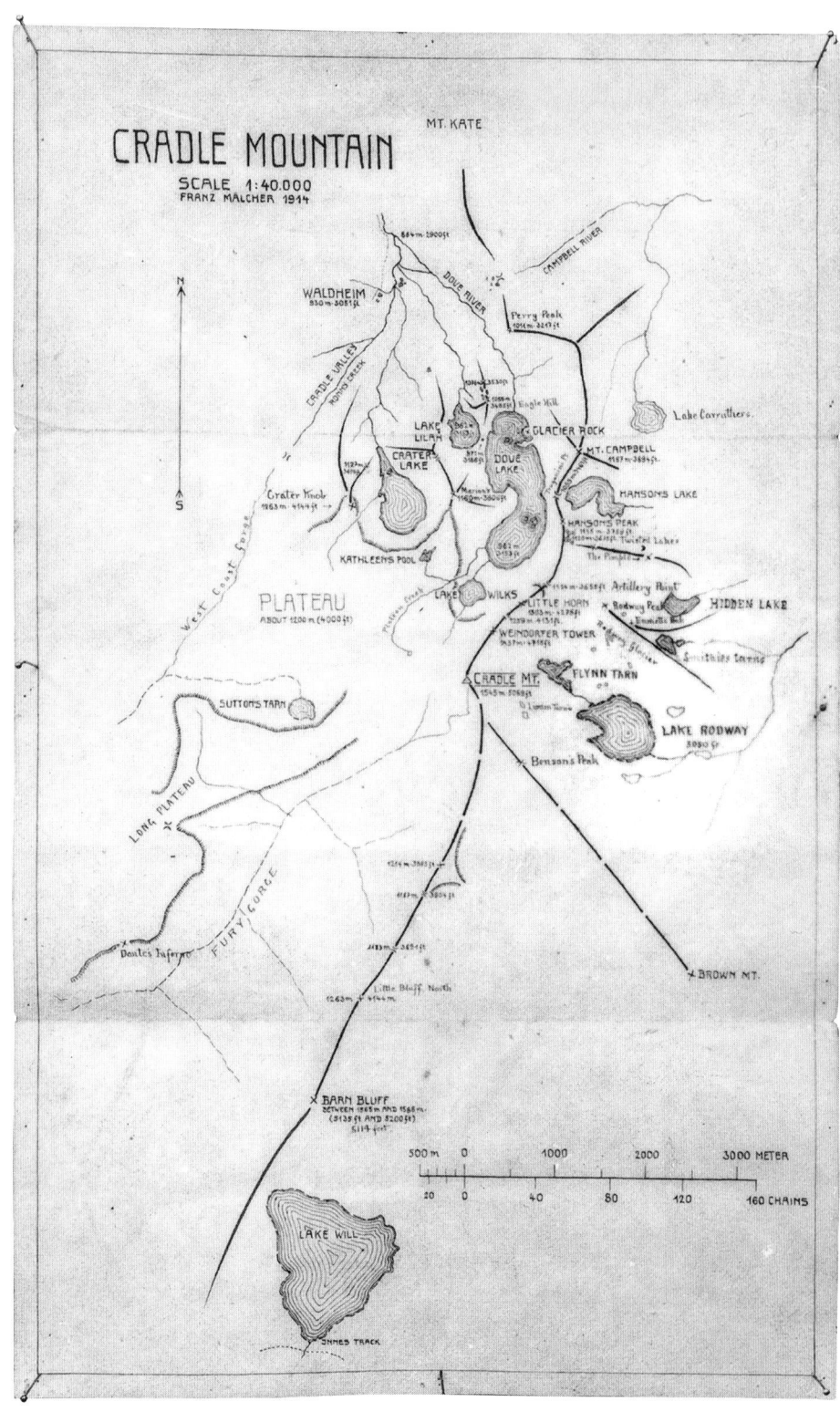

Hand-drawn master map of Cradle Mountain, 1914 (Franz Malcher)

A CRADLE MOUNTAIN LOVE STORY

KINDRED

KATE LEGGE

THE
MIEGUNYAH
PRESS

CONVERSIONS
1 inch = 2.54 centimetres
1 foot/feet = 30.48 centimetres
1 yard = 91.44 centimetres
1 mile = 1.6 kilometres
1 acre = 0.4 hectares
1 pound (weight) = 0.45 kilograms

THE MIEGUNYAH PRESS
An imprint of Melbourne University Publishing Limited
Level 1, 715 Swanston Street, Carlton, Victoria 3053, Australia
mup-contact@unimelb.edu.au
www.mup.com.au

First published 2019
This edition published in 2022
Text © Kate Legge, 2019
Design and typography © Melbourne University Publishing Limited, 2019

Typeset in 11.5/14 pt Bembo by Cannon Typesetting
Digital image restoration by Mark Hanlin
Cover design by Pfisterer + Freeman
Printed in China by 1010 Printing International

 A catalogue record for this
book is available from the
NATIONAL
LIBRARY   National Library of Australia
OF AUSTRALIA

9780522878929 (paperback)
9780522874525 (ebook)

For Jack and Tom and all of theirs

CONTENTS

BEGINNINGS

Many years ago a well-travelled girlfriend told me Cradle Mountain in north-west Tasmania was her favourite place in the world. I promptly pencilled a note to self: go see. But life tugged in different directions, favouring another's preference for shiny resorts far from the rugged, unpredictable wild. Then in 2015, weeks shy of our thirtieth wedding anniversary, my husband announced that he had 'run out of puff' and I had the opportunity to ramble wherever I pleased. His choice of platitude was apt. We had just returned from a family skiing trip that had concluded with a spectacular dust-up on a walking trail beside an icy river where our hot, angry breath smoked in the chill air. *I know I walk too fast.* Our adult sons insist they were terrified of being left behind as youngsters in shopping malls and streets. They wanted to put *me* on a leash.

Since my father was wired to the same speed, there must be a nature–nurture element to the rhythm of gait; the further the distance, the better. During primary school I'd regularly accompany a neighbour-hood family on strenuous bushwalking holidays through the coastal dunes of Wilsons Promontory, Victoria's first wilderness preserve, a thumb of land jutting into Bass Strait. We'd walk for hours before blocks of chocolate would be squared between us to fuel another feat of exertion. I relished the freedom of momentum as we crested hills with a whip of weather in our faces, traipsing through the salted landscape, borne on an adventure that left us deliciously spent by day's end. I also treasured the emotional breather of plunging into nature. Outdoors meant time away from a fraught home. The silvery torsos of ti-tree woven through the scraggy green scrub soothed me.

When my marriage frayed, each of our sons took me for a weekend gambol. The youngest knew of my hankering to visit Cradle Mountain, and since his fiancée was working in Hobart, he booked a trip. Within minutes of arriving at the lodge perched on the rim of the Cradle Mountain–Lake St Clair National Park, I left them to unpack while I hurried to the front desk for the walking tour to Crater Lake advertised on a blackboard in the foyer. Keen to get my bearings, I was anxious not to waste the last hours of light on this wintry June afternoon. The receptionist informed me nobody had turned up so the walk had been cancelled. 'But what about me?' I begged with a plaintive refrain that was even starting to grate on *me*. The lodge's veteran guide appeared from a back room to explain that given the lateness of the hour and the overcast weather, it'd be a push to get there and back. My disappointment must have told on my face for he tilted his head quizzically. 'Are you a good walker?' he asked.

As we drove into the park along the narrow, single-lane entry road, I kicked myself for having dragged the poor man out into the cold when I wasn't really sure I *could* stay abreast given I had no knowledge of the steepness of the terrain or the pace we'd need to set since there'd been snow the night before and it was sleeting now. When will you learn, I chastised myself, conscious that shy of sixty was a little late for personal epiphany, let alone the hard yards of reform. We parked at Ronny Creek, a name that meant nothing to me then for I was oblivious to the cast of men and women whose names are written on the tarns, vales, peaks and knolls. The path towards Crater Lake is a gateway to the Overland Track for serious walkers who spend up to a week traversing the route from Cradle Valley in the north of the national park to Lake St Clair at the southern end. Drifts of snow coated the marshy buttongrass heath of Cradle Valley. As we climbed upwards, the citrus of lemon boronia and mountain berry plants cut through the chill air. We stopped to catch our breath, admiring the fringes of Suttons Forest, another stranger I would get to know, where mossy trunks of King Billy pine, myrtle and beech trees, possibly predating all of my known ancestors, formed a dark bower over a waterfall tumbling downhill from the lake above. Determined not to linger too long here, for I could always return tomorrow, I inched ahead of my guide, who by this stage was panting a little at my heel.

When we reached the stony shores of Crater Lake in the last light of this grey day, I stood humbled by the grandeur and melancholic key, pitched to the mood of my soul. We sat on a crescent of white pebbled shore contemplating the architecture of sheer cliffs, whose tips were veiled by wispy clouds against a metallic sky. Dark-green myrtle and beech forest carpeted the lower slopes closest to the smooth, fathomless pool of water. We didn't speak. I felt something shift inside me, the stir of a breeze, the push of a shoot through thawing earth. Above the southern rim of the lake, where the path forks right for those continuing on the Overland Track, the guide joked that we could probably reach Lake St Clair and return before nightfall at the rate I walked, but we turned left, skirting Wombat Pool and Lake Lilla before wending our way back to his four-wheel drive in the now deserted car park. Enquiring at the front desk the next day, I was told the guide was not at work. My son laughed. 'He's probably had a heart attack!'

That morning I was on my own. I set out early, crossing the Pencil Pine Creek that borders the park, its water stained tannin from the buttongrass. Tightening the flaps of my waterproof jacket against the drizzle, I followed the boardwalk that traces the serpentine curves of the Dove River, swollen from rains and melting snow. On the forest floor, decaying trunks tapestried in mosses with an embroidered ruffle of orange lichen lay higgledy; overhead, windy gusts shook the crowns of trees. Out of the forest and into the open heath, the spiky-leafed spears of exotic grass trees appeared as surprise guests amid yellow gums, myrtles and native pines. Most visitors drive or ride the shuttle buses that ferry around two thousand people a day at summer's height in their hurry to reach the picturesque jewel of Dove Lake, a basin of tranquillity nestled below the ribbed pinnacles of dolerite that form Cradle Mountain's distinctive shape, its ragged peaks often obscured by clouds. The Roaring Forties blow from the west coast, smack into the mountains, where the sudden drop in temperature unleashes buckets of rain. I didn't encounter another soul on my tramp except for the occasional wombat snuffling through the boggy buttongrass, or the lonely cark of a raven above, a snapped twig or rustle in the undergrowth telegraphing news of creatures scouting for food or nests, and in this eerie solitude, my thoughts fell captive to the humbling sense of intricate forces at work over spans of time too vast to imagine. When the boardwalk delivered me at Ronny Creek, I veered to the right instead of retracing yesterday's steps and wound up at the door of a rustic wooden chalet.

Set beside a sheltering forest of myrtle, beech and pine on a crest overlooking the tumbling spray of Loose Leaf Creek, the building is a modern replica of the forest home built by Gustav Weindorfer, an Austrian immigrant, and his Tasmanian-born wife Kate. Both mad botanists, they fell for each other over the piano—he sang, she played—while classifying the native plants they'd collected on excursions through bush, heathlands and coastal shores. She climbed mountains, at a time when few women dared; he grew up at the foot of the Austrian alps. Their passion lit an urge to save a corner of the planet when they climbed the Cradle summit in January 1910 with Ron Smith, who names the creek, and one other bushman. Kate became the first white woman to reach a rooftop monopolised by lizards and eagles. Their 'Eureka' yell of discovery stirred the impulse to share this extraordinary panorama. Others might have kept such wonder secret, hidden from the world's intrusive glare. Gustav and Kate shouted for others to see the glory, sketching out loud an off-the-cuff idea for a tourism venture in a national park open to all.[1] The pair opened for business in 1913, welcoming a trickle of thirteen guests to the original chalet crafted from King Billy pine palings split by hand. The only relic of Gustav's fine carpentry in the shrine that stands here now are the carved clothes hooks behind the wooden doors.[2] I didn't know this arcane detail then, but what I felt in my bones was the urge to write about this couple since my acquaintance with their pluck, ingenuity and far-sightedness fuelled a yearning to know more.

In the gift shop next to the lodge where we stayed, I bought a slim monograph dedicated to Kate.[3] One book led to another as I entertained the idea of writing a literary fiction tracing their silhouette in a landscape I kept walking in my head as I worked by day penning magazine articles for *The Weekend Australian*. At times scribbling profiles of here-today, gone-tomorrow people, I increasingly found myself accessing the digital archives of the National Library to scour Tasmanian newspapers from the early twentieth century for any snippets or insights into the Weindorfers for a story I thought I might tell. The more I learnt of them, the more I felt compelled to share them, just as they sought to do with the landscape that wrapped its arms around them. Fiction, no matter how true to their likeness, somehow denied them the credit and recognition they deserve. They'd met as naturalists in Melbourne at the turn of the twentieth century, a time that suited them, for they felt the yearnings for nature that had earlier inspired American wilderness prophets like Henry Thoreau of Walden Pond and John Muir, the founding father of Yosemite. The Weindorfers were freaks of nature. Scientists *and* dreamers. Custodians of the natural world, they trod lightly in this hauntingly beautiful scape, intrigued by the geological scripture of glacial lakes formed millions of years ago and trees thousands of years old, borne by an unshakable faith in the restorative power of the wild. Here was a place where, as Gustav phrased it, 'there is no time and nothing matters'.

They called their chalet Waldheim, German for 'forest home', a hub that attracted photographers and, more importantly, a who's who of botanists, zoologists, ornithologists, entomologists and geologists— scientists of every stripe intrigued by the diversity of species, many unique to this place. They carried cameras, tripods, instruments, nets and blotting paper, seeking mammals, blowflies, deciduous beech, frogs and Triassic fossils like the mountain shrimp that dwell in the crystal-clear streams. They mapped and fathomed, surveying rocky strata, reading between the lines of nature's bible, hoping to illuminate the past and the future.

Death cut short Kate's role in a joint undertaking that could not have taken shape outside of their togetherness, while Gustav lived to see the Waldheim guest book grow fat with superlatives, singlehandedly spearheading the crazy-brave plan they had nurtured as a couple. At summer's peak, he could plate up a two-course dinner for twenty-five ravenous guests after guiding a party up the summit and down, once scurrying back to the top of nearby Barn Bluff, taller than Cradle, to retrieve a visitor's camera.[4] He was an indefatigable walker. How could I not fall for him?

They both sensed intuitively the significance of the Cradles long before the machinery existed to enshrine places of world heritage value. To my mind, they personify an ancient tradition that historian Simon Schama celebrates in *Landscape and Memory*.[5] They grew so rooted here that they became the 'genius loci' or 'spirit of the place'. They believed in Thoreau's maxim that from nature comes the tonic and barks that brace mankind. John Muir only dwelt in Yosemite briefly, with the rest of his years spent proselytising its preservation. Once Gustav built his forest home, he stayed. Though he toyed with the heresy of selling his timber during a desolate stretch, he was spared this sin by a serendipitous collapse in prices, ensuring his legacy was unsullied by the stain of sawdust. Instead he worked tirelessly, initially with Kate beside him, to foster awareness of the biodiversity and splendour at every turn.

American photographer Ansel Adams, who caught Yosemite's cathedral spaces with his lens, once reflected that Half-Dome Rock is 'in the last analysis' just a piece of rock, and yet we are humbled in its presence. 'There is some deep personal distillation of spirit and concept which moulds these earthly facts into some transcendental emotional and spiritual experience.'[6] Yosemite is often called 'God's garden'. Gustav hailed the Cradles as an 'El Dorado' for botanists. Science was their altar. While he and Kate were loosely attached to the Anglican Church, the communion they felt in the presence of natural wonders was grounded in a different faith. They saw nature as a book to be studied: 'to analyse and recognise out of the superabundance of appearances and the individual occurrences the eternal law of the whole and the ingenious arrangement of things'.[7] They devoured every word written in the rocks, plants and gnarled pines, awakening a nation not then wise to the treasures within its shores.

My father was a historian. I chose the rogue profession of journalism much to his disapproval. I do not possess the rigorous training of his discipline, but as a chronicler of current affairs, I bring a lighter touch to this moment in time. I've been influenced by Clare Wright's account of Eureka[8] and Hazel Rowley's memoir *Franklin and Eleanor.*[9] For both these women understand the truth that history is messier than the power of one, that relationships give rise to extraordinary events and extraordinary people. I'm indebted also to historian Tom Griffiths, whose recent book *The Art of Time Travel: Historians and Their Craft*[10] quotes Ian Hancock, one of my father's contemporaries, acknowledging R. H. Tawney's injunction 'that good historians need strong boots' so they can walk the streets, the lanes, the corridors, the libraries or, in this case, the landscape where the ghosts of past lives linger.

I've walked the Cradles in all seasons, climbing the summit on a glorious day in May, heart in mouth and on all fours, unsure how Kate clambered up that escarpment of boulders perilously poised, wearing her long skirt and broad-brimmed hat. In autumn the deciduous beech trees endemic to Tasmania turn the lower slopes ablaze with their small yellow and claret-coloured leaves, ridged like crinkle-cut chips; months later, doonas of snow whiten the ground while ice crystallises branches and crusts frozen ponds. Still the buses crawl back and forth disgorging scantily clad tourists with their iPhone cameras along with veteran walkers rugged up for serious hikes. Upwards of 280,000 visitors come here each year.[11] I wonder sometimes what Gustav and Kate would make of the crowds swelling in number along signposted tracks kept tidy by a bevy of park rangers in the landscape they nurtured for posterity. This is my homage to them. This is not history. This is a story. Not his-story or hers but theirs. The story of their love and their legacy.

From the kitchen of the chalet, 2017 (Penny Viney)

The Gorge, Mt Buffalo, 1910

1

AWAKENINGS

Kate Cowle drew a calming breath as she scanned the crowd beneath the decorative corniced ceilings of the Royal Society library,[1] the soft, cultured voices of fellow members of the Field Naturalists Club of Victoria reassuring as she drank in the scent of the leather-bound collections of scientific reports and journals lining the polished wooden bookcases, each one opening a door into the earth's mysteries. A meeker creature would not dare take the podium before such august company. There'd surely been several dress rehearsals in the Clarendon Street kitchen of the East Melbourne terrace house where she and her two sisters lodged under the same roof as veteran naturalist Alfred Hardy, a public servant in Victorian forestry, whose recreational pursuit was freshwater algae, though he also hunted giant gums on bush safaris.[2]

Among those present on the evening of 10 August 1903 was Austrian immigrant Gustav Weindorfer, one of the club's most enthusiastic participants, attending almost every excursion and authoring several reports on botanical excursions and two lengthy papers on the fertilisation of flowering plants by wind and insects.[3] He'd recently volunteered to lead a Christmas camp-out to Mt Buffalo, the first to include women since the club was founded in 1888, though they had long been welcomed into its mix of professional scientists and passionate amateurs harbouring pet obsessions with pond life, mollusc shells, butterflies or birds.

Energetic, industrious and restless, he'd left the Carinthian alps on a youthful surge of adventurism, begging a fare from his older sister, bound for a country he'd roved in books.[4] Handsomely European with a Van Dyke beard, moustache and thinning dark hair hidden by his trademark Tyrolean hat, he was twenty-six, eleven years younger than Kate, and marking time in a low-paying clerical job while he wished for a career in botany. The club expanded his small circle of German-speaking friends, taking him on weekend rambles to collect specimens in the Dandenong Ranges or the bayside ti-treed heathlands or Victoria's high country. In the company of fellow members, Gustav strode forth to meet native Australian flora face to face in the tradition of Baron Ferdinand von Mueller, the German-born inaugural director of Melbourne's Botanic Gardens, who roused this country to the wonder of its native plants and forests and, as a measure of our gratitude and respect, was rewarded with a full-dress state funeral upon his death in 1896. Von Mueller's deputy, Johann Luehmann, yet another German and co-founder of the Naturalists Club, sponsored Weindorfer's nomination in 1901.[5]

Gustav and Kate were both newcomers. She was inducted a year after Gustav by another foundation member, Charles French, an entomologist and horticulturalist who was enchanted by tree ferns and who worked in the herbarium that von Mueller established.[6] Tasmanian-born, she'd left Hobart after a cruel string of deaths that

Gustav Weindorfer, 21, before sailing for Australia   Kate Cowle as a young woman

had taken her younger brother, her mother, her father and then her stepmother. Buoyed by a comfortable inheritance from her father's estate, she shifted to Melbourne with her older sister, Carrie, and a younger sister, Laura, the three of them 'spinsters', carving their independence in a cosmopolitan setting where there was scant chance of indenture as maiden aunts to the progeny of their married siblings. Kate had been educated in Hobart. She could play violin, flute and piano as easily as she handled cows or horses, at fourteen riding with her father for two days, and over 60 miles, from the north-east town of Branxholm westward to St Leonards.[7] With a prominent nose, generous lips, enquiring brown eyes and dark hair worn high, her face was strong—fine boned but hardy. Already acquainted with her through club excursions, Gustav warmed to her exuberance, her competence, her musical prowess (since he loved singing) and her quick study of plants. Here was someone with an eye for identifying, classifying and preserving specimens that matched his own delight at this activity.

Kate was the only woman to present a paper to the club in 1903.[8] Eminent biologist and anthropologist Professor Walter Baldwin Spencer spoke the following month, indicating the calibre of the forum that she addressed, unabashed by her lack of status or professional qualifications. This was the strength of a club where hobbyists drove scientific enquiry. Modestly titled 'Notes of a Visit to Mount Roland', her presentation led listeners on a tour of the landmark that peers like a rocky raven, wings hunched, over the shoulder of Sheffield, a small town in Tasmania's north-west. 'Mount Roland is bold and rugged, its northern end being an almost perpendicular escarpment,' she began.[9] The 65-strong audience knew little if anything at all of this place, for few of them had travelled across Bass Strait, let alone climbed a mountain, whereas she'd grown up with this dramatic thrust of basalt visible from her father's farm at Kindred. She'd climbed the 4047-foot peak first in January and then March that year with several of her brothers and sisters. She wondered if the smoothing of the rocks at the foot of the mountain was the handiwork of an ancient sea, although she and her companions found no marine fossils in the stones they scrutinised.

For the first thousand feet, the track wound through a forest she populated with personalities, using formal Latin taxonomical terms with the colloquial names of stringybark, peppermint gum, musk, silver wattle, honeywood, purple berry, prickly box, white iris, stinkwood.

Mt Roland, Tasmania (J. G. Branagan)

Higher up, her favoured realm of tree ferns, mosses and lichens coveted attention. Over the ravine towards the top, she'd counted snowberries, native pepper, Gordon lily, asters, like wayward children to be marked on the class roll as all present. She was at ease in a landscape most Australians viewed as dun-coloured bush, unable to distinguish the strands entwined within. 'From the top of the mountain there is a fine view of the surrounding country and hills,' she concluded, 'and even the most ardent botanist or geologist must pause to admire it, with that silent outreach of the soul toward eternal beauty.'[10]

That silent outreach of the soul toward eternal beauty.

If Gustav had not already fallen in love with Kate's wanderlust on field trips, her vivid account that night spoke to him in a vernacular they made their own. Fear of heights or inclement weather didn't bother her as she sashayed upwards in ankle-length skirt, high-collared bodice and beribboned hat, noting the purple heath and dwarf beech, artichoke and yellow thyme colouring the summit. A black snake caused some excitement when it crossed her path in January, but not even the terrific storm she encountered two months later discouraged her. 'The thunder echoed from crag to crag with a deafening roar, the rain came down in a torrent,' she told the gathering. Descending through a dense mist, her party lost a pile of specimens they'd left to be collected on the way down.[11] She nonetheless exhibited several, along with photographs and rock samples, to illustrate her talk. During the conversazione afterwards, several men commented, admiringly, upon the difficulties to be met collecting in such rough country.[12]

Her paper was published in the club's September journal. So was one Gustav had delivered in July comparing the alpine flora of Europe and Australia. His more theoretical paper, parading considerable research, quoted New South Wales government botanist Joseph Maiden's pamphlet on the flora of Kosciusko as well as geologist James Stirling, who'd spoken on 'The Physiography of the Australian Alps' at an 1889 conference of the Australian Association for the Advancement of Science.[13] He'd been in the country barely three years yet wrote like a seasoned observer, his appetite for exploring at any altitude insatiable. The report of a club excursion to Shoreham on Melbourne's Mornington Peninsula in November 1902 crowns him as the 'most energetic' of the group, 'walking over to Dromana and returning much pleased with his collection' then taking a coach to Bittern, from where he 'walked along the railway line to Frankston in search of the flora we'd noted from the train on the way down'.[14]

At school he'd excelled in the subjects he enjoyed: forestry (a subject deeply rooted in the German curriculum and psyche) and agriculture. Notes kept by his first biographer, George Bergman, estimated Gustav's library in Melbourne at 500 volumes.[15] Letters during this period pester his parents to post new German texts on botany. Upon disembarking from the *Darmstadt* in Western Australia's port town of Fremantle, his first glimpse of eucalypts upset him. 'The country looks dreadful,' he wrote home. 'The gum trees, at all times wretched creatures, stood sadly in the drought stricken country, rattling their long leaves.'[16] Melbourne's cooler climate, with its Great Dividing Range, suited him better. Soon his mother was teasing him for calling the Australian alps 'our Alps' in a sign of shifting loyalties.[17] He'd visited the Victorian high plains of Bogong and Omeo at Christmas in 1902 with botanist Dr Charles Stanford Sutton, a Carlton medic who became Gustav's lifelong friend and bushwalking buddy, and another naturalist, Francis Barnard, a pharmacist seduced by ferns and insects.[18]

Kate and her siblings on a ramble near Forth River (*left to right* Dan, Blanche, Charles, Bertie, Kate)

Sutton and Barnard co-authored a botanical account of their trip, leaving Gustav to contrast the Eastern Alps of Europe with Australia's high country. His comparison of tree lines, climate, the bursts of growth between snowfalls, the alpine colours and vegetation confirms a methodical mind and also a romantic lilt. That questing Germanic streak, probing why the flora is so different, determined that Europe's denser pine forests afforded more protection than the Australian forest, 'where the Eucalypt trees, with their high slender trunks and open crowns, are further apart, thus providing no mutual protection against the ravages of wind and snow storms'.[19] His view of our natives is softening here, and though he can't help acknowledge European alpine flowers as more beautiful for the reds and blues, he found that the whiter, yellower scheme of Australia's alpine flowers nonetheless presented 'an indelible picture which every Australian may justly regard with pride'.[20]

Impatient to return to Victoria's peaks, he volunteered to lead the club's Christmas camp-out to Mt Buffalo, a big event—historically, because the park had only recently opened for tourism, and logistically, since the distance from Melbourne was 200 miles. But culturally this was also a milestone for women, who'd been invited along for the first time in a small, triumphant rip to the canvas ceiling. Early rumblings of concern at getting the right mix proved groundless. For weeks in the lead-up to departure, Gustav had been fussing over details, borrowing extra tents as numbers firmed, tying loose administrative ends.

Buffalo Falls, 1900 (Nicholas Caire)

The morning of Thursday 24 December 1903 broke hot and sultry as Kate Cowle arrived at Melbourne's Spencer Street railway station, joining eleven other women who had signed up for history. These young travellers were educated, comfortably off, and though there'd be an element of roughing it, they were on holiday, bound for the highlands. Among them was feminist Dr Gert Halley, the first female medical graduate of the University of Melbourne and the eldest of three daughters born to former club president and veteran naturalist J. J. Halley, a Congregationalist minister who had been chief spruiker for the 'domestication of science', hurrying his male brethren to embrace the higher education of women: 'sooner or later we shall have to open without distinction of sex, the doors of all our intellectual and scientific societies'.[21]

Gert's sister Una, who'd married botanist George Coghill, a businessman, club treasurer and avid beetle collector, was also on board, along with her husband, who was co-leading this field trip with Gustav. Railway porters at Spencer Street station, carrying luggage and escorting passengers to their carriages, were pulled up short when Kate, Gert, Una and others in long skirts and ruffled blouses claimed the seats reserved for field naturalists who were, naturally, presumed to be men.[22] The party of twenty-two excursionists would be among the earliest wave of tourism to Mt Buffalo since the proclamation of a national park in 1898. Enterprising local guides from mountain families—fierce rivals in fact—had built hospices at its foot beside the Eurobin Falls and above on the plateau to lure Victorians into this mountain garden of humbling, tumbling waterfalls, grassy plateaus, lyre birds, a haunted gorge, a gigantic teetering Leviathan boulder, and the intoxicating promise of new specimens and scenic grandeur. An apocryphal story—sometimes sourced to the travel writer known as 'Telemachus', who wrote of the 'picturesque' Buffalo, and other times attributed to Australian landscape photographer Nicholas Caire, who crawled around this mountain with his camera and tripod—tapped into a new curiosity. 'Did you see any snakes in the mountains?' someone asked. 'No, no snakes, but I saw glory.'[23] Caire found glory with his picture of a young man perched on a rock in the Buffalo gorge, seeming as small as an ant tucked inside an immense stone cleavage. The photograph hung in railway carriages as a promotional lure for this bush Parthenon, beckoning the adventurer in every heart.

Buffalo Gorge, 1900 (Nicholas Caire)

The glory of the Buffalo Ranges had tested the brush of Russian-born artist Nicholas Chevalier. His painting of these mighty mountains was the first local artwork purchased by Melbourne's National Gallery in 1864.[24] A man in his bullock dray travels a dirt road in front of a timber hut dwarfed by slopes of tangled green forest rising into muscular shoulders of bare rock, drifts of ice smoothing their peaks. Gilt framed on a museum wall, this was as close as most Victorians got to the grandeur of the Ovens Valley and the ranges beyond. Unless they could saddle a horse, lug a swag, boil a billy, peg a tent and set a compass, they had no chance of roving so far or returning safely. Apart from prospectors, cattlemen, hunters or zealous botanists like von Mueller, few had any cause to travel here. There was no impetus. The tradition of recreational hiking popular in Europe had only a toehold here.

Towards the turn of the century, the idea of experiencing nature gathered momentum in America and Australia. Once seen as remote, unreachable and often forbidding for the fearful elements that lurked within its darker recesses, untamed land was being recast by a convergence of technological changes—transport, photography, urbanisation—and by personalities with the spunk and foresight and sensibility to seize a moment.

Railways hungry for passengers opened new routes, encouraging recreational escapes from cities and towns, where rattling motor car exhausts and dusty streets wearied spirits. Photography was enlisted to unfurl scenic panoramas. Instead of standing back behind an easel to capture the sweep of a landscape, the photographer shouldered in among peaks, gorges and waterfalls. Pictures of the sublime pulled citizens in close, heightening the drama even as these images peddled the notion of seeing it for themselves. Photographs propelled people into the wild, but the first tracks were laid by the prophets or pioneers who'd found a way into these untouched places and felt such a deep communion here that the urge to share was irresistible.

John Muir unveiled Yosemite to the world after a period spent shepherding in its valleys and groves during the 1870s awoke him to the significance of this place for science and soul. Photographer Carleton E. Watkins, whose photographs of the sheer, smooth, monumental Cathedral Rock helped persuade the US Congress to proclaim Yosemite as a national park in 1890, was led there by Muir. The essays Muir crafted preaching national parks as an imperative for the future of humanity became a bestselling book when published as *Our National Parks* in 1901.[25] 'The tendency to wander in wilderness is delightful to see,' Muir wrote. 'Thousands of tired, nerve-shaken overcivilised people are beginning to find out that going to the mountains is going home; that wildness is a necessity; and that mountain parks and reservations are useful not only as fountains of timber and irrigating rivers, but as fountains of life.'[26] President Teddy Roosevelt heard his call.

Northcote Crevasse, Mt Buffalo, 1910

In early 1903 the President and his muse spent several days camping under Yosemite's night sky. These experiences are transformative. Like the slow-moving glaciers that had sculpted Yosemite's garden, the emotional and spiritual impressions of a place etch a groove. During a visit to the Grand Canyon in May that year, Roosevelt pleaded with Americans not to skin any part of the country, 'whether it is the forest, the water, or the scenery', but rather to 'handle it so that your children's children may get the benefit'.[27] Sweeping an arm towards the sheer clefts and pink-tinged minarets of the desert landscape before him, he begged: 'Leave it as it is. You cannot improve upon it.'[28]

These tremors were felt on our shores. Mt Buffalo was not the first national park gazetted in Australia. The Royal National Park south of Sydney in New South Wales swiped that honour in 1879. But the Buffalo story parallels Yosemite's journey, and though the cast of characters is more unwieldy, there was one man who fell so deeply under its spell that he could not rest until the secret got out. Dr John Wilkinson met Buffalo's magic while camping in its midst, travelling on horseback under the guidance of local cattleman Ted Carlile, the son of a prospector, who knew the trails and topography backwards. Wilkinson had settled in the nearby town of Bright to practise medicine, but he could not let go of the places he'd seen or the taste of man's insignificance in their presence, where you could be forgiven for doubting 'there was anyone else in the world'.[29] He joined forces with flamboyant commercial traveller William Staker, a mountaineer also mad for its wonders, and they set up a ginger group to promote Buffalo, initially as a destination, later as a reserve. They heavied the railways for regular services as far as Bright; Carlile built a hospice on the plateau, sourcing alpine ash on site and carting everything else—chairs, roofing iron, mattresses—up the steep, narrow track on the backs of pack horses. They commissioned Caire to photograph the glory, selling his pictures to fund their campaign, and 'Telemachus' to write about it in *The Argus*, Melbourne's major morning paper, rejoicing when a park was declared finally in 1898.[30]

The Victorian naturalists were spirited to Buffalo, while the destination was hot with the flush of public debut. Already engaged in the park movement, club members had agitated for the protection of Wilsons Promontory in 1898. This was the air Kate and Gustav breathed: talk of national parks, landscapes, vegetation, specimens of native grasses, the

Ted Carlile's hospice on the Buffalo plateau

health of waterways. Here they were at the birth of tourism ventures in scenic places that were therapeutic and spectacular, and that held the promise of scientific enquiry. Who knew what was possible?

Within the towering eucalypt forests of the Dandenong Ranges east of Melbourne, the German-born photographer J. W. Lindt had built a guest house called The Hermitage. He used local timber for the quaint gabled buildings surrounded by a lush fernery. Gustav visited here in 1901, a year after the railways opened a line to nearby Ferntree Gully.[31] Surely impressed by Lindt's enterprising way of welding nature and tourism, he must also have admired his dashing past. Lindt emigrated here in his late teens, working as a rouseabout in western New South Wales before fate handed him a studio job in Grafton on the state's north coast. His studies of indigenous Australians in the nearby Clarence River district were his ticket to British New Guinea with the Royal Geographical Society, and he later travelled through the South Pacific to the New Hebrides, Vanuatu and Fiji, where he photographed fire-walking ceremonies. Lindt subsidised these forays with formal portraits of society sirs and madams in his Collins Street studio. He retired to the Black Spur, concentrating his lens on giant mountain ash and sprawling tree ferns. Some evenings he entertained guests with lantern slides of faraway islands, telling stories of tribal communities or his escape from an active volcano on the Vanuatu island of Tanna. Lindt spun together the traits of buccaneer, anthropologist and artist, and in later years incorporated a naturalist streak. Von Mueller designed the garden he planted in his bush retreat.[32]

Gustav and Kate possessed similar qualities of adventurism, industry and zeal. His hasty departure from Austria—on a fare borrowed from his sister Rosa and without farewelling his parents—flung him into the unknown. He'd read precociously, devouring Australian anthropologist Alfred Howitt's stories of indigenous societies when he was eleven years old; in his late teens, he bought Wolfgang Siebers' 1895 German travelogue *Nach Australien*, illustrated with coloured ink drawings. The map reproduced in its pages includes Tasmania, where, strangely, the only highlighted point of interest is 'Mt Cradle'.[33] Gustav had felt torn between staying put and the fire in his belly as his ship steamed from the port of Genoa in May 1900. 'On the outside you try to be calm but on the inside your heart is pulling on your innermost fibres,' he wrote in a German newspaper report of his voyage.[34] The desire to delve into nature's beauty had set his course.

Given his hunger for botanical books, Gustav was likely aware of the German naturalist Alexander von Humboldt, whose six-volume work *Cosmos*, published in 1849, identified the subtropical forests of the great southern continents, including Australia, as the crucible of a botanical diversity sure to fire the aesthetic imaginations of all who dared to travel and observe. They would discover new species, but more importantly they would decipher the relationships between plants, soil, climate, rainfall, elevation and other geophysical data. Humboldt was held in high regard by Baron von Mueller and, no doubt, by his assistant, Johann Luehmann, who'd led Gustav to the Victorian Field Naturalists, where learning firsthand from nature was a core principle. Humboldt's belief in travel beyond the perimeters of Europe—to observe and compare and make connections that illuminate nature as a harmonious whole—shoehorned a generation of Germans and Austrians out of their comfort zones and into the wild.

Kate too was heeding a siren call for independence and learning. She had no professional vocation beyond a thirst for nature, fast preoccupying her, and emboldening her confidence as she revelled in the opportunities of studying outdoors in a new city on the mainland.

Rubbing up against the busy minds on show at naturalist gatherings was a tertiary education of its own. On board the steam train bound for Buffalo were ornithologists, entomologists, botanists, fossil-hunters, lovers of pond life, wives, husbands, daughters, single women like Gert and Kate, all of them excited by the promise of a place heralded as 'the garden of the gods'. At Wangaratta they changed to a covered truck, 'rather dirty and decidedly rough', which delivered them at Porepunkah, the end of the line. There they switched to horse-drawn traps for the ride through ripe grain fields in the Ovens Valley, on the final stretch towards James Manfield's hospice at the foot of the Eurobin Falls.[35]

The Manfields were in cut-throat competition with Ted Carlile, who monopolised the plateau. The naturalists had chosen the former as host and guide, filling his four-roomed home, with the overflow of men accommodated on improvised beds of wire netting stretched over logs in the barn. Never one to loaf, Gustav forged ahead that evening to the plateau, climbing another 3000 feet, his signature recorded in Carlile's visitors' book on Christmas Eve.[36] Lindt's Hermitage and the Buffalo hospices run by Ted Carlile and his wife Mary and the Manfield family were start-up enterprises that set him thinking.

The Hermitage guest house, The Dandenongs (J. W. Lindt)

Early on Christmas morning, the rest of the party rose early to join him. George Coghill could not resist straying from the track to search out new plants 'and various old friends in unusually rich garb', thrilled to pocket several rather good longicorn beetles found on the flowers of an aster.[37] With his head down, eyes hoovering the ground, he ascended the mountain top unaware, 'and it will be many a day before I forget my first glimpse' of the 'tundra' country with its rich pickings. Their camp was struck within 50 feet of the gorge, offering uninterrupted views of Bogong and Kosciusko. The women bunked together in a slab hut, the men in tents.

Kate fossicked for mosses and lichens while Gustav roamed restlessly, making fastidious notes of every plant he met. He charted the shift from Silurian rocks of the early Palaeozoic period to the granitic formations where the saturated black soil nurtures alpine blooms, questioning why and how these species flourish at such lofty altitudes—'As if their proud relatives in the valleys had banished their dwarfed sisters to the barren heights of alpine regions'.[38]

He shared Coghill's thrill at the 'tundra' country, 'a green carpet interwoven with the greatest varieties of colours', where the felted buttercup and the pale, straw-hued marsh marigolds have disappeared to make room for violet kunzea, native orchids, mountain milkwort and the delicate petals of *Gentiana saxosa*, 'its single white flowers pencilled with lines of a tender blue'.[39] He observed nearly three hundred species, surprised to meet 'one of our few Victorian conifers' growing luxuriantly along a creek in the Haunted Valley alongside purple-flowering round-leaf mint bush and 'the pompous Pimelea ligustrina'. Not yet naturalised as a British subject, he knew his backyard better than most native-born Australians, ascribing human quirks to plants he now knew intimately enough to have favourites, hailing the *Grevillea victoriae* as 'one of our most beautiful proteads'.

The bird twitchers, quieter in their pursuits, were just as euphoric at rare shows of nest-construction, watching spine-billed honeyeaters carry bark to pillow their bed in a broad-leafed acacia tree. They reported a scarlet-breasted robin's castle in the crevice of a huge granite boulder, containing three eggs, while two junior Pennant parakeets were housed in the hollow of a dead gum. Wherever bowers were boggy and wet, the beautiful lyrebirds tolerated hushed spectators, and a brown kingfisher was caught swallowing a fair-sized lizard in the noon heat.[40]

A Buffalo orchid (Alice Manfield)   A bird's nest among rocks at Mt Buffalo
                                           (Alice Manfield)

Pond-life specialist Octavius Sayce captured two species of sessile-eyed crustaceans in a bottle of water from a creek in the Haunted Gorge: one an isopod belonging to a family of considerable morphological and physiological interest that had been recorded only at Mt Kosciusko and sites in Tasmania; the other an amphipod closely related to an old-world genus; both of them 'blind inhabitants of subterranean waters' worthy of further study.[41] Each small shard of biological knowledge was another piece of the mosaic—for how else can we understand evolution and adaptation? Were it not for heavy rains that turned creeks into swollen streams, the haul might have been greater, but foul weather 'really added very much to our enjoyment,' George Coghill recalled. 'The rolling billows of mist in the near and distant valleys sometimes reminding us of snow and often of the sea, more than compensated for any discomforts.'[42]

The Buffalo trip confirmed Gustav's energy and purpose. On Sunday 28 December he was off again, with Dr Sutton, on horseback, riding 30 miles over the Kiewa Valley to Mt Bogong, 'majestic and imposing in the distance', and too temptingly close to ignore.[43] Disappointed by the variety of plants, they nonetheless collected armfuls and on their return stumbled upon clumps of a rare orchid, arriving back at the foot of Buffalo on New Year's Eve. They spent the evening arranging specimens. Merriment reigned above at the gorge camp, where Kate joined the rest around a fire, playing charades, singing, reciting poems, even making speeches, their giddiness elevated by an open sky and the sense of being cheek by jowl in nature's maw.[44]

Having missed his chance of a New Year's Eve kiss, Gustav beetled back up to the gorge on 1 January to bid farewell, learning that Kate had sprained her ankle on a long ramble to the Horn and Leviathan Rock. Reference to his 'flying visit' in the club's post-mortem report seems to suggest indecently brusque concern for her injury, but Kate could look after herself.[45] She'd learnt self-sufficiency from losing so many close kin, and her equanimity would serve her well in years to come. Mr Here, There and Everywhere had up and gone from the camp on his own jaunts. His hyperactive whirl piqued Kate's warming to a man who was always hotfooting it somewhere.

She stayed on with the others for several days, clothes sodden after days of soaking rains—'slippety-slop down that mountain we went'.[46] Unfussed when they found the Eurobin Creek had swollen to a raging torrent, they searched for a log high enough to form a bridge where they could safely ford. At the Manfields' hospice below, there were fires and dry garments, nothing ever quite as heavenly as the warmth of shelter and food after an invigorating, chilly descent. When the train

Camping Days, Manfield's hostel (Alice Manfield)

pulled into Spencer Street station, Gustav was solicitous enough to meet them.[47] He was falling for Kate. But she had to compete with a louder passion knocking inside his breast. His report of the trip confirmed the seductive pull of a landscape resembling the Carinthian alps of his European homeland, only here in the new world there was a sense of virgin territory, unexplored by botanists, offering the chance to make his mark at last. Enchanted by the white flowering snow aciphyll he'd found on Buffalo's cooler slopes, he marvelled at 'the eternal peace' of alpine regions, 'where we can see expanding at our feet the proofs of the creative power of nature during unaccountable ages'.[48]

Adopting English as a second language stiffened Gustav's eloquence. His musings on nature lack the lyricism of John Muir's elegant prose, but both men borrowed the metaphor of nature's book to teach others the merits of reading closely between its lines. They were unable to resist the allure of mountains and the truths that lie beneath their crust, in their creases and upon their slopes. Sometimes Muir sounds as obsessive and itchy-footed as Gustav. 'I have been down from the upper rocks for three days and am hungry for exercise already,' Muir wrote of Yosemite, describing his method of study as 'getting in touch with Mother earth; jumping from rock to rock, feeling the life of them, learning the songs of them, panting in whole-souled exercise, and rejoicing in deep, long drawn breaths of pure wildness.'[49] In an extraordinary coincidence, their paths almost crossed. Muir came to Melbourne the week of the Buffalo camp-out, arriving on Christmas Eve just as the naturalists were shunting through the Ovens Valley. Slipping into town quietly without prior warning or publicity, he'd sailed from California to test Baron von Mueller's boast of eucalypts taller than America's beloved redwoods.[50]

Von Mueller had written of a mountain ash 500 feet tall, 'as high as the great pyramid'. Interest in Victoria's giant timbers had been goaded by a hunt for the very tallest in nature's grasp as part of the state's Centennial Exhibition in 1888.[51] Instead of a mechanical contest harnessing newfangled technology, here was a search for the heftiest trunk protruding from our forest canopy. Nicholas Caire had photo-graphed a large-butted gum said to be 464 feet, which he named 'the Baron', but it was later measured at a salutary 219 feet.[52] The director of Melbourne's Botanic Gardens, William Guilfoyle, doused Muir's competitive angst. Victoria's *Eucalyptus regnans*, otherwise known as mountain ash, were unlikely to eclipse the towering height of redwoods and sequoias. He sent Muir off to see Caire, who showed the American his photographs. On Christmas Day, Muir travelled by train to the Black Spur to visit J. W. Lindt at The Hermitage, charmed by his secluded hostel 'in the heart of the forest primeval'. Ever the tree-whisperer, he made friends with 'new treefaces' including 'magnificent Beeches, five to six feet in diameter'. After an evening thunderstorm and heavy shower, he rose to a 'charming morning, calm, cool, bright, glorious sunshine … the sun shone on the wet leaves … [and] cooled air full of fresh ozone. How the tree ferns enjoy it!'[53] Lindt led him through the forest, where they found a few eucalypts 250 feet high, and a handful 20 or 30 feet taller. Muir counted growth rings where he could, concluding that even the very large trees were not older than 200–300 years. He left for Sydney on 29 December, the day Gustav was climbing Mt Bogong, jumping from rock to rock, bloom to bloom, listening, looking, learning, 'nature there presenting us with an awakening spring, which has again and again filled the hearts of men with greatest delight'.[54]

They missed each other by a matter of days, just as Muir in his younger years had travelled within 60 miles of Henry Thoreau, these spheres of influence filtering through books and pamphlets, papers and ideas rather than conversations in the flesh.[55] Muir, now in his sixties, had achieved his apotheosis. Still a young man, Gustav's ladder to nirvana lay ahead. He too would sacrifice his life to a glacial landscape populated by ancient native conifers, but he had yet to set foot there.

———————

The brains and boffins of Melbourne's science community frocked up for the presentation of the inaugural Mueller medal at the two-storeyed Royal Society Hall on the evening of Thursday 21 April 1904.[56] Newly minted with the Baron's profile on one side and a waratah flower on the other, the silvered bronze tablet was funded from the pockets of the Victorian Field Naturalists and was to be awarded every two years for distinction in scientific research. Gustav got there early in the hope of shaking hands or rubbing shoulders with heroes such as anthropologist Sir Walter Baldwin Spencer, who would present the honour to Alfred W. Howitt, a botanist, anthropologist, explorer and geologist whose fifty years in the field read like a boyhood fantasy, travelling in remote country, and studying and living with indigenous communities to record their language and customs. Best known in Australian households for leading the expedition to rescue Burke and Wills, he thrilled the Royal Society audience, recounting how he'd found the third explorer, John King, 'in the last stages of exhaustion' near the South Australian border.[57] Looking back on his career, he felt as if he had lived several lives. British born, he'd arrived at the Ovens goldfields with the roar of miners' cradles 'echoing like the waves upon the shore'. Next he'd gone droving through the margins of the Mallee, surveying for pastoral land in South Australia's sandy deserts and seeking minerals in Gippsland, only commencing his prolific botanical and anthropological studies in his sunset years. He rode with a book open on his saddle, observing nature as he went. Gustav had read Howitt's writings as an eleven-year-old boy in short pants. When his mother heard of this glittering evening, she understood the thrill: 'This will have been a great moment in your life to see Mr Howitt personally and to hear him speak.'[58] Howitt's reflections shook loose his caution and doubt. Von Mueller and Howitt were Gustav's idols, big-picture men unafraid of horned beasts. An avid reader of *The Wide World Magazine*, brimming with 'true' tales of Burma, Central Africa, the Amazon River or the Khyber Pass, the new Australian often considered leaving Melbourne for Samoa or Noumea because embracing the unknown was how great men made their name.[59] Listening to Howitt girded his impatience with his dreary, dead-end day job clerking for a Melbourne-based firm of Austrian shipping agents. He earned a pound a week clawing meagre social status from an honorary position as chancellor of the Austro–Hungarian Consulate.[60] At night he schooled himself in Australian botany, writing on flora for the local press and the naturalists' journal, collecting specimens for his herbarium, posting plants to European gardens and institutions, just as von Mueller had done, and exploring wherever his legs carried him so that he might read the landscape and learn. He sent ferns and mosses to the Vienna Court Museum for Natural History; a classically prepared collection of 320 species of Australian plants went to the Austrian Museum of Natural History; he packaged living tree ferns for the director of the Austrian Court Garden at Schönbrunn Palace, the former imperial summer residence in Vienna.[61] Germans and Austrians were a significant force in Australian botanical life, and the similarities between them are inescapable. Industrious, meticulous, earnest, they gathered, collected, labelled and documented our landscape, teaching us to do likewise.

On Christmas Eve 1904, Gustav went west with Dr Sutton in tow for an adventure in the Grampians. Another arduous journey, first by train to Stawell, where they arrived at 11 pm, then a two-hour ride through the valley where the Little Wimmera flows to a homestead at the foot of Mt Cassell, one of the outliers in this range. Up with the currawongs early as usual, they climbed all day, at times bashing their way through dense underscrub in heavily timbered country. On top of 'Goat Rock', they were mesmerised by 'the view sublime', the fertile river plain below, far off the basin of Lake Lonsdale, mountains pleating into the Mallee lands.[62] Disappointed by floral specimens (while nevertheless identifying an impressive 250 species), they collected seeds while Gustav determined that this area formed the westerly outrunner of Australia's south-eastern forest flora belt, a theory he would develop further.

The naturalists set a ferocious pace. Home on 30 December, they were off again on New Year's Eve, east to Gippsland, first by train, then a five-hour haul in a three-horse wagon along the Walhalla Road, 'dinned' by the sound of lyrebirds as they forded the Latrobe River, before setting out the next morning for what they thought was Mt Erica, the nearest peak of the Baw Baw Range. Smoke from nearby bushfires hung so thick that they didn't see the mountain until right on top, where they dropped their burdens 'under a boulder as big as a house that had conveniently fallen on to a smaller brother', forming a shelter. Though the stone bed was hard and a solitary blanket thread-bare comfort from the night's chill, at least rising before dawn posed no hardship.[63] These were pioneering trips: tracks were missed, routes retraced. Sutton later wrote that what they thought to be Mt Erica, based on local intelligence, was not the Mt Erica on the maps but a peak 6 miles to the south-east of it.[64]

Kate didn't elbow an invitation to these camp-outs, for the pair were not married or even engaged. Impatient with social strictures, certain conventions nonetheless restrained them. But her disappointment must have shown in her rapacious thirst for his account of what they had seen and found, needing little interpretation if he slipped into Latin names or the detail of foliage and stipule, pedicels and lobes, for this was their language. Had he mentioned his vain search for *Pultenaea rosea* in the Grampians, she would have felt his disappointment, just as she would have cheered at the sight of magenta storksbill, a perennial herb endemic to Australia, its pink petals reminiscent of a geranium or iris. Kate's yearning for nature's discourse equalled his own. He began visiting the Cowle sisters at their East Melbourne terrace in the evenings. Surrounded by the specimens they'd each collected, Gustav patiently demonstrated taxonomy's tricks of classifying plants, and then pressing and flattening them between blotters. Sometimes he'd bring sheet music, which Kate would play on the piano, the sounds of his rich, deep baritone voice tickling the pleasure of fellow lodger and naturalist Alfred Hardy.[65]

The couple shared a knack for identifying a rare plant or discerning unique features from its relatives, and while these skills can be acquired through diligent application, the jet of desire thrusts them to another level. They'd both spent childhoods in the country, accumulating an awareness of insects and birds through observation and experience. Her father's diary describes Kate nursing an albatross that her brothers brought home from the Mersey River, unflustered by the wild bird.[66]

Whereas Kate enjoyed the lifeline of siblings at hand and a generous inheritance from her father's estate, Gustav relied on his wits in a new land. The pangs of ambition gnawed at him. He had no strings to pull or credit to borrow, relying solely on a prodigious energy and thirst to spur him forward within botany circles. He became the go-to reference guide within the club, asked to identify specimens collected during an excursion to Victoria's Mt Wellington in June 1905.[67] A plant he'd plucked from a swamp near Wandin in the Lilydale district, 25 miles from Melbourne, was christened *Pultenaea weindorferi* 'in honour of the finder who during the last few years has done much to extend our knowledge of the habitats of Victorian plants'.[68] The paper he wrote on 'The Flora of Victoria' was published in the Commonwealth's *Year Book* for 1905.[69] Two paragraphs into his essay, Gustav cheekily suggested it was time von Mueller's 1887 bible on Victorian plants be updated, since new species had been recorded but not compiled into a supplementary key.

The Cumberland Mammoth, Marysville (Nicholas Caire)

His writing foreshadows the emerging science of ecology, with its focus on climatic conditions, geology and geography. He argued that heavy yearly rainfall in Victoria's south-east since older geological periods had thwarted new forms of vegetation, weakening the number of endemic species compared with other states. Linking the state's flora to plants in New Zealand, South America and especially Tasmania, he grasped for the then novel theory of a supercontinent. Most striking was his plea for stringent safeguarding of forests from careless tree-felling along river frontages, home to *Prostanthera lasiantha*, *Bursaria spinose*, *Hymenanthera banksii*, *Acacia dealbata*, *Cryptandra* and many others. 'By the wanton destruction of these trees, and the denuding the banks of their undergrowth, their constant erosion takes place,' he warned, so that 'many species of our native flora are likely to entirely disappear. It would be therefore highly advisable that all water frontages be reserved throughout the State, and the destruction of shrub life on or near the edges of the rivers strictly forbidden.'[70]

He introduced readers to 'magnificent forests' of Australian beech, blackwood and dogwood, sweeping them alongside gullies and creeks where tree ferns thrive, their broad, light-green fronds shading watery crevices: 'Vast forests extend along the sources of the mountain rivers, which flow towards the south and southeast. In many of them the axe of the wood cutter has not begun the work of devastation, and it is to be hoped that these remnants of our once extensive forests may be reserved before their destruction.' He was hostage now to their beauty: 'Here Casuarinas develop their beautiful and interesting forms, there the gracefully symmetrical Exocarpos stretches its slender branches.' Even the Mallee was embraced, for those who saw monotony were missing the subtlety and show of its parts—'the scrub is very far indeed from being destitute of charms.' Its sandy ridges are natural flower gardens for goodenias, pimeleas, asters and grasses such as *Panicum*, *Agrostis*—he names them all. 'At the fall of the first rain the barren, dusty plains become, as by magic, covered with a green carpet, gaily decorated with a wealth of flowers.' Several he considered ideal for domestic gardens, 'but, like so many others of our native plants, [they] have been hitherto greatly neglected'.[71]

At home in our backyard, having tramped up mountains and across plains, Gustav stumped up bravely for the job of government botanist in 1905, perhaps hoping his zeal would make up for weak academic

credentials, but the era of the passionate amateur was in the tightening fist of professional scientific discipline. British botanist Professor
A. J. Ewart, with teaching and research experience from Oxford and
Cambridge, landed the double-header gig combining the bureaucratic
job with an inaugural chair in botany at the University of Melbourne.
When Ewart addressed the Naturalists Club in March the following
year, he spoke of 'being among strange faces and surrounded by a
strange flora'.[72] This would have stuck in Gustav's craw, even though
he was a new boy himself, but he'd been gone for months by then,
mesmerised by the next new horizon.

He and Kate were planning a future together in Tasmania. They
had spoken of using her inheritance to buy a farm.[73] Kate, at forty-
one, was eleven years older than Gustav. Her younger sister Blanche
had set a precedent by marrying a younger foreigner, Canadian-born
architect Stephen Priest. Even so, Kate's younger brothers, Dan and
Charles, circled paternally, crossing Bass Strait to meet their sister's
beau. Gustav's parents could not scrutinise her suitability up close. They
studied a photo of Kate that Gustav had sent, enchanted by her wise eyes
and the energy of her smile, suggesting this gave her a certain dignity.
In those days of stilted poses, Kate's unadorned features were strong
and plain. The only beauty that endures the cruelty of age is character.
Her parents-in-law seemed over the moon that their son had found a
woman both 'loveable' and 'practical'. His mother's comment that 'Kate
will now be your mother' was awkward shorthand for transferring the
baton of female influence since there was no tinge of reproval in their
delight.[74] Not prone to flowery emotion unless rhapsodising an alpine
posy, Gustav's diaries recorded events, staccato style. Always noting the
weather, he neglected to take the temperature of his heart. Here was
a woman with the spunk to take the path less travelled because she
possessed the means and maturity to see this chance at his side as a
once-in-a-lifetime ticket.

Her credentials were impeccable. She'd climbed Mt Roland and
Mt Buffalo, but foremost she was a botanist, someone as enthralled as
he by collecting plant specimens and exploring wild parts. He was her
clover. Not only could she keep up with his free-swinging stride, but
she felt a similar lust for communing with nature on top of the world.
How lucky was she to slip earth's tether on the arm of a partner as
hardy as he was fine, who could recite poetry while whetting the stone

of his axe before shouldering its blade into the grain of the wood, a man who thought deeply, read widely, roamed everywhere, a spirit prone to shirk conformity, who could sing, cook and conjure from a candle's flame an addictive brew of coffee. He came without property, furniture, social standing, or the security of family nearby, but the traditional scaffolding of matrimony counted for nothing beside the promise of a character who'd coloured her tomorrow in vivid swirls. Here was a soulmate, a self-starter, as able to thrive with the barest of necessities as an alpine plant clinging to a scintilla of soil on a windswept slope brushed by the clouds. She loved his European sensibility, his fierce intellect, and the excitement of adventuring together in a tiny island state awakening slowly to the lure of the wild.

They must have spoken of mountains. Gustav had seen photographs of Cradle Mountain by photographer Stephen Spurling III published in Tasmania's *Weekly Courier*.[75] These dramatic images of country, untouched and unexplored, were the first tugs piloting Gustav and Kate towards fate's port. Lindt's Hermitage and the Mt Buffalo's hospices germinated possibilities in the meadow of their courtship as they looked into the distance. Not far from Kate's family farm, now run by brother Dan, the Cradle's peaks seemed tantalisingly close, though the distance in miles disguised the dangers and difficulties of getting there.

Gustav resigned from his positions in Melbourne, sailing for Tasmania in early November to labour on Dan's farm, absent unusually from meetings of the naturalists, where he'd been expected to speak as the leader of recent excursions to Sandringham and Braybrook.[76] An apologetic letter was read to members in December expressing 'the pleasure he had experienced during the past four years … and regretting that he had not had the opportunity to bid farewell'.[77] He left the mainland as peremptorily as he had farewelled Austria, for prudence and caution are the enemies of fleet-footed roamers.

City Shoes & Mountain Boots

2

MOUNTAIN HIGH

The sweltering heat of high summer in the Australian bush sets even those with the steeliest nerves scanning vigilantly for the first waft of smoke, alert to sudden wind shifts that remind them who is boss. A happier anxiety crowded the hearts of the Cowle clan on the eve of Kate's wedding to Gustav Weindorfer on 1 February 1906. Family members bustled inside the homestead of the eldest sibling, Pressland, who lived in the potato-farming district of Stowport, inland from the seaside town of Burnie on Tasmania's north-west coast. Several of them had given up hopes she would ever marry. Press, as he was known affectionately, was scheduled to walk Kate down the aisle of the small, weatherboard church at 3 pm the next day. Her best friend and younger sister Laura had the honour of attending as sole bridesmaid in a gown of fawn voile.[1] Hand-written invitations welcomed guests afterwards at Killara, Press and Eva's homestead, to view the couple's wedding gifts and toast their union with refreshments.

The women scrubbed and cleaned, polished the silver, laid the best china ready for sandwiches and cakes, shooing children from the kitchen, where they lingered for treats. When the sweat trickled down their foreheads, they sought relief outside in the shade of the covered veranda. Kate hung the creases from her ivory voile dress sewn with lace and silk. She shook out her tulle veil embroidered with lover's knots, finer than those she could feel twanging inside herself. She too had grown accustomed to the prospect that, at forty-two, she might never be a bride, yet here she was on the cusp of exchanging vows with a handsome, charming, younger foreigner, without having met his parents or visited his homeland. Though she had performed in public, she didn't enjoy being the centre of attention quite as much as the man she would be taking for a husband. Surges of excitement and the last-minute pangs of doubt that typically accompany life-changing moments played with her composure.

Farmers had been monitoring a grassfire lurking near the Emu River for several days. Midway through the thrum of wedding preparations at Killara, a fierce squall sprang up, fanning the flames into a fearsome front that bore in a south-westerly direction.[2] Cries rang out summonsing the menfolk as gusts strengthened the blaze now burning towards the Cowles' property. Gustav joined his brothers-in-law and neighbours in a fight that would last throughout the night.[3] Killara was spared but the fire roared towards the Jennings' place next door, where men pulled down outbuildings to starve the flames of fuel. Others rescued the feeble, elderly Mrs Jennings, conveying her across potato fields to safety. Hungry sparks soon set upon the little church, neighbours converging there to carry wooden pews out into surrounding paddocks; men ripped burning planks from the exterior to secure the building from flying embers. A newspaper story on the conflagration credits a 'young lady visitor from Victoria', possibly a wedding guest, for alerting firefighters to the lick of flames underneath the church's foundations.[4] She joined others fetching buckets of water from a nearby tank. The report cheered the community's grit: 'Nothing that could be done for one another was too much to ask.'[5]

The church survived, but two homes on Jacklyn's Hill burned down. The owner of one property lost everything except for a chicken coop, inexplicably left standing amid blackened ruins, while his neighbour mourned the loss of house, furniture and a prized collection of military relics.[6] The next day, flintlocks taken at the battle of Waterloo were salvaged from the smouldering ashes, while Gustav and Kate's wedding went ahead in the drawing room at Killara, half an hour later than originally planned, soot scrubbed from faces and hands, the wedding party and guests exhausted but exuberant, eyes stinging still from the smoke that scented the air.

With vows exchanged, a gold signet ring slipped onto the bride's wedding finger, and their marriage certificate signed—Kate's profession

noted as 'Lady', her status 'spinster'—the burden of society's expectations lifted from her shoulders. The couple left the wellwishers, mostly
Kate's relatives, at dusk, travelling by horse and cart in a shower of
confetti through a smouldering haze. Kate wore a tailor-made skirt and
coat in navy blue, adorned in a white Paris hat trimmed with roses.[7]
They spent their first night as man and wife in a guesthouse near the
beach at Penguin on the north-west coast. Her finery would hardly suit
the honeymooners' true destination though. Turning their backs on the
silver service of a Hobart hotel or even a tour among the Tasmanian
lakes, they chose instead the wild, uninhabited crag of Mt Roland, at
the northern edge of Tasmania's Great Western Tiers mountain range.
Kate's chief concern, conveyed in a scribbled note to her sister Blanche
prior to the wedding, lay not with the cake, or her dress, or the flowers,
or the order of service or the possibility of a fire, but with the glitch in
arrangements for getting to Sheffield, the town nearest this peak: 'We
cannot get through to Sheffield on the Friday so would you mind if we
stay with you. We could both sleep in my little room, in Gustav's bed,
[then] go on by the morning train.'[8]

Gustav had written home of how he could see the snowclad peaks
of Roland and Black Bluff from the Kindred farm, where he'd been
toiling for two months since arriving in Tasmania. He must have told
his parents of Cradle Mountain since they wondered if the couple
might extend their honeymoon to see this spectacle 'since you wrote of
how you want to spend these weeks in the lap of nature'. Mt Roland
had been in Gustav's thoughts since Kate had spoken of this rugged
escarpment in her report to the Victorian Field Naturalists Club.

Smoke from the flames they had barely extinguished hung heavy
over Sheffield when they arrived by coach to buy supplies before riding
by buggy to the homestead owned by the Perkins family at the foot
of the mountain. Getting up there with even a minimum of comforts
would have posed enough logistical problems, but Gustav and Kate
were bent on botanical rummaging everywhere they roamed. They
brought 800 blotters and portfolios, guns to hunt their dinners of
kangaroo tail soup, wire netting to craft beds, a tent of course, fiddle and
flute for entertainment, potatoes, jam, hams, six billies, three frying pans,
blankets and clothes, their provisions carted up the mountainside by
Gustav with help from John Perkins and his brother Bert, who served

as guides and porters since their property backed onto the foot of the mount's surest yet steepest ascent. The Perkinses left their dog Brit with the honeymooners, and the kelpie did his duty sounding the alarm when a tiger snake slid through the grass.[10]

To climb so high, sleeping out under the stars, exposed to the elements, takes a heart that is completely smitten, for during their five-week jaunt they encountered winds that blew their tent down, bouts of incessant rain, mosquitoes in such pesky numbers they up and shifted, even a brief snow storm, not unheard of in early March, forcing them to shelter in a gorge, where they lit a fire for warmth, before going back down to their camp. Yes, they met a snake, but more startling than a slithering reptile was the glory of the mountain's grasp, as well as rare gems such as the five new styphelias they found growing at the top.[11]

Most of the time they spent here they were alone. There was birdsong, the drone of insects, sounds of foraging animals—echidnas, wombats, opossums and kangaroos, all fair game, for meat had to be sourced from somewhere. Occasionally hunters announced their presence with dogs and guns;[12] the Perkinses visited once or twice, and a day after the snow storm, they crossed paths with a lively group of picnickers enjoying the views from the gorge, and taking tea with these nine ladies and ten gentlemen provided a welcome breath of conviviality to enliven the solitude.[13] Blissfully happy to forage and gather, they spent their days collecting and arranging specimens, exploring ravines and creeks, Gustav often hunting at night alone. Twice weekly he'd hike down and back to replenish their stores, fetching fresh reams of blotting paper for preserving plants, leaving Kate behind at camp for hours on end.

Their joy up there together spills from the pages of three letters they wrote for the local newspaper in pidgin Irish brogue under the pseudonyms of Mike O'Flannagan and his trapper mate Pat Heggarty. The first was published on 19 February in *The North Western Advocate and the Emu Bay Times*, written probably when the newlyweds were tent-bound days earlier, cold and wet, barely able to kindle a fire, perhaps indulging in a tipple themselves. Heggarty began by telling O'Flannagan he'd been on his way up the mount, 'wid me billy can on me back, me gun on me shouldher, besides a few odds and inds', a drop of whiskey in his inside pocket, of course, 'whin be chansht oy larnt a honeymoon couple had seized the summit'. He's witnessed some strange sights over the years but 'niver in me loife before av honeymoon in thim sterile ragions. Shure there's no telling pwhat nixt, for Roland may be only a shtep to Mount Wellington, to be followed by Cradle Mountain.'[14]

Whether this correspondence was a true collaboration or an inspiration of one more than the other, the letters crackle with humorous blarney, their composition confirming an awareness of how peculiar they must appear to outsiders, an oddness the couple embraced with a carefree, swaggering pride. Cradle Mountain makes an appearance, signposting the dream that would define them. O'Flannagan and Heggarty each stole a visit separately, eyes on sticks, bewildered and intrigued, as if the camp was Aladdin's cave. Instead of a makeshift shelter, Heggarty was staggered by 'an advance posht av civilisation'.[15] O'Flannagan 'had a sly glance into the tent and saw a bed looking like a comfortable couch and by the look of their tucker … they do not intend to visit the "Cradle Mounts" too soon.' Overcome by 'that savory shmell o' cooking … they were making all sorts o' dishes', he kept his distance in the bush, watching them set to work on a bulging knapsack. 'Shure! I thought it was a kangaroo but it made me heart aisy when I found I was misthaken … I now find why those two sthay on the mountain. The contents of the bag were "plants" of all sorts, which they dried between paper and put under heavy stones. Then there came across to me the swate tones of a fiddle and flute. Och! It fairly broke me up and I came away with the thought that those two knew how to find happiness even in "sterile regions".'[16]

What floored these characters more was the gun-toting lady mountaineer whom Heggarty came across while her man was down country: 'The lovely bride aither spinds the toime washin' and ironin', or sits wid her shoulder agin a boulder wid a six-shooter in her pretty pfist.' He would have doffed his hat and maybe offered her a shot of his whiskey but feared that if he went for his pocket, she'd think he'd gone for his gun and beat him to the draw. 'There ud be that six shooter pointin' at me eternally loike a nadle to a magnet … Oy can fale thim lead pills from very sympathy.' When O'Flannagan ribbed him over his groundless fear—'she wud have messed ye, Pat'—Heggarty agreed but pointed out that in his ducking and weaving to get away, he would have copped a bullet sooner or later from her stray aim.[17]

Gustav's frequent trips down the mountain for supplies gave him opportunity to post these letters. He tried to let his parents in on the ruse but the joke is lost in translation. They can't get their heads or tongues around the brogue, mystified by the humour of it all.[18] Australian lingo often puzzled them. *'Was ist eigentlich ein "Billy"?'* they'd asked once.[19] An inveterate scribe, Gustav felt compelled to communicate his experiences from the moment he left Austria bound for Australia, and he soon made friends with local editors, boldly pitching them stories. Sometimes these were published under pseudonyms. Kate didn't keep a diary, but her letters betray a mischievous talent for sketching characters and mimicking accents.[20] When O'Flannagan told Heggarty he doesn't like shooting roos in 'close saison', Heggarty chided him: 'And yes don't loike kangaroo out av "close season". (Moike darlint', don't use thim Frinch woruds) …'[21]

For every 'beautiful day' and 'glorious morning' during their mountain high, there were miserable cold, wet spells in camp. Battered by a terrific storm in late February, 'the fire goes out and can't be made again'. Cheerfully resourceful, they warmed water for their coffee over a candle flame.[22] Secluded from the judgement of others, they did as they wished, skin to skin with the landscape around them, so that the watering hole nearest their camp was soon christened 'our creek'.[23]

From the nethermost reaches of Roland, on a clear day they could scan effortlessly across to the western horizon, where the curved saddle of Cradle Mountain and the clenched fist of Barn Bluff beckoned through the purple haze. Cradle had been front of mind for Gustav since savouring the *Weekly Courier's* pictorial spread in June the previous year. (His botanist's eye had gone straight to the giant grass trees, *Richea pandanifolia*, that the *Courier's* photographer Stephen Spurling III had caught like a huddle of tall, faceless space invaders marooned in a verge of eucalypts,[24] the man in the photo, standing beside them, easily overlooked in the presence of their strange spiky-headed stalks.)

Heggarty and O'Flannagan eavesdropped on the couple. They knew the honeymooners had Cradle Mountain red-flagged on a map. Fresh from the thrill of Mt Buffalo's opening to the public, with its hospices, guides and train travel luring people into the wilderness, Kate and Gustav must have canvassed possibilities for a venture of their own, in the way that couples will kick around a plan that may never be executed. The picnickers on the plateau were a sign of change afoot.

Here was a tipping point. In a country reigned by the tyranny of distance, there was too much ground to cover on foot for walking to

Giant grass trees in Cradle Valley, 1905 (Stephen Spurling)

appeal as a recreational pursuit. But even Heggarty gleaned an idea whose time had come, fancying himself among the converted. 'Oim intrested in thim spicimints the honeymooners are collectin' ... Ye mines they belongs to the "Field Nataralist Club", thin more power to thim, says oi, for so do I to some extint.'[25]

But O'Flannagan was spot on when he reckoned Kate and Gustav would not be going to the Cradles any time soon. They had a farm to buy first, and to this end they rose at 5 am on 21 February for a flying trip to Kindred, hoping to negotiate purchase of a portion of Lauriston, the family estate that Dan Cowle now ruled, arriving there after dark with portfolios of plant specimens to deliver for safekeeping. A bargain was not struck, and the next day, under heavy rain, they returned to Mt Roland, glad at least their tent had withstood another storm.[26]

Letters from Gustav's parents make clear their relief that he would be returning to agriculture, a worthy profession, never suspecting that the farm would be a means of subsidising a much riskier proposition.

'The botany you will probably put to one side to concentrate body and soul on farming,' his mother writes advisedly.[27] Their warmth towards Kate was layered with an immense gratitude, for she provided the wherewithal to coax him into productive labouring on the land. Kindred, with its chocolate-brown volcanic soil and proximity to the mountains, was a prize the couple coveted. But as they packed up camp, 'eating all day to get through provisions', the search for a property still lay before them.

John Perkins sent his eldest son, Dick, and daughter Annie (nineteen and seventeen) to help ferry the honeymooners' odds and sods down the mountain in sugar bags slung over their shoulders. Kate rewarded them for their troubles with gifts: a book for Annie and a doll for Dick.[28] This disruption to long-established gender stereotypes stuck with Annie well into her nineties, when she vividly recalled Kate's quirky reversal of tradition and the hardship of sore feet as they clambered up the steep, rocky slope in boots too thin and worn for the task. Pain and disappointment are like fluff to the Velcro of memory. Children polish the highs and lows and forget the benign lulls in between. 'They weren't proud or anything,' she remembered of her brush with the Weindorfers that summer. 'We liked them. They were good to us.'[29]

Kate and Gustav did not conceive a child on their honeymoon. At forty-two, her chance of falling pregnant was a low-percentage game requiring divine intervention. But the Cradles nested within them. The mountain's name is often attributed to the shape of a miner's cradle, a masculine tool of trade, but early references spoke of 'Crib Rock', alluding to its distinctive rock-a-bye baby shape and a maternal, domestic symbol. One of the pioneering ramblers through Cradle country was the former Deloraine police superintendent Dan Griffin, who chronicled his journeys as 'The Tramp'. In 1897 he wrote an article declaring that 'in all probability', Cradle's name was derived from 'the old fashioned cradle of the gin-case pattern—the sort the first Tasmanians were rocked to sleep in when bassinets, perambulators and such like things were not known in the colony'.[30]

An all-rounder with a deep inside knowledge of the racetrack, Griffin was a legend in the district. His familiarity with the high country had brought him out of retirement in the winter of 1905 to join the second search party sent to bring home the body of the young trapper Bert Hanson from Cradle Mountain. Weak from starvation and fatigue, the teenager had been left in a huddle when he couldn't walk another step, his loyal kelpie shivering at his side, while his mate Tom Jones staggered on for help. This tragedy had intrigued Tasmanians. The story confirmed fears about such a forbidding, remote location. Hanson's body was not found until the snow melted in September.[31] The Weindorfers knew the pitfalls of inclement weather, but they loved the thrill of their wits on edge and the reward of sights that were worth every peril.

No sooner had they come down the mountain than Gustav was conniving his return. They'd gone to stay with Kate's sister Blanche and her husband Stephen Priest at their seafront home in Devonport, inspecting farm properties that were either too big or too expensive, and entertaining the dinner table with stories of Mt Roland's crannies and crags. Two weeks after their return to the lowlands, Gustav was marching his new brother-in-law, who was close in age, up and down the summit in one spurt.[32] The next day he drew a map, conquering it on paper. From their first camp-out together on Mt Buffalo, when Gustav left the party to climb Mt Bogong, Kate must have sensed his absences were as set as the cut of his chin. After another bout of farm-shopping, he bolted again, this time with Press Cowle and a Mr Boden, who was best man at the wedding. Toting heavy swags, they went off tin prospecting on the Hampshire Hills; they walked for miles over the next few days—double or triple that in Gustav's case because he left them at camp to go further, deeper around Mt Housetop, Blythe River, Laurel Creek—until they all eventually emerged, footsore, 16 miles above Stowport, where Press lived. Arriving home at 7 pm, they were greeted by the news that 'dear Kate [was] not well'.[33] She bounced back from whatever ailed her, but the tread of his comings and goings amid her lapses of ill health left a faintly discernible trail through the fresh growth of their entanglement.

Within a few days, they shook hands with Dan Cowle on a deal that sold them 100 acres of the family holding. Work began feverishly on refitting the existing cottage with linoleum and wallpaper, while Gustav built huts for the pigs and the poultry—'*baute schweinestall ... began gefluegelhof*'—his diary suddenly lapsing into German, as though he sought the comfort of an old shoe in response to their new confinement.[34] But the furrows of a fenced-in paddock would not contain a leg stretcher like Gustav.

Daring to be different hazards the chance of being misunderstood. Suspicion would tail them always. Gustav's German accent, his love of garlic and coffee, Kate's plucky nature, their independence from each other, their obsession with plants—all would be fodder for loose tongues in small rural communities where bloodlines knew each other's skeletons and families could trace connections through a fine mare that one person's father sold a good while back to another's cousin. While Kate's provenance was impeccable, Gustav was an unknown quantity, heightening the scrutiny of them both. But there are wildcats who linger in the backwoods of every place, and the Weindorfers would seek them out just as their laser-sharp eyes could identify a rare specimen by the tiny hairs at the base of its pedicel.

In the front garden at Roland Lea (*left to right* Gustav's parents, Pauline and Johann Weindorfer, with Kate and Gustav), 1910 (Ron Smith)

3

KINDRED SPIRITS

American-born King O'Malley lit up the remote west-coast towns of his Tasmanian constituency. His sombrero was bigger than Gustav Weindorfer's Tyrolean pork-pie hat, and he grew a thicker thatch of hair, but otherwise these men marched to a rhythm each might have recognised in the other when they met at the Kindred Hall on a Tuesday evening in November 1906 for one of the largest political meetings ever held there.[1] They had each crossed from one side of the world to the other, starting afresh in places too small for a cartographer's grid, where they'd made their presence felt. Both men were prone to bold ideas, bandying colourful, persuasive rhetoric to get others on board, deaf to naysayers. They were prepared to fling their hat over the fence before deciding how best to retrieve it. O'Malley joined the Labor Party after his election in 1901 to Australia's first parliament as the member for what was then the federal seat of Darwin, named after naturalist Charles Darwin, who'd visited Hobart on board the *Beagle* in February 1836. West-coast prospectors in this remote corner of the state warmed to his flamboyant sermons, delivered from the balcony parapet of a Queenstown hotel, selling them his sworn belief that their sweat and grit should be rewarded with better services, roads and communication.

He'd arrived in Kindred unaware that the Methodist Church was holding its annual Sunday School anniversary, but the clash of venue was soon sorted. Once the social event was done, Gustav took the chair, introducing O'Malley, who spoke for two and a half hours spruiking his pet schemes, among them a Commonwealth-owned 'people's bank' with branches tied to post offices across the land. Australian historian Manning Clark regarded O'Malley as 'picturesque', strong in urging the people to shape their own destiny but weak when it came to how that should be done.[2] Loudly populist, he railed against 'stagger juice' with the vehemence of a former drunk, relying on the punchy slogans he'd earlier employed selling insurance and real estate to rivet constituents. According to the local newspaper's 'Kindred correspondent', conceivably Gustav Weindorfer, the visiting MP 'made a lasting impression among the voters here'.[3]

Kindred was the hilly hub of a fertile farming district, boasting two churches (Methodist and Anglican), one school, a local hall, a railway siding and a daily mail service from Forth, 5 miles away and its nearest neighbour. Within months of settling here, Gustav carved out a role for himself, frequently being elected to chair meetings. Unafraid to assert himself, offer opinions or ask, 'Why not?', he was alert to novel inventions, and bent on improving services with the verve of O'Malley. When the two shook hands that night, he didn't let slip an opportunity to buttonhole the King on the urgent need for telecommunications in Kindred.[4] Shortly afterwards, an officer was reportedly dispatched to assess the district, but nothing happened. Gustav again pestered O'Malley, engaging in another bout of shadowboxing with authorities until finally *The North Western Advocate and the Emu Bay Times* quoted the deputy postmaster general promising that telegraph poles were on their way. A win for Gustav, this was the first of many campaigns that would take him from the small fry of Kindred's municipal affairs to guardianship of the treasures in its backyard.[5]

Kindred was so-called because initially everyone living there was related. A kindly, caring community spirit shone through when rural tragedies struck, as they often did with brutal force. Residents rallied to raise money for the local farmer who severed a limb in his thresher machine and for the family who lost a baby girl dropped by her toddler sister while their mother ducked out to milk the cow. Horse and trap accidents often tipped riders and passengers headlong on the poorly metalled roads.

The Cowle family's property, Lauriston, was regarded as the pick of the district. Dan's potatoes regularly made news. A 4-pound whopper he harvested was displayed proudly in the Devonport window of *The Advocate*.[6] The Weindorfers lived across the road from the original

weatherboard homestead built by the family patriarch. Helped by sister
Blanche's architect husband Stephen, they renovated an old cottage,
with the extensions hewn and hammered together by Gustav. Perched
atop a small rise, their home was next door to the one-roomed school
house and the Methodist church, with its cemetery of headstones
commemorating pioneer settlers. They bought dairy cows, planted an
orchard including walnut and cherry trees, seeded paddocks of white
elephant potatoes and Algerian oats, and dug vegetable gardens of
green beans, peas, raspberries, gooseberries, garlic, onions and lettuces,
establishing their agricultural credentials on the acreage that Kate had
bought for them with her inheritance.[7] Her late father had been a
shrewd operator, selling goods and services to mining communities
then investing smartly in sought-after Devonport land, a port city on
the make, and at Kindred, where the soil was good enough to eat. One
of nine siblings, Kate shared Gustav's frugality. While he laboured, she
took an early lead managing bank overdrafts and the mortgage.[8] They
called their farm 'Roland Lea', conjuring their closeness in spirit to a
place that loomed in their courtship and honeymoon, seeing the farm
as the meadowy doorstep of this escarpment, merely a skip and a hop
away. In truth, the trip was a day-long journey by horse, rail and foot.
But the heart collapses distance when the destination is worth every

The Cowle family homestead, Lauriston, at Kindred, built in 1881

jolt. On a hill at the rear of their home, weather permitting, they could crane for an uninterrupted view of Mt Roland in the south-east and, further southwards still, Black Bluff.

From the small Austrian town of Michelhofen in the alpine ether of Carinthia, where Gustav grew up, his mother, Pauline, joked that he would soon know Mt Roland as thoroughly as she knew 'the Michelhofen hills', yet she fretted when she heard he was off to explore Black Bluff at the end of 1906, betraying her anxiety that he would never settle, contentedly, on one pursuit: 'I just do not understand how your farm work still leaves you time for botany and climbing the snow covered Black Bluff.'[9] She hadn't seen him for a decade—though they corresponded almost weekly—and had lost sight of her son's capacity since he'd left Austria to flourish on his wits and mettle. Though they spoke German, his parents were of Italian and Slovenian heritage, a mix common in Carinthia, lying near Austria's southern border, where the Pyrenees and the Tauern mountains were well patronised by walkers and skiers. His father, Johann, who had served in the Austro–Hungarian civil service, also composed music in a kitbag bulging with surprises. His mother enquired whether her son had put the piano in the living room or the library, keen to picture the layout of their house. Gustav asked them to send him agricultural texts from Germany and pleased his parents with local plaudits for his produce and novel methods.[10] He presented a paper on German potato-drying experiments to an April meeting of the Ulverstone branch of the board of agriculture, later scoping potential for potato distilleries and potato flour, and becoming one of the first dairy farmers on the island to import the American-designed Babcock machine (1892) for testing milk quality.[11] Gustav offered to lend his to the board so that it could lease the device to members.

The couple stirred up Kindred and its surroundings. Kate formed a choir at the Anglican church, their congregation.[12] Gustav had converted from Catholicism in his homeland after being physically bruised by church officials during a military parade, thereby clearing a prerequisite in her father's will.[13] While Kate was less of a force on the public stage, she often played piano for social events and fundraisers, and opened their home to young, single, female teachers at the school, where the children made lively neighbours.[14] Once the Weindorfers' dogs were busted stealing the students' lunches, their bulging girths giving the game away.[15] This was a time for bedding down, so that they might take hold in the soil like the plants and trees prospering around them. Sundays were devoted to their herbarium collections, and sometimes excursions to nearby landmarks. Botany was their first love, farming a necessity, but one they plied innovatively.[16]

They spread know-how through the community and got plenty in return. Gustav invited locals to Roland Lea for a pruning demonstration by an orchardist, since fruit-growing was new to the district,[17] while his assiduous lobbying for communications technology bore results when the telegraph poles were delivered, finally, in April 1907.[18] They lay by the roadside for weeks so that horses shied on approach, and Gustav had to give one more nudge to get them shunted into the ground. The last pole was dug in at the end of May amid Empire Day celebrations, when the Union Jack was hoisted in the school yard for students to salute as they paraded by in columns of four.[19]

Chuffed by all they had achieved, Gustav and Kate invited his parents to visit, prompting an ecstatic 'Hip, hip, Hurrah' from Johann and Pauline Weindorfer, who in their excitement replied by return post in a mix of German and English: 'so *dass wir* the following night sleeping and awake uninterrupted dreamt of the "little island", so mild in winter and so warm in summer, *aber, aber*,—so unspeakably we feel inclined to pack and get our tickets for the journey on the White Star line or on the German mail steamer to the lovely home of our beloved children in Australia.'[20]

Wanderlust was embedded in the Weindorfer gene. His father's exploits, under the pseudonym 'Max Winter', in colonising territory along the East African coastline on behalf of Germany resembled the plot of Joseph Conrad's novel *Heart of Darkness*. Gustav himself probably knew little of the story that was uncovered in 1954 through the diligent digging of his first biographer, Dr George Bergman, who kept the shadier details of Johann's 'Babylonian exile' secret to spare surviving members of Gustav's family embarrassment.[21] Bergman's correspondence, kept at the Mitchell Library in Sydney, reveals that Johann fled Austria in 1885 to escape retribution for embezzlement or gambling debts that had occurred on his watch as a civic official. Though this was not a criminal offence and the money was later repaid, the shame was considered so great that those caught had the choice of suicide or vanishing. Johann chose the latter. He abandoned a ship bound for America and threw his papers into the sea at Trieste, sailing instead to

Zanzibar.[22] There he joined forces with a notorious empire builder, Dr Carl Peters, who spearheaded the German East Africa Company's efforts to acquire territory with Venetian beads, bales of American cloth and unseemly haste. The Emperor Bismarck's flag would be flown amid beating drums before the inky signatures on treaties had dried.[23] Weindorfer senior ran German East Africa Company stations up and down the Somali coast for seven years, calling himself 'Papa Winter' and even attending a reception for British explorer Sir Henry Stanley. He then shifted to Berlin, where he stayed until an imperial pardon allowed his return to Austria in 1903.[24] Bergman speculates that the discovery of this skeleton possibly explains Gustav's abrupt departure for the other end of the earth, prompting his sister Edith's doubts that he would ever return home. 'Our family has a peculiar skill to scatter in all directions,' she wrote soon after his arrival in Melbourne.[25]

Johann was seventy-one and Pauline sixty-six when they arrived at Roland Lea in February 1908. They'd warned the couple not to put them into harness on the farm because of their age, but once ensconced in the district, they lifted the cultural tone. Johann mentored a local pianist, Florence Trebilco, even scoring an ode to Cradle Mountain, the destination that danced in Gustav and Kate's thoughts.[26] Kate's musicianship must have won Johann's respect, for a piano—then rare in farming households—was in his eyes as necessary as a hand grinder for coffee beans. Evenings often revolved around the ivories, Gustav and Kate partners in song—in a previous life she'd performed duets with her late brother Freddie at the Devonport Hall, comfortable on the piano stool before an audience. Once settled in this nook, his parents felt at home.

His mother's wish that agricultural pursuits would tamp her son's restless surges possibly inflamed them in the paradoxical way that resistance often fans its antithesis. The couple kept in touch with their extended family of mainland naturalists, a mobile band with backpacks and blotting paper who had the means and motive to ramble inter-state. Gustav had hatched a plan with his botanist colleague and bush brother Dr Charles Sutton, the Carlton GP, for the two of them to visit the Cradles and Black Bluff over the Christmas period in 1908. This twosome had become a habit before his marriage to Kate, who agreed to stay behind with the elders at the farm. The country was inhospitable, with few paths apart from an old, rough track laid in 1826 by the

Van Diemen's Land Company (VDL) for bullock dray traffic. Unknown hazards may have discouraged them from including Kate in the party, however ready she was for the challenge. Surveyors employed by VDL to hack a way through a corner of this region in the foulest of weather chronicled the excruciating hardships they faced, at times proceeding barely 500 yards an hour. Their reports, published in 1832, describe a landscape that had not been much disturbed in the decades since.[27]

Few Kindred farmers explored far beyond their post-and-rail fence. There was, however, an exception living close by. Ron Smith, seven years Gustav's junior, was a man with a nose for exploring and a pair of legs to rival Gustav's own. His grasp of the remote hinterlands entered his bloodstream almost by osmosis through the tales and trials of his extraordinary father, James 'Philosopher' Smith, a prospector likened once to a Tasmanian Moses, a man 'happiest amongst the trackless wild'.[28] Ron lived at Westwood, near Kindred, on land cleared and farmed by his famous father, who had struck gold, but more profitably tin, after years of crisscrossing mountains, rivers and forests in search of mineral ore. Stashing provisions in a bolthole at Black Bluff, the Philosopher would roam the north-west, going for days without a meal if he was on the scent of a quarry. He unearthed a substantial tin deposit near the summit of Mt Bischoff, which became the richest tin mine in the world. His respectful sobriquet bowed to his learning and temperament.[29] Ron, who was named after the Tasmanian botanist Ronald Campbell Gunn, inherited his father's curiosity in what might lie over the next ridge.

He had known Kate since his childhood, though she was eighteen years older. In a place where the local paper reported every carriage accident, families knew the district's doings. The Cowle family would drop in at the Smiths' to break their regular journeys from Devonport to Kindred. Ron remembered Kate and her sisters singing around the piano.[30] Gustav must have heard stories from his wife of Ron's legendary father. Hard-wired for rambling, Ron had visited the Cradles twice already.[31] The two men bonded over a landscape that had seeped into their being. In 1897 Ron had clipped and filed an article on Cradle country written with finesse by a bushwalking lawyer known

as 'Peregrinator', who'd wondered of such melancholic beauty: 'Is it
not the voice of the great Creator … telling his Child, man, that earth
is not his rest?' *Earth is not his rest.*[32] There were scant maps and no
blazed trails; few of the landmarks and creeks bore names, and apart
from several newspaper accounts of previous ascents to help them steer
a course, walkers were on their own. Anyone heading to the Cradles
would have been glad of Smith's intelligence and counsel.

Gustav left Roland Lea with Dr Sutton on the morning of 4 January
1909, in a horse-drawn 'pagnel' (a two-wheeled cart), carrying six
portfolios, 1500 sheets of blotting paper, food for a week, a change of
clothes and a compass.[33] They climbed the hills leading to Wilmot,
15 miles ahead, through thickets of sassafras, blanket wood, musk,
Christmas bush and dogwood, stopping briefly at noon to feed the
horse and fuel themselves before starting out for Middlesex cattle
station, 22 miles further. Deep ruts and rocks in the soft mud made
even trotting difficult. A fallen tree blocking the way was impossible to
shift so that the only solution was to unleash the horse, unpack the cart,
then lift the vehicle inch by inch over the log. An 'obliging wayfarer'
who must have loomed like a miracle, since few travellers had cause
to be there, helped out.[34] Night closed in. They knew by the fencing
that they'd reached the station, but they couldn't find the manager's
hut, despite a bright moon. Frank and Louisa Brown ran the small
stock operation, providing shelter and occasionally fresh meat from
a slaughtered sheep. Cattleman and rouseabout Tom Perry acted as a
guide to the Cradles, leading pack horses in and out of the valley. Like
the Perkinses at the foot of Roland, these satellite families provided
staging posts for the trickle of passers through—prospectors, hunters,
loggers, ramblers, anyone with a purpose in these parts. Travellers
brought news, yarns, company—and in the case of Dr Sutton, a rare
medical house call—in return for a roof and a meal.

When the two botanists set off across the sward-covered plains,
they were as delighted by the fair weather as by the pink-flowering
Trachymeme humilis, yellow everlastings and white asters wherever they
set their feet.[35] The dark-green waratah bushes had done blooming,
their scarlet pistils stripped naked, but the pair rejoiced at the sight of
a rare pink flower—*Oenothera tasmanica*—that the government's chief
botanist, Leonard Rodway, who was known to Gustav, later confirmed
hadn't been spied in Tasmania for sixty years.[36]

Cradle Mountain mirrored in the still waters of Dove Lake, 1929 (Gustav Weindorfer)

Collecting as they went, they spent the evening preserving specimens under the cover of a roughly hewn paling hut with a fireplace and two wooden bunks. Since the previous day's hike had afforded them the briefest impression of Cradle Mountain, they woke in a hurry, for this was their chance at the summit. The shroud of clouds a curse, they trooped through the valley, pausing at the clear, pebbled stream that flows from Dove Lake beneath the Cradles into Dove River, scooping seedlings of King Billy pine, turning this way and that to admire the citizens of this native garden, catching the scent of pale pink boronia and the denser, sweeter smelling buds of its kin *Boronia rhomboidea*: 'At the river's edge swayed merrily the white flowering pine leafed daisy—Olearia pinifolia—quick rushing streams almost hidden in the long grass run in all directions and little stagnant pools, bordered by thick sphagnum beds … In our eager search for specimens we did not notice that a thick fog had surrounded us and we had passed the saddle which connects the ridge we ascended … it was necessary to retrace our steps and we succeeded in getting a glimpse through the broken clouds of the little horn … enabling us to preserve a proper direction.'[37]

On the plateau, they were greatly amused by the cushion plants, deceptively voluptuous-looking mounds of green, seeming as soft as a pillow yet hard as nails, for survival on this barren, windswept cleft binds the plants so densely that they are rock-firm, prickly to touch, cleverly conserving warmth and moisture when snow falls and temperatures plummet. Once a cushion forms, others piggyback, so the velvety green may be mottled by miniature daisies or sage. At the foot of the crags, the sky cleared for a moment: 'To the south west appeared the bold mass of Barn Bluff, to the east is an endless chain of blue hazy mountains, the Western Tiers, Mt Roland and Mt Claude and in the north Black Bluff.'[38]

They began at the western end, using both hands to haul themselves over the boulders, but rain and fog closed in around them, and as the hour was late, they were forced to descend, losing direction, retracing their steps, consulting their compass and bearing north. The creeping snare of disorientation, as fatigue and chill took hold in heights with

Cushion plants on the plateau below Cradle, 1929 (Gustav Weindorfer)

precipitous cliffs and fading light, was dangerous—Bert Hanson's mountain grave a haunting reminder. Gustav and Sutton were soaked through by the time they found their way back to the valley, but foul weather had thwarted them before, never diminishing the itch to keep going. Like two boys on an outdoor scamper, their mood was buoyant, ecstatic at times, for the diversity of plants and trees sculpted by the fierce climactic extremes was too much for their greedy eyes to take in but all the more reason to return sooner.

Circumnavigating the great glacial basin of Dove Lake, they marvelled at the celery top pine, weather worn and covered in lichen, keeping to the high bank until their progress was 'brought to a stop by an impenetrable forest of pines and beeches filled in with a thick undergrowth. This upper part of the lake with wooded islands, white beaches, dense and silent forests and the huge mountain sides casting gloomy shadows make an unforgettable picture and with a resolve to solve the mysteries by penetrating that dark forest on some future happy occasion we turn our backs on it all, and following the lake waters along the Dove River, gain again the shelter of our hut.'[39]

Tom Perry returned with their horse for the trek back to Middlesex, where they ate ravenously before starting afresh. They veered north-wards this time through an open gum forest to a mine on the Lea River at the foot of Black Bluff, where they met the owner, Walter Malcolm Black, another point of light in this wilderness. His paling hut displayed gentility, with shelves and books, and his back story would have warranted a place among the spines arranged there. Educated at the prestigious Victorian private school Geelong Grammar, he was the son of wealthy grazier, the late Archibald Black. Upon his father's death, he sued the estate, being granted a windfall out-of-court settlement on the condition he stayed away, although the sins deserving exile were not recorded.[40] He'd done as requested, drifting through western New South Wales, trying his hand at gold prospecting, before taking over the Black Bluff mine. The Tasmanian bush was veined with characters who twinkled as brightly as the lode of mineral resources underground. Black built an 11-foot punt out of King Billy pine with Tom Perry, who'd helped renovate his hut, for boating excursions on Lake Lea. His grey horse, Blue Spec, named after a 1905 Melbourne Cup winner, often wandered loose with a bell around his neck. For the five years he lived there, he kept meteorological records and dabbled in botany.[41]

Gustav and Sutton bedded down at Black's, and in the morning the three of them scaled Black Bluff. The harsh exposure to cold south-westerly winds limited the variety of plants on the summit, but spirits soared, for the cloudless day afforded a panorama denied them by the fickle weather of Cradle Mountain. From the top they could see the island's north coast from Table Cape to beyond Tamar Heads and the peak of Ben Lomond. 'The scarred sides of the famous Mt Bischoff were clearly made out, lying nearly due west; to the south mountains of all shapes and sizes, ranging up to 5000 foot in the Cradles, display a picture which, with the blue sky over us and the far blue sea to the north, is undoubtedly as fine a view as a tourist can imagine.'[42]

As fine a view as a tourist can imagine.

At day's end the botanists paused to admire red Tasmanian Christmas bells hanging over sheer rocks that were inaccessible to man, reminding them of nature's tenacity in the tiniest handful of soil.

Kate must have envied Gustav when he returned home, invigorated by all he'd seen, picking out particular flowers and mosses for her benefit, declaring the Cradles 'a veritable flower garden, a true Eldorado for the botanist', a phrase he'd parade later in a more scholarly account of the region's flora.[43] The two lengthy articles he penned for the Launceston *Examiner* whetted readers' interest in the forests and flora of a region still seen through the grisly pall of Hanson's death. But the notion of tourism was being touted. An article appeared in February canvassing Middlesex as 'a tourist destination'. The author mentioned his encounter with Gustav and Sutton at Lake Lea as proof of the region's appeal, quoting their sworn testimony that the Cradles surpass Victoria's Mt Buffalo in scope and beauty.[44] The visionary leap from remote mountain outpost to tourist destination was prescient. Kate and Gustav felt the rumblings of a rare opportunity. If they had read extracts of John Muir's essays on national parks, they would have had good reason to believe the interest in wild places would grow as cities expanded and railroads and trails opened them 'not only to the determined traveller rejoicing in difficulties but to those (may their tribe increase) who, not tired, not sick, just naturally take wing every summer in search of wildness'.[45] They had their own anecdotes as testimony—the picnic party atop Mt Roland; the excursions to Buffalo; the swell of interest in outdoor recreation—confirming their mutual passion for walking, climbing, birdsong, flora, fauna, sights that silence the urge to speak, and their unshakable sense that the risks were worth the glory. Kate might have held her breath when Gustav recounted his and Sutton's dance with mist and fog, the very demons that bedevilled Hanson, turning in circles to find their way down. Her eyes must have shouted, 'Take me next time.' She had felt the thorn of sacrifice and compromise that then was overwhelmingly a woman's lot, instinctively accommodating the urges of a man she knew couldn't be pinned like a scarab beetle in a glass case.

Covering for his absences, she had remained in the background helping organise the church social, gathering wood, weeding gardens, tending the animals, looking after her parents-in-law, being aunt to her siblings' children, possibly still hoping for her own, in every way a loving wife. They were a feisty team. Within the short period of their own personal history they had settled in Melbourne, married, moved to Kindred, grown a farm. Now that he'd met the Cradles and was surer of his way up and over the plateau to the crags, they began planning an ascent for the summer to come, his parents, Pauline and Johann, comfortable enough in the routines of Roland Lea to manage the farm while they were gone.

In the meantime, Gustav shifted the pots on his various burners, juggling crops, herbariums, mountaineering and local politics. He'd become a lightning rod in the local shire's squabble over the spoils of council boundaries, emboldening him to test the mood for a new political force. In a salute to O'Malley's spunk, he launched a Kindred branch of the new Tasmanian Liberal League, the forerunner of the modern Liberal Party, its platform fuzzier than the sharper craving for an alternative to Labor.[46] Gustav advanced to the state council of this ginger group, meeting powerbrokers, learning the ropes and pulleys of democracy, as keen for political innovation as he was to master the Babcock milk tester. Kate generously performed on the piano at socials under the new party's banner.[47]

Towards year's end, as the days lengthened, the couple invited Ron Smith to join them on their trip to Cradle Mountain.[48] They met for a 'botanical ramble' to arrange provisions and where they would stay, plans that were roughly sketched since they were prone to unpredictable elements—foul weather, a wrong turn, a sprained ankle, a snake bite, pea soup fog—anything could slow them down.

———————

Before dawn on 28 December 1909, the party of three assembled in the driveway of Roland Lea with a checklist for their departure. Gustav secured the harness of their horse, Jolly, and repacked the cart to spread the load. Ron rode his bicycle. From the veranda, the elderly Weindorfers watched them go, waving until the party disappeared from sight. As a blistering sun climbed higher in the sky, they called a halt for rest in the cool of a shady copse before pushing ahead on a track that climbed more often than it dipped. They arrived at Middlesex station after nightfall, bunking in with the managers, Frank and Louisa Brown. Louisa was surely glad for female company. She shared her bed with Kate while the three men slept on the dirt floor in the other room.[49]

They woke to a dismal drizzle with a dusting of snow, the kind of morning 'tourists would prefer to be rolled up in blankets near a roaring fire than to tramp God's wide world over which all elements of heaven seemed to have let loose in one of the last spring cleaning storms,' Gustav wrote later, the 'T' word tripping off his tongue, creeping into his lexicon.[50] But these three were hardly average sightseers, and the thought of Gustav lounging in bed instead of seizing the dawn was inconceivable. Mine-owner Walter Malcolm Black turned up at the station inviting them to visit. Kate sat astride his reliable grey plodder, Blue Spec, while the others tramped, returning in the late afternoon for a dinner of freshly butchered sheep.

On 31 December 1909, the trio rose early, loading two packhorses with tents and provisions for their trudge to the Fury Mine at the north end of Hounslow Heath. Staying beside a creek banked with daisies, irises and lemon-scented boronia, they caught a haul of mountain trout, crisply fried for their evening meal. A tent fly was hung to curtain a private space inside the hut for Kate's benefit. For two days they roamed the course of nearby waterways, gaining views to the bottom of Fury Gorge, a deep river chasm where the forested slopes below them appeared 'unlit by any ray of light'.[51] That afternoon the men went off alone, scaling a ridge to gain their orientation, describing the north-ward land towards the sea as a 'primeval forest'. They arrived back in

The Fury Mine hut (*left to right* Walter Black, Gustav and Kate), 1910 (Ron Smith)

time for tea, cooked by Kate, who must have wondered once or twice what she would do if they didn't return. Intent on covering as much ground as possible, the party decamped to a site at the northern shore of Crater Lake, and closer to the mountain.

Black hiked in from Black Bluff to join them, his kelpie in tow. Hefting a swag on his back, he helped carry food and gear up and over the valley, skirting a small fire on the heath. Flocks of currawongs descended on the smoking ground to pick off scorched insects.[52] The torque of gnarled gums reminded Gustav of giant creepers woven tightly around an invisible crutch. He worried that they had chosen an inhospitable place, always reading the book of nature closely for clues. Luckily the weather was kind. They pitched tents 150 yards from the lake's edge—Black and Smith shared a small silk tent, the Weindorfers in the largest—fashioning mattresses from beech and lemon thyme boughs before turning in: 'through the silent darkness of this supreme mountain solitude stole the murmuring sound of rippling water leaping from rock to rock, gladly escaping from the sombre shadows of the lake to the sunshine of the valley.'[53]

Gustav and Kate interpreted the stone tablets that nature set before them in a library where the eye could not keep still, the question 'Why is it so?' never far from their thoughts in a landscape so peculiarly shaped. Just as John Muir intuited Yosemite's geological history through the smoothness of its vast rock cliffs, Gustav examined Cradle applying the same fine lens, questioning the name Crater Lake for its misleading suggestion of volcanic activity, convinced its immediate surroundings did not disclose proofs of such an interference: 'Nearer lies the explanation that this basin has been formed rather by glacial than volcanic action.'[54]

Crater Lake, 1905 (Stephen Spurling)

Morning broke with the loud, harsh cry of the currawongs, the squawking of inquisitive parrots and the shrill call of white cockatoos. It was a perfect day. They took Smith's advice in choosing a path over the ridge between Crater Lake and Dove Lake on their way to the foot of the crag. Though the sky was clear, the temperature above would be nippy and conditions could change in a flash. Kate wore layers of woollen underwear beneath her ankle-length skirt, with a jacket over her long-sleeved blouse, a wide-brimmed hat and stout, leather lace-up boots. The men's trousers allowed for a freer stride, even with puttees protecting shins, their hobnailed leather boots coated in beeswax and fat scraped from animal hides to weatherproof them. They carried packs with a billy, bread, jam and tea for picnic stops along the way. Gustav—always at the helm, a step or three ahead—found the swiftest path up, warning the others of loose footholds as they clambered over stones that reminded them of broken earthenware crockery, halting occasionally to study a plant or gaze above at a white gull with a scarlet-coloured beak soaring in the sky. On the plateau, where they crowded around a cushion plant, Kate enthralled by its deceptive voluptuousness, one of the party fancifully suggested these plants were like upholstered poufs where the lofty spirits 'knelt in reverence to the silent mount's superior age'.[55]

Close up of a cushion plant mosaic

By noon the climbing demanded hands as well as feet over boulders that ranged in size 'from travelling trunks to house-like dimensions', proving troublesome to navigate.[56] Progress was thwarted by large crevices between the boulders, some of them iced slickly and impossible to grip, with none of the handrails often provided by tree branches or sturdy shrubs anchored to earth. Sometimes they retraced their steps only to find they'd abandoned a better track for a worse course.

Once over the lip of the crags, they rested below the saddle that gives the mountain its cradle before the final 100-foot climb up the south-eastern slope to the highest pinnacle. Collecting snow in the billy, they boiled water using bleached branches and roots from the sparse, low-growing vegetation for kindling. Gustav studied the rocks encircling them. There had been scant geological surveys of the region, with assumptions of Cradle's height largely guesswork, the history of its evolution untold. Over the decades ahead, science would fathom the miracle of dolerite found in South Africa, India, South America, Australia and Antarctica, through new discoveries about the fate of Gondwana. When the supercontinent broke apart, the immense strain on the earth's crust forced the intrusion of magma into thick sills between sequences of older rocks, eventually cooling to form the dolerite columns exposed through 180 million years of weathering and erosion. Gustav had long been intrigued by the riddle of flora shared by South America, Antarctica and Australia, proffering theories on ice drifts transporting seeds from one continent to another.[57] As they drank billy tea in the basin below the Cradle, he speculated on the fault lines calibrating a huge pillar of rock that stood 20 feet above its neighbours. Seismic disturbance had twisted upper sections of the rock, estimated to be 5 feet in diameter, on its axis, the breaks resembling the knuckled joints of a giant's finger.[58] Smith and Kate were distracted by grasshoppers and lizards in a search for wildlife on a day where the elements aligned, urging them onwards and upwards to the top.[59]

The men reached the summit first after a further hour of exertion, cheering Kate's arrival soon afterwards at the highest point, which was marked by the broken remains of the wooden trigonometrical station erected by surveyors in 1854. She must have relished the honour of beating her fair-skinned sisters to this rooftop. Even while hushed by an overwhelming sense of insignificance, there was exhilaration in the accomplishment, and she had thrice passed the test with Mt Buffalo,

View of Barn Bluff from Cradle's dolerite pillars

Mt Roland and now the Cradles, placing her in a league of one, the pride of her husband in their joint achievement meaning more than applause from any other quarter. Up this high, pulses racing from exertion, each was equal to the other.

They spent three hours identifying those peaks they knew, such as Barn Bluff, Black Bluff, Mt Roland and St Valentine's Peak, wondering at the others, squinting at the strip of Indian Ocean to the west and the blue of Bass Strait in the north, counting the lakes dotted about like tiny mirrors sewn into embroidered fabric. Gustav's enthusiasm bubbled in geyser spurts as he drew on their experience of Mt Buffalo to imagine how this great wilderness could be shared, for tourism, for science, for all. He tossed around ideas for a national park, an accommodation hostel, one idea on top of the other like the boulders of the crag they stood upon, overtaken by the urge to showcase what they could see, not simply for profit or personal gain, since their appreciation of the natural sciences dampened hubristic ambition in favour of the universal benefits.[60] The view was sublime, but far above the picturesque sway of this place was their sense of the knowledge embedded here.

Kate and Gustav had been shaped by a convergence of events and experiences not unlike the subterranean pressures altering the earth's crust, readying them for a vision others could not realise. Smith was sympathetic to the scheme outlined on the summit, while Black hung back, reticent, wondering how they would pay for the venture, his energies given to extracting ore from the ground. Tourism was barely an asterisk in the state's budget, its revenue columns entirely dependent on mining, timber and agriculture. Black's quizzical mindset was the majority view. Before leaving the mountain top, Smith took photographs. They each signed a piece of paper and put this record into a photographic film tin that they stuffed inside a crevice of the trig station's wooden base.[61] This was an occasion that warranted ceremony, however slight. The handful of white climbers who'd conquered the summit had come, then left, confident they would not forget what they saw from this peak, but had turned to other dreams, other mountains, the demands of careers and family. Smith and the Weindorfers could not leave it alone.

Instead of retracing their steps for a speedy descent, the party struck out in a westerly direction, determined to explore as much as they could of the surrounding topography before dark, Gustav's step springier than

usual, Kate behind him, swept along in his wake. Doubts that might
have flickered through her mind about the soundness of their plan or a
nagging suspicion the dream might subside once back on the lowlands
did not stand a chance. A man of action, Gustav sped forth, for if he'd
dithered on the journey he'd taken to this point, to this place in a
corner of a rugged island so far from his birthplace, he'd have missed
his window. The very next morning, he and Ron went searching for a
suitable site to build an accommodation house mirroring the hospices
he and Kate had seen at Buffalo.[62] On the north-west slope of Cradle
Valley stood a rocky rise overlooking open grassy country on one
side, a shadowy, moist forest of pine, myrtle and sassafras trees on the
other. A creek that would supply good water tinkled over rocks on
its way to the Dove River. Mentioning the stream in an article he
later wrote, Gustav quoted a verse by Alfred, Lord Tennyson: 'For men
may come and men may go but I go on forever.'[63] The veneration

Gustav and Ron Smith lugging packs to a hut outside Cradle Valley, 1910 (Ron Smith)

they'd felt up high strengthened in the days ahead as they bathed in the creeks and pools, rambling across vales and heathland, acquainting themselves with the smaller peaks nearby. Ron determined he'd buy land too. 'The mountains, the lakes, the valley and the surrounding forest with the great extent of Hounslow Heath nearby and Barn Bluff and other mountains within easy walking distance appeared to us to make the place ideal for spending a holiday,' Ron remembered of that day. 'We hoped the Government would eventually recognise its value to the state … and proclaim the place a national park. At the time we only thought of it including Cradle Mountain.'[64] Ron would not build on his land for another decade, but Gustav and Kate's haste was white hot, fired by the hospices, guides and transport services flourishing at Buffalo.

When Black departed, the trio walked with him as far as Dove River, where they caught an impressive haul of mountain trout. Secured to a string under water to stave off blowflies, the fish were almost snatched by a canny lobster missing one claw.[65] The days were hot, the nights warm. Ron killed a wombat near a pool they later named after the sturdy native, fashioning a very efficient Coolgardie safe out of a sugar bag and sticks hung on a branch to preserve the meat from flies. They skinned the animal, pegging its hide to the soft bark of a gum, declaring the meat 'tender, tasty, and satisfying'.[66] The freedom of self-sufficiency and a spell of fine weather emboldened their confidence in the mountain's embrace, chasing away the moodiness that settles under a lead-grey sky in dark, damp forest glades heavy with an ambiguous allure. When they passed near where Hanson's body was found, they dwelt on the uneasy truce between the mountain and those who roam there. 'Calm days little disclose to the unwary hunter the lurking dangers of these lofty heights, when nature's unchained forces drive home to man the iron fact that he is nothing but a transient atom in this great universe,' Gustav wrote.[67]

Finding themselves low on provisions, Ron tramped 9 miles through the bush to collect supplies they'd left behind at Fleece Creek—flour, sugar, tinned meat, jam and butter—and was delighted by the kindness of Kate and Gustav when they surprised him on his return with a picnic at the top end of Cradle Valley, where the tangled branches of the mountain beech join the stately sylvan pine. Below them the water from the lakes converged to flow through the valley, prompting Gustav

Gustav and Kate at camp near Crater Lake, 1910 (Ron Smith)

to ask whether mighty rocks now eroded by water or by glacial action once barred the escape of these waters.

They shifted camp to a hut outside the valley, where gaps in the walls and an opening above the doorway provided a little too much ventilation. Giant leeches burrowed through their socks on the walk there. The shack appeared to be free of resident critters, apart from a young tiger cat hiding under the floor, who gratefully accepted crumbs of cheese from Gustav before the trio tucked into a batch of fried 'puffalonies'—pancakes made from flour and water.[68] He and

Kate collected a vast array of specimens, as well as seedlings—native deciduous beech, King Billy pine and pandanifolia for planting at home to test their adaptability nearer the coast. After almost two weeks in the valley, Smith left for his Ulverstone farm at 6.15 am on a Tuesday morning, walking the Dove Valley track, which was wide enough for a loaded packhorse. This path had only recently been cleared by Wilmot farmer Bob Quaile, who owned a stock run at Daisy Dell, near Middlesex station. Yet another kindred spirit, his horsemanship and wagonette would later play a crucial role in conveying tourists, baggage and provisions through boggy terrain to the forest house already shimmering in the Weindorfers' thoughts. Smith took four hours to reach the Browns' homestead, where he'd left his bicycle, and another five hours to complete the 41-mile journey from the valley home to Westwood. Gustav had the cheek to celebrate the speed of Smith's return odyssey as 'surely exploding the idea so often met with, that the Cradle Mountains belong to an outlandish place far away from any civilisation'.[69]

When Tom Perry arrived by horse days later to collect the Weindorfers—hundreds of plant specimens carefully pressed, seedlings stowed—their reluctance to leave was salved by the promise of return. After overnighting with the Browns, they loaded the cart and hitched Jolly for the ride to Kindred, their hearts deep in an enchanted forest heaving with possibility. Thrown together by the jolts of ruts and rocks, they revisited the places they'd christened in a private iconography of trails and waterways from Wombat Pool to Brewery Creek. Kate's portfolios bulged with mosses and lichens gathered from ancient trunks of pine and myrtle; both of them wondered whether the native King Billy pine would flourish in a warmer bed; Gustav mused on the forbidding cliffs ringing Crater lake, imagining the slow-moving, rock-encrusted glaciers grinding valleys, scouring cavernous basins, the timelessness quietening them. The last verse of Henry Longfellow's 'Suspiria' skipped off his tongue:

> O great Eternity!
> Our Little life is but a gust,
> That bends the branches of thy tree,
> And trails its blossom in the dust.[70]

The silence between them was broken by thoughts that wouldn't be still, sketching a thousand different scenarios for the land they would buy, the guest house they would build, the logistics of managing the farm, the tracks they would blaze for tourists, the road that would surely be built, the wildlife they'd befriend on cold nights in front of a crackling fire. Convinced surveyors and government officials would see the merits of a destination that had captivated them, they counted the mainland naturalists who would be sure to visit their hideaway, not for a minute discouraged by the obstacles and the difficulties of this extraordinary venture, because whoever dares look down risks stumbling.

4

WELCOME TO COUNTRY

Truganini wore thin rags, her bare feet sinking through waist-deep snow drifts, when she struggled by Cradle Mountain to the Middlesex Plains with a small party of indigenous Tasmanians in 1834.[1] She'd helped persuade these north-western kinsmen to abandon hunting grounds at the behest of London-born George Augustus Robinson, a lay preacher and leader of the so-called 'Friendly Mission' bent on removing tribes of first peoples to Flinders Island for the purpose of 'civilising' them. Tiny in stature, with the tightly coiled hair that set Tasmanian Aboriginals apart from the mainlanders, Truganini is celebrated as a heroic warrior or less flatteringly cast as Robinson's patsy, promising her kin 'plenty damper, sugar, blanket' and the potent lure of protection from Governor Arthur's martial law to end hostilities between blacks and whites.[2]

Born and raised on Bruny Island off the state's south-east coast in the D'Entrecasteaux Channel, she'd witnessed a spate of unimaginable violence. Her mother had been murdered by whalers, her sister abducted into sexual slavery by sealers, her uncle shot by soldiers, and her betrothed murdered by timber-fellers who'd chopped off his hands with a hatchet.[3] She met Robinson in 1829 when she was eighteen and, with her husband Wooreddy, served as his guide and interpreter on fatiguing and perilous journeys like the one through Cradle Valley. Robinson's account of this expedition in a letter to Colonial Secretary John Burnett describes the reluctance of these poorly clad men and women to cross the mountains, where for seven days they travelled through snow, bitterly cold and miserable.[4]

Gustav Weindorfer knew this story. Years after his initial trip with
Kate to the summit of Cradle, he'd begun trawling through published
records to research the history of the highlands for the Launceston
Royal Society. Finding 'the material to hand was too meagre for such
a body', he'd abandoned the project, offering the bits of information
he'd dug up to Charles Whitham for a history of Western Tasmania
published in 1924.[5] He'd read *The Lost Tasmanian Race*, an account of
Robinson's mission published in 1870 by the compassionate teacher
turned author James Bonwick, who documented the deplorable treatment of indigenous people at the hands of settlers, whalers, courts,
police, governments and even Robinson, for the pilgrims experienced
'unwonted misery' on the 'frightful journey' around Cradle Mountain
in wintry depths. Gustav quoted Bonwick's description of Robinson's
passage through Cradle Valley in his covering letter to Whitham:
'the ill-clad, ill-fed, diseased and way worn men and women, including
the merry little Truganini, were sustained by the cheerful voice of their
unconquerable friend and responded most nobly to his call while their
legs as we are told were cruelly lacerated in threading the thorny scrub
and clambering the sharp rocks.'[6] The prickly scoparia that grows
on the slopes and the floor of the valley draws blood—Gustav once
described the plant's 'sharp pointed leaves' as 'man defying'.[7] More
concerned to pinpoint the route these travellers took—speculating the
party must have crossed at the top end of Cradle Valley or 2 miles lower
down by the Dove River—than to unpick the tragedy of their plight,
Gustav annotated the mention of Truganini with a joke: '(I understand
she was called 'queen' so you see I had royalty here before—GW)'.[8]

Bonwick had met Truganini (there are various spellings of her name)
in 1863, three decades after the last tribes were brought to Hobart:
'Her eyes were still beautiful and full of mischievous fun ... 30 years
earlier she would have been captivating to men of her colour and not
uninteresting to those of white skin. Her mind was no ordinary kind.
Fertile in expedience, sagacious in council, courageous in difficulty,
wisdom and fascination of the serpent, the intrepidity and nobility of
the royal ruler of the desert ... a savage maiden trained in wilderness ...
without doubt she was personally attached to Mr Robinson and strove
earnestly to serve him.'[9]

Robinson is painted as a thick-set man with florid complexion,
and though his conciliatory efforts to secure peaceful surrender came

from a good place, 'like any great or good man [he] had certain weaknesses of character' that truth compels the historian or biographer to confront.[10] Gustav too had many imperfections. He was a man at a time when males, even Europeans, were stiffly bound. His scientist's precision made him less disposed to deal with the mire of emotion. His lack of interest in the early occupants might also be understood through the prism of early twentieth-century ethnography, which cast natives as fossils. Evolutionary theorist Edward Tylor wrote them off as 'representatives of Palaeolithic man', while for naturalist John Lubbock, 'the Van Diemener and the South American are to the antiquary what the possum and sloth are to the geologist'.[11]

This derision infused *National Geographic*'s early coverage of Australia. A fan of the magazine, Gustav wouldn't have frowned at its focus on the country's flora and fauna in a 1916 edition titled 'Lonely Australia', where indigenous people were dismissed as 'a remnant of bygone days'. A photograph of 'South Australian black fellows' ran with the caption: 'These savages rank lowest in intelligence of all human beings.'[12]

It is strange all the same that a couple so curious about geology, history and botany did not search or wonder at the footprints of those who had visited Cradle Mountain tens of thousands of years before them. The forced removal of Tasmanian blacks wiped these first people from the consciousness of later generations, enabling a great forgetfulness. Archaeologists and anthropologists did not apply their carbon-dating tools to the caves and middens in the Central Plateau until the 1970s, discovering a Pleistocene site in the Forth River valley not far from Cradle Mountain, which proves a sequence of occupation from about 34,000 BCE, when glaciers existed on Cradle Mountain plateau only 3 kilometres away.[13]

Tasmania's indigenous people did not keep written records, save for the charcoal drawings on the roofs of their bark huts or the layers of animal bones, shells and thumbnail scrapers buried deep underground, telling us how and where they lived. Before Robinson's passage through these parts, surveyors and explorers like Henry Hellyer reported on the existence of indigenous inhabitants. Employed by the VDL Company to explore the north-west corner of the island, Hellyer tuned his antenna more to mineral and pastoral prospects and the tricky art of surviving in the wild than to signals from indigenous families rearing children and hunting for game. In a gripping account of climbing to the summit of St Valentine's Peak near Black Bluff in 1827, he describes coming into contact with these clans, though he did not see them in person: 'We found two native huts and marks of many fireplaces in the neighbourhood as if their spot had been lately occupied by a large body of natives. In one of the huts I saw a drawing of the moon done with charcoal upon the inside of one of the slabs of bark which formed the hut and regarding it as evidence of there being artists among them I cut out the piece and placed it carefully between two other pieces of bark in my knapsack. I sketched two figures of the moon with charcoal on the bark of the hut and put the date of my visit.'[14]

As he made his way north, crossing the Emu River, he glimpsed more huts, as well as trees from which bark had been stripped for shelter: 'We picked up green boughs by the embers of their fires that had not been gathered two days; we supposed they were not far off and might have used the boughs for mosquito fans. We saw several trees with steps cut in the bark and at twenty miles from the sea picked up the shells of very large lobsters and crayfish which they had roasted.'[15]

Fellow VDL surveyor Joseph Fossey, who travelled nearer Cradle Mountain, also met ample evidence of the first people's occupation when he mapped a road westward from Launceston through Hounslow Heath: 'From the numerous huts that present themselves it is a part of the country to which the natives frequently resort and on the heath I came so near them that I distinctly heard their call for the assembly of forces.'[16]

These reports were published in an 1832 history of VDL that concludes with an appendix of correspondence between Governor Arthur and his British masters agonising over how to manage increasing violence between white settlers and the original inhabitants: 'I cannot divest myself of the consideration that all aggression originated with the white inhabitants and that therefore much ought to be endured in return before the blacks are treated as an open and accredited enemy by the government.'[17] After wrestling with various solutions, all of them bound to fail, he noted that 'It is distressing and painful to banish the natives from their favourite haunts', but ultimately this is what he did, commissioning Robinson to round up stragglers in the hope that if they were segregated and 'civilised', then survival may follow.[18] But dismal Flinders Island was no sanctuary, and the blankets and shelter were never going to shield them from disease or give them a reason to thrive. Those who endured were later settled at Oyster Cove, near Hobart, until they also perished. Truganini died in 1876.

Gustav was familiar with the VDL history since he'd cited its report of the road through Hounslow Heath in his letter to Whitham, but he made no reference to the surveyors' reports of the blacks who lived here, being more interested in the tracks the company had laid than the men and women pushed out by the wheels of the carts. He'd also read the botanist-explorer Daniel Bunce's 1854 'Reminiscences of Twenty-Three Years' Wanderings in Tasmania', where the pages on journeying by the Cradles through to Middlesex Plains described a remarkable indigenous rendering of two VDL oxen carts that had travelled this road: 'It appears some natives had observed this and a short time afterwards one of the company's servants passing that way found in one of their crudely constructed huts a piece of the bark off a tree with a rough drawing of the whole scene. The wheels of the carts, the bullocks, and drivers with whips over their shoulder all distinctly depicted in their rude but interesting manner.'[19]

Again Gustav chose to edit this anecdote from the bibliographical summary he forwarded to Whitham, citing only Bunce's descriptions of landscape punctuated by 'two remarkable high points one of which is called Ribrock and the other Barn Bluff', his postscript explaining in brackets that Ribrock must be Cradle Mountain.[20]

Nevertheless, the Weindorfers were more keenly aware of our indigenous heritage than most Australians in the early twentieth century. Kate had collected Tasmanian Aboriginal flints, which she had exhibited at a Naturalists Club meeting in Melbourne. Others brought along a pair of corroboree sticks from Victoria's Western District, a stone tomahawk from Gippsland, a rock found under the skull of an Aboriginal near Hamilton, and a message stick from north-western Australia. These relics, plucked on botanical rambles, were presented as a record of the past rather than as testimony of a living culture.[21] The couple became friends with Clive Lord, director of the Tasmanian Museum, where curators put Truganini's skull on show, ignoring a plea she'd made before her death. Exhibited from 1904 to 1947, the display encapsulated a view of first peoples as an extinct species.[22]

Enthralled by a glacial landscape formed millions of years before humans had set foot there in an incomprehensibly vast chronology that collapses black then white occupation into a blink, Kate and Gustav could not see the people for the trees. Gustav saw man as a transient atom in this timeless place. But our guilt and regret and remembrance scratch for attention, raising questions about the people who walked in the mountains before them, because ignorance is no longer an excuse. Whenever I speak of the Weindorfers' accomplishments, listeners frequently ask about the first inhabitants. Although Gustav and Kate appeared to give slight consideration to the earliest visitors before Truganini's traverse, he at least studied nineteenth-century documents to get a fix on who had been there and when, conveniently sidestepping the emotional maelstrom of their abuse because this was a fact he could not alter and was not drawn to dwell upon.

There is also the aftertaste of his father's activities in the late nineteenth century as a senior servant of the German East Africa Company swiping land from African chiefs with a similar bag of bribes, only they were beads and silk instead of blankets and damper. Gustav rarely mentioned his father's colonial scramble for African territory, according to Smith, who spent long days in his company, knowing little more than the vague fact of Johann's engagement in Zanzibar.[23] He cared more for exploring glacial footprints, the region's botanical heritage or the route Truganini took. There is little in his diaries or her letters to suggest that the Weindorfers encountered any clues in the landscape hinting at the customs and rituals of the Cradles' former occupants. The heavily timbered forests that grew over former sedge land when the ice melted greatly reduced the game available for hunting, while the cold alpine heights were hostile hunting grounds, encouraging a pattern of seasonal visits on the journey between coast and hinterland.

Many years after the 1910 camping expedition that led the Weindorfers to build a home in the valley, Gustav and Smith went out exploring at a high elevation on the forest-covered south-east slope of Perry's Peak. They kept to the short, low, rocky ridges where the vegetation was not as dense, until they came upon a small ledge 3–4 feet wide, sheltered from weather by an overhanging rock. Inside, lying a little away from the rock wall, was an old trunk of a tree fern, which they thought to be *Dicksonia antarctica*, a few feet in length, less than a foot in diameter, worn smooth on one side. The ledge terminated and they were forced to retrace their steps, finding another route home, both puzzling in the months and years afterwards as to how the tree fern got to this place so high up, since none grew there, even at lower

Cradle seen from Truganini Point, on the shores of Dove Lake, 1929 (Gustav Weindorfer)

levels: 'and it was equally hard to imagine that any human would do such a pointless thing as carry the trunk for miles and put it there in the dense forest.'[24] The possibility this ledge had sheltered indigenous visitors was not even contemplated. This spot was roughly 3 miles distant from the chalet Gustav and Kate built in the valley, but Smith was never able to find it again, despite numerous attempts to hazard his way back through dense forest and broken country.

From the Cradle summit overlooking Lake Wilks and Dove Lake (J. G. Branagan)

In Truganini, these white custodians at least had a presence to salute, even though she hailed from the coastal south of the state. Gustav kept alive the account of her passage through the valley, weaving the story into his encyclopaedic commentary whenever he accompanied visitors on walks, alerting journalists, such as *Daily Post* editor Leonard Hubbard, to Robinson's account to give it wider public currency.[25] His precocious decision to name a landmark in her honour, many decades before the nation sought to atone for our sins, was gracious and respectful. Truganini Point lies beyond Glacier Rock on Dove Lake. Gustav christened knolls and tarns in an egalitarian spirit, choosing to distinguish veteran guides, surveyors and pioneers, dear family members and friends, visitors who followed long after the first people but who loved this land just the same and kept their footprint almost as small.

5

FOREST HOME

Kate pressed her nose against the window of the carriage, willing the gauzy fog to lift so that the mountains might declare themselves as the train snaked south-west towards the Tasmanian port of Strahan. She was adventuring with sister Laura on a rare trip, just the two of them. If the weather calmed enough, they would ride a motor launch around the sweeping bends of the Gordon River, curious to see a wilderness they'd heard spoken of with hushed rapture. At every stop, someone they knew clambered aboard—the wife of the geologist at Mt Lyell mine returning from Melbourne with her three children, then Bishop Mercer, who was in a hurry to find a seat. Beyond the platforms, the waratah, sassafras, pines and deciduous beech with their bright-red new growth were even older acquaintances Kate nodded to as the train flew past, too fast for her to identify the only stranger in a wild gully far below. In a letter written to Gustav from the Bay View Hotel the morning after they'd disembarked in pouring rain, she described the mystery plant as 'a fairly high tree with yellow spikes, either of buds or flowers'. 'I was wishing you had been with us but you would have wanted to get out and walk and explore,' she teased, wiser now to his restless ways, but feeling his absence. 'I miss you dreadfully.'[1]

Walking about Strahan on this misty December morning in 1911, she imagined she was in the Cradles, the undulating countryside patched with buttongrass, aromatic boronia and prickly heath reminding her of the mountain valley where they would start building an accommodation house in the new year. This was now their offspring, every vista described in terms of its likeness to stretches of the country they were getting to know intimately, so that Guildford Junction, where the train idled briefly, was similar to Middlesex Plains, 'the same gum trees in clusters and copses with waratah, needlebush, pink mountain berry and thousands of daisies'.[2] Promenading along the Strahan esplanade, the sisters were invited to tea by the wealthy merchant Frederick Ormiston Henry and his family, who'd cashed in Mt Lyell shares to erect a grand Federation brick home set on 5 acres overlooking the bay with a tower and widow's walk. Kate was more impressed with his case of butterflies and minerals and the native plants in the garden, since she and Gustav were on a mission to spread indigenous flora through beds and plots everywhere.[3] Two years earlier, he'd written to *The Australasian* of his success at Kindred transplanting native trees and acacia from seeds and saplings collected on bush rambles, promising readers that their beauty outrivalled many exotics. 'The pity is … that we Australians often regard our native flora as weeds and a nuisance, that we pay high prices for imported plants or rather aliens which in many cases in their native lands are nothing more than weeds,'

Gordon River (Stephen Spurling)

he chided.[4] Once an alien himself, he'd sunk his roots into our soil so comprehensively he felt beholden to awaken fellow countrymen and women to home-grown beauty, as Baron von Mueller had done before him. Outsiders had a paradoxical knack for lifting European scales from our eyes.

Strahan's Bay View Hotel belonged then to Danish-born, German-educated entrepreneur Louis Emil Sadewasser, who owned the launch the sisters hoped to ride down the Gordon River once the weather cleared. Sadewasser, like Gustav, had quickly become a civic prod in his small Tasmanian community, winning a seat on the local council, using his craft for search and rescue, ferrying tourists and parliamentary delegations, and hosting official receptions for visiting dignitaries in the formal rooms of his imposing two-storey hotel.[5] In March 1909, he'd squired the Liberal leader, Alfred Deakin, through the unspoiled beauty of the King River Gorge in the gentle light of the morning sun.[6] J. W. Lindt, Louis Sadewasser and Gustav Weindorfer enticed us into our backyard, awestruck by the scenic grandeur lying fallow. The Gordon's serpentine course through wild forests and fern glades seduced early tourists. 'Wait till you have seen the Gordon!' one traveller gushed of the boughs bending marvellously low from the mighty banks as if to kiss their reflection in the stream. A decade into the twentieth century, chafing tensions between the timber-getters and the nature-lovers were barely discernible above the silent coursing of water and the plash of a silvery tail rippling its skin.

The success of Sadewasser's business must have heartened Kate and Gustav as they prepared to turn the first sod of Cradle earth. They had no blueprint beyond Gustav's experience of Austrian alpine chalets, their knowledge of Lindt's Hermitage and their exposure to the Buffalo hospices. Neither of them had hospitality training, though Gustav had served briefly as a waiter at the German Club in Melbourne. He would be architect and builder, while Kate would run the farm, which they'd keep initially as collateral on a line of credit, renting for a period before selling eventually when tourism earned them an income to rival the price of potatoes and oats. The couple would charge for accommodation, meals and the services of Gustav as guide and packhorse, carting luggage in and out of the valley, while guests would be required to bring nothing more than warm clothes, stout boots and a pair of legs. This was the plan. Its execution, though, was tested.

Soon after Kate's return to Kindred, her husband set off for a solo trip up the mountain. He would ready the site they had chosen on the north-western slope of the valley where they would labour and sweat to birth their pioneering start-up. Interrupted only by the vagaries of snow and rain or the urge for a smoke, Gustav seldom paused to rest, excavating foundations, judiciously selecting trees and fallen logs of King Billy pine to split into palings by hand. Every task was executed laboriously, with tools and materials that could be slung over a pack-horse along the 4-mile track from the valley's entrance. Even before the stillness of the valley rang with the blow of axe and hammer, the couple were becoming known for their botanical expertise and daring embrace of a remote corner of wilderness. Letters arrived from Lebrina in Tasmania, where the former Kindred schoolteacher William Carnie had been posted, wanting identification of a plant he'd not seen before, while another missive came by sea from Cambridge, Massachusetts, headquarters of emerging botanist Frieda Cobb, who begged seedlings and samples of the roots and trunks of varieties of deciduous beech growing on the north-west coast.[7]

Kate signed up for Gustav's absences when his lips first caressed her hand. Standing in one spot was physically uncomfortable for this peripatetic wayfarer. While she was content initially to give him a long rope, neither of them had expected that patterns of togetherness would be pared into solitary periods that were easier for him than for her, since every day spun with the promise of tomorrow, while she muddled through familiar routines at a place she'd known since a girl, managing a cantankerous farmhand resentful of her authority. This was the unavoidable seesaw of matrimony. She surely could have learnt to split palings straighter than the labourers Gustav borrowed from Bob Quaile or the Browns at Middlesex, but given the scope of the grunt work required in this rough country, he was the sturdier bet. They wrote to each other almost daily, her letters delivered to Middlesex station or the packing-case post office nailed to a tree near Daisy Dell, updating him on the sale of their white giant oats, the rollcall of neighbours ill from diphtheria, the recalcitrance of the farmhand and the antics of animals wild and tame, all of whom they adored: Jolly their horse, cunning in her way; kelpies Bixie, Fuschs and Flock, who stayed with one or other of them whenever the couple were apart; the birds they imagined as winged couriers, singing telegrams to Gustav at Cradle or visiting Kate

Gustav and his dog Flock (Fred Smithies)

in her Kindred garden. 'An Egypt came quite close to me yesterday and I think brought me a message from you,' she wrote.[8]

His horizons had broadened beyond the straightening of the farm, whereas her focus centred on courtesies and pleasantries she'd be glad to relinquish once the chalet opened for business. In January 1912, she informed him that the rector had asked whether Gustav would be attending Sunday service to meet the new curate. 'I felt constrained to go,' she conceded, oiling the mechanics of community—a duty from which he'd been spared. Noticing the curate and his wife looking forlorn, she'd stepped in: 'No-one having asked them to dinner, so of course I did.'[9] Her letters to him have been preserved, while his correspondence to Kate has vanished, though his daily diary entries shed a light on life in the valley, and his voluminous exchanges with Ron Smith, a compulsive archivist, reveal much of what he thought and did. A tinge of sadness crept into her confessions these first months they spent apart, particularly when night fell with no children underfoot to distract her from her longing for him. She invited the nearest neighbour, Irene Medwin, for company. 'I stayed alone until Friday and then got tired of the silence of the house after dark so sent a note to her to come over in the evening. She came promptly and goes home during the day after helping me milk in the morning.'[10] Kate had not expected to live alone as a married woman. Sister Laura made do with a self-contained apartment attached to the home of their married sister Blanche, connecting her to the squeals of nephews and nieces. Kate had brother Dan and sister-in-law Marion close by, but she missed Gustav, the intimacy, the banter, and his sonorous baritone accompanying her piano whenever they made music together. His isolation was greater, though she felt the lonelier at Roland Lea, for despite community, family and neighbours in the vicinity, she was without her 'dear boy' for weeks on end. When the Weindorfers searched for a housekeeper several years later, there were no takers because eligible candidates balked at the lack of transport connecting Kindred with nearby towns.[11]

Their unusual arrangement intrigued many in the district, who were perplexed by what on earth this couple had found up there to warrant enduring the discomfort, the cold and the separation anxiety. The value of gold or tin or even possum skins they understood precisely, but the wild with its scenic and scientific wealth filled no columns in their ledger. Gustav was shielded from the glances and raised eyebrows Kate met from shopkeepers, members of the congregation and the local busybodies who left grubby fingerprints on envelopes as clumsy proof they'd tampered with the couple's handwritten confidences: 'Laura says all the letters they received from me while at Waldheim were either quite open or horribly dirty with finger marks where they had been opened and stuck down again. I wonder why they are treated so—someone must be very inquisitive.' The Kindred farmhand made known his bafflement at the master's absence. 'It beats him how you can stay out there all alone,' Kate briefed Gustav. 'He would not care to stay a day alone out there.'[12]

Bushmen like Walter Malcolm Black were in on the secret: 'I note you are going to make the mountains home, a place of delight among the winter months and there is no reason why a person should not be just as comfortable there and less circumscribed than in the suburban portions of smellful cities or in the uninteresting outskirts of rural ones.'[13] Black belonged to an unincorporated brotherhood of believers who mainlined the opiate of nature. The Weindorfers befriended them one by one as they slowly announced themselves and their plans, with several of these new friends becoming pivotal to the fledgling forest enterprise.

Waldheim porch under snow, 1929 (Gustav Weindorfer)

Beside herself with anticipation, Kate counted the sleeps in child-like fashion until the day she would join her 'boy', making lists of the articles he'd requested—flour, carbide, nails, bread, fat that she'd rendered, blankets, bacon, tins of powdered milk, vegetables pulled from the Kindred garden. Always 'hungry for news of you', she watched the distant skies to keep track of the mountain's weather. 'I knew you were having plenty of snow because it was quite low down on Roland, Claude and Bluff, and today the Cradle looked like a white mound.' The kink of her widow's walk meant she could see the heights he roamed from her lowland perch. 'I let Flock smell your letter and she licked it all over. She is a dear little companion, follows me everywhere.' Flock's presence at her feet conjured her husband. 'I should be lonely without her. It is nice to feel there is some living thing full of affection to welcome me in the morning and follow me all day … It seems such a long time since I heard your voice. With heaps of love, ever your affectionate Kate.'[14]

By December of 1912, the chalet was sound enough to receive a handful of visitors, including Ron Smith and Kathleen Carruthers, who had recently married. Watertight but still draughty, it comprised three rooms: a large open-plan living and dining area, and two bedrooms. The shared space was so cavernous that several pine logs propped the ceiling to prevent it from sagging. At its heart was the mighty fireplace, not yet finished, so they sat on the floor dangling their feet into the pit below for warmth.[15] Two small bedrooms and a hut slept up to ten people in bunks and on chaff-bag stretchers that were heaven compared with camping on hard ground. Hefty blocks of wood had been cut into chairs. Smith recalled that there was plenty of food and firewood so that everyone was warm and nourished, most of all Kate and Gustav.

Smith and his wife struck out one day for the southern slope of Mt Campbell, east of Dove Lake, where Bert Hanson had died seven years earlier, his headstone a cairn of rocks. Poking around nearby, they found the skull of the dog that had refused to leave the trapper's side. In a story that had riveted Tasmanians, the kelpie's loyalty shone out, epitomising the trueness of such an animal, so contrary to human self-interest. While the loyal kelpie had perished, Hanson's mate had staggered on for help, becoming the sole survivor. Smith brought the smooth white grail of bone home with him, quietened by the thought that not a soul had visited the monument in the seven years since the lad's demise: 'And what a change from our sad thoughts when we returned to the cheerful warmth and flickering light of the great fire in the fireplace at Waldheim and the hot coffee, already an institution and Weindorfer's cheerful conversation and active movements as he busied himself helping his wife who was equally busy and cheerful.'[16] The lighthearted banter of Gustav and Kate fixing meals and catering for their guests was a yin to the yang of inhospitable weather. No sooner had the first lot of friends gone than another party descended, among them the Tasmanian surveyor Joseph Wilks and his wife Edith, who became the fourth white woman to reach the summit. Word was spreading through the scientific community. The couple started to receive a trickle of letters from botanists, biologists and ornithologists interested in their bush laboratory.[17]

These were glorious months of promise as Gustav's head spun with plans for improvements and extensions. Kate loved being there, handing him shingles for the gabled roof, watching him work, salving a splintered thumb, rustling up treats for them to savour during rest breaks. As the day for her departure loomed, she couldn't hide a wistfulness settling inside of her. They would be parted for two months as Gustav battened down and completed finishing touches before the onset of winter. In late May he scribbled a diary entry in German acknowledging his wife's melancholic mood, which he hoped to remedy by bringing her with him to the Cradles more often.[18]

Wald is German for forest, while heim means home. The English language has no equivalent compound noun. The couple christened the chalet in his mother tongue to accentuate the foreignness of an enterprise that was neither hospice nor hostel nor hotel, as Australians called these lodgings. Lindt had chosen 'The Hermitage' for its reassuring appeal to local patrons. The name 'Waldheim' foreshadowed a tilt towards the European recreations of hiking, skiing, bobsleighing and skating in a vast outdoor arena where health, wellbeing and physical activity were an intrinsic part of a holiday package. Architecturally the chalet resembled Austrian alpine dwellings with its steep-pitched shingled roof and decorative sapwood fretwork. If this at first seemed discordant with the Australian wilderness, the palings—initially pink in appearance, the sapwood trim paler still—soon weathered grey, blending into the surrounding copse of native conifers. Fashioned from the forest's King Billy pines, the building grew as if it were a third cousin of the trees that prospered there. The glass in the windows was the only visible manufactured material. Upright trunks robed in bark stood as pillars, three on either side of the standalone porch, weaving classical elements of design into the façade. Smaller saplings had been whittled and pinned to form a diamond frieze adorning the exterior.

Inside, the struts and beams and walls were knotted boughs. The ambience, even in these early days, sang of warmth, cosied by their chattels; books, gramophone records and periodicals were always in evidence, as were sprigs of nature—seedlings and feathers plucked by the botanists to dry or to study. As one guest declared of this finely

Waldheim grew into its forest bower, with a fenced garden sprouting cabbage-sized lettuces.

crafted abode, 'Waldheim is like nothing on earth.'[19] This Austro–
Australian hybrid was endemic to Cradle, much like the King Billy
itself. 'Instead of the usual painted box with tin roof and unsightly
milieu we have here an artist's fabric,' another visitor wrote admiringly.
The Weindorfers' creation had a personality that spoke of the forest and
the midwifery of the couple responsible for its birth. In their words,
'Waldheim is not to be mentioned in the same breath as the usual barn
that goes under the name of accommodation.'[20]

For the mantelpiece, Gustav hove a solid pine plank 3 inches thick.

Gustav and Kate planned to open for business in December 1913.
After wintering at the farm, they could not wait to get busy for their
debut season, riding to the valley together—their mood joyous, the
cart groaning with provisions. His diary entry for the day of departure
twice records the fact this was a 'glorious day'.[21] They stayed overnight
at Moina with William Hitchcock and his wife Caroline, the managers
of the Bismuth mine who were becoming fast friends, part of the
bush fraternity of men and women loosely connected by the tourism
venture sprouting in their midst. The wives in particular yearned for
female company. Caroline Hitchcock, like Louisa Brown at Middlesex,
welcomed Kate's visits, bringing news that didn't register with the
men or a bouquet from her garden at Roland Lea. For six and a half
weeks, Gustav worked fiendishly, expanding the original structure to
eight rooms. With the hut for spillover, they could now sleep sixteen
comfortably. He fitted shelves and a cupboard in the kitchen; hung
bedroom doors; roofed the porch; sealed holes and cracks in the double
walls; secured spouting for water collection; and finished the chimney,
resourcefully using flattened petrol tins to fireproof the timber flue.[22]

For the mantelpiece, Gustav hove a solid pine plank 3 inches thick.
Each end was supported by three trunks, bark intact. Large stones
smoothed by the river were laid around the hearth to announce the
bedrock of communal gatherings. Kate softened the interior with
cushions she'd stitched, tidying the cupboards for crockery and cutlery;
fistfuls of lemon boronia or whatever was in season sprouted from two
brass vases at either end of the mantel, which soon became crammed
with small things: photographs, bird bones, china ornaments. In the new
bunkrooms, Gustav stretched wire over the beds for mattress support.
He split more shingles, built a kennel for the dogs and cleared a narrow
track from the entrance of the valley to their doorstep, signposted by
white crosses on trees.[23]

The inglenook fireplace

Kate's fiftieth birthday dawned on 19 July, with knee-deep snow and a bare pantry. Despite strenuous hunting expeditions around the valley, they had no meat until Gustav snared a ringtail possum on the evening of the next day.[24] The art of nesting absorbed them completely. They took long walks through the valley getting acquainted with every clump and spinney and stone. When he trudged to the station or further across the plains to the mail tree, Kate kept house or went on botanical saunters with a dog for company. The collection of firewood was a constant imperative, as was hunting, the skins sold while the meat was stewed for dinner. Nothing was wasted, not petrol cans or string or jam tins.

At the end of July, in the thick of winter, Kate dragged herself towards the day of her departure. She hated leaving. Perhaps she had a sixth sense of life's precariousness, for this was as close to the clouds as she'd soared. Here they were in a botanist's paradise, living on the edge, snug at night, miles from another soul, alone with their thoughts, their private patois, their jokes and each other. They loaded the plant specimens and seedlings they'd collected over weeks of rambles and rounded up the dogs for the walk to Middlesex, where the horse and cart were stabled. Overnighting with the Browns, they parted the next morning, Kate in a loaded cart bound for Wilmot, with Bixie on board. He kept Flock, traipsing the whole day to Waldheim's door, where his mood slumped as he cleaned up, cooked, chopped wood, pegged out the skins of possums and a tiger cat, and resumed making the stairs to their porch. 'Camp dull and lonely without Kate,' he wrote in a rare admission of blue.[25] The wind howled through the mountains that night, but he hadn't an inkling of the ferocious storm about to hit Wilmot as Kate left Tilley's Coffee Palace for the last leg of her trip home.

'I had only gone a few miles when I encountered one of the worst storms I have ever been out in,' she wrote later. Gale-force winds and pelting rain caused havoc throughout the north of the state: power went out; the Mersey River flooded; boisterous waves swamped Devonport, smashing the SS *Oonah*'s bow into the timber pier, damage bills tallied everywhere.[26] Kate had survived storms on Mt Roland, even Mt Buffalo, but driving a horse and cart through the eye of this one proved her stoicism. 'Leaves and limbs were blowing about and every moment I expected a tree on me as they were rocking and swaying.' She caught up with the salesman for Singer sewing machines, who was 'awfully scared', and the two of them went along together, Kate's hands aching raw with the strain of checking Jolly's bolt, helping each other around two trunks blown like toothpicks across their path.[27] She was drenched through and glad to pull in to Ron and Kathleen Smith's house at Westwood for a hot meal of baked lamb and apple pie. The next day at the farm she reported trees strewn everywhere, fences down, newly ploughed paddocks in a mess. She aired her wet things in front of the fire Gustav had laid ready for her before they'd left. The house reeked of mice, and their cat Bobbie was plump from the cull. 'I got such a longing for a cup of coffee that I ground some beans through the mincer', his ritual now hers, the aroma and taste of his brew bringing him physically close to her, a reminder whenever she flagged after these solo trips of how lucky she was to have a life aloft with him.[28] His German words now part of her vocabulary, she told him she had 'been living on eggs and *schwarm* ... I wish my boy was here. Heaps of love Kate. P.S. I heard lots of pretty chicks singing in Quaile's land away in a gully when I had a last look at the Cradle from the hill this side of Bull Plain.'[29]

The month of August seemed interminable. Kate couldn't keep the tears from her eyes when after almost two weeks of silence she held a letter from him in her hands. Sitting on the steps in the sun to read it through twice, she felt 'a little nearer to you and it was nice to know what you did each day'. Neighbours were solicitous. Mr Jensen gave her three large rock cod—'but I could not enjoy them for wishing you were here'—and a magazine with news of the discovery by an American archaeologist of the lost Incan city of Machu Picchu in Peru.[30] Bixie was not faring well. Kate worried he was too old and stiff for the mountain winters. But the acacia in her birthday garden was a picture, and she'd begun making lists of all he'd need when she next came, several items requiring trips in the cart to Ulverstone. The farmhand was down with mumps; she'd oiled the harness and washed the cart; the fowls were laying erratically, producing five eggs one day, none the next. Vegetable beds needed weeding. 'I do not know where to start first … scents of violets, Boronia and acacia intoxicating but it seems sad without my dear boy.' She sewed mattress ticking for the beds at Waldheim; the animal skins had been dried 'carefully' ready for sale, and not one was mildewed.[31] She'd done Frank Brown's skins too. He'd been good to them and one favour deserved another. When loneliness sharpened the thorn of his absence, she'd reach for her music. 'Today has been a dull miserable day. I felt so sad missing my dear boy that I went to the piano to try to cheer myself up.' She played Beethoven or Brahms and the Austrian songs now part of her repertoire, imagining his fine voice holding the tune. 'Well I must say goodnight to my dear, dear boy; how I wish he could be beside me. With heaps of love from your loving wife Kate. P.S. The little sassafras is blossoming beautifully.'[32]

Gustav smarted at the solitude too. Cabin fever brought on by incessant rain, warm melting snow and the dregs of winter sloshed through August's veins. He baked a 'brownie' with cocoa and flour and soda, proud of his culinary skills. Never short of chores or the urge to do them, he pegged skins and fussed over fiddly interior jobs, always reading to escape his confinement, 'snow melting, slush, mush, dirt, wet rain everywhere'.[33] He visited the station for company, meeting Black, who was in search of the same. Quaile's man Jim Rowlands came to help; two men from Lorinna appeared in the valley in search of pine, and they invited them to stay overnight, visitors a treat.

Inclement weather forced Kate to delay her departure, with everything packed and ready to go: nails, blankets, fresh bread, even a pollard cake for Flock that she'd made, hoping 'little Flick Flock has

Forest home, 1922 (Stephen Spurling)

not forgotten me'. There were flowers for Mrs Hitchcock, 'some salad greens for you', her maternal instincts showered on others with these small gestures. The squaring of her shoulders was just as necessary a preparation for this journey along unmade roads through stretches of silent country. She feared fresh snow covering the ground might lead her astray on the approach to Middlesex station—'I had been rejoicing over the warm rain yesterday'—but the longing to see and to hold 'my dear boy' overwhelmed any qualms at setting out. 'It seems such a long time that we parted.'[34]

A general store had opened in the tiny dot of Wilmot, the last township on the road to Cradle, selling ironmongery, drapery, boots, clover seeds, shelves of every product on a farmer's list. Commercial newcomers to the district were further spokes in the primitive tourism wheel, connecting one outpost to another, abridging the distance for travellers by breaking it down into friendlier chunks. '*Marcus maxim lavat*', Gustav wrote in a draft for the first tourism brochure to be published by the Tasmanian government, muddling the Latin proverb *manus manim lavat*, 'one hand washes the other'. But his translation captured the gist: 'One hand makes the other said the old Romans and so it is with the tourist trade.'

Naturalist friends from Melbourne played their part, volunteering as guinea pigs for the opening season. Dr Charles Sutton and George and Una Coghill, who went on the Buffalo camp-out, confirmed they were

coming in January 1914. Kate sent them details of how to get there—
the train from Devonport to Railton, a coach to Sheffield, and coach to
Wilmot, where the Tilleys were on hand to convey them for a fee via
horse and trap to the Middlesex station. From here they would walk
the last 6 miles. 'I did not mention our price as I thought we might
want to make a reduction for friends and I suppose we will not charge
the doctor at all unless he insists on paying,' she told Gustav.[35] Tariff
rates were set initially at 8 shillings per night for board and lodging,
2 shillings for Gustav's service as guide, and another 5 shillings each way
if he carted luggage, limited to 200 pounds, from Pencil Pine Creek.

Dr Sutton had been to the Tasmanian Government Tourist Bureau's
Melbourne office to appraise them of Waldheim and the Weindorfers;
staff there had no idea of the chalet's existence.[36] News filtered slowly
as railways and government agencies cottoned on to brochures and
guidebooks encouraging traffic to scenic destinations. This was the
point of Gustav's Latin phrase. He most needed the hand of government for advertising. The couple approached the Hobart photographic
studio of Spurling & Son to purchase their hand-coloured postcards of
Cradle Mountain.

Stephen Spurling III, the young scion, had taken the pictures that
had seized Gustav's attention in 1905. Spurling's father, who ran the
studio, was delighted to hear of their tourism venture and requested
particulars 'as we occasionally get inquiries from people desirous of
making a trip'.[37] His enthusiasm was qualified by his knowledge of the
effort required to land there: 'You seem to have made the path smooth
enough for the mountaineering class of tourist and we will do our best
to send along any who may have a fancy to see this beautiful locality.'[38]

This was the fine line they straddled in their mountain eyrie.
Mountaineers and botanists primed for rough conditions would come
regardless, but how to entice the rest? Pencilling notes on the back of
an International Harvester catalogue, Gustav and Kate tentatively conceded the spurs of journeying to Waldheim as they polished the plusses
in their draft for the government's proposed promotional booklet:
'Cradle Mountain district is not the place for holiday makers intent on
lazing away the days in easy chairs with books and iced drinks. Rather
it is a spot for those whose energetic souls long for a brief respite from
the cares of civilisation and the daily newspapers and to spend their
holiday in the wholesome open air among unspoilt nature. For those

whose bent is walking … there are no made roads and one direction is as good as another.'[39] The bracing and exhilarating highland air 'much appreciated for its stimulating effect on the respiratory organs' was an ambrosial tonic that could be inhaled from the slopes or the valleys depending on the visitor's appetite for exertion in 'virgin' territory, 'untouched by human hands'.

'The creeks and lakes are full of native trout which being utterly unsophisticated fall victim to the fisherman who can if he be an artist set to work with the finest of tackle and enjoy the delight of scientifically playing his fish.' Summer's climate of hot days and cool nights promised flowering alpine meadows and clear, smooth lakes with sandy shores for picnics and bathing. In autumn shooters would find 'game aplenty', with kangaroos, wallaby, wild duck and wattle birds, 'but it is not organised slaughter for the hunter must be prepared for some rough scrambles'. Those brave enough for the rigours of winter could sample snow-shoeing or skiing, the 'effortless swing and glide over an unbroken surface of crisp snow and the music of the skis as they break through the crust with their peculiar creaking noise' a novelty, while

On top, 1911 (*left to right* Gustav, Kathleen Carruthers, Dr Charles Sutton, Kate) (Ron Smith)

long, sweeping hills were 'unrivalled for lugeing or bob sleighing', and for the skater there were 'shallow reed fringed pools covered with smooth clear ice'.[40]

Guests unafraid of heights could clamber upwards to the rocky, windswept plateaus then surge for the peak: 'The access is easy and practically free of dangers (except for those who look for them).' As if to counter Spurling's concern that Waldheim was a niche destination for summiteers, the draft brochure assured its prospective readers that even the most formidable-looking crags of Cradle had been conquered 'by ladies who had never before accomplished any mountaineering feat'. From the top, the visitor enjoyed a panorama of lofty mountains—Barn Bluff, the Ducane Range, Mt Pelion—'alternating with yawning abysses and densely wooded valleys'. Here was the birthplace of the great rivers—the Fury, Pieman, Forth—roaring towards the north-west and western coasts. The 'geologist, naturalist and scientist' were summonsed to 'a district of remarkable interest' where they could feast on species endemic to the western highlands and the dolerite rock of the Precambrian era. They could trace glaciers' footprints in mirrored tarns, sombre gorges and moraines, 'these silent witnesses of the everlasting force of nature'.[41]

Deft at fudging the negatives, the couple deleted a paragraph mentioning the harsher climate in winter, when 'harmless little streams' swelled to 'raging torrents which not being bridged only experienced buccaneers are able to ford safely'. Best not to frighten the skittish. 'Up to recent times a man setting out to the Cradle Mountain was anxiously expected to return,' they conceded, allowing a curt bow to Bert Hanson's surrender to hostile extremes. His memory would not daunt their efforts to inflame yearnings for the wilderness stretching in every direction beyond Waldheim's front door, while once inside there was no wanting for comfort. Here 'is the last word in luxury', they purred. 'Even the most fragile visitor could not complain of having to rough it here.' Why then had nobody thought of welcoming tourists here before? they asked rhetorically. 'The answer is simple because there was no one there who had the daring thought to enter upon a business which up until now was fraught with failure. But the tide has turned.'[42]

Kathleen Carruthers and Gustav gaze at Barn Bluff from the Cradle summit, 1911 (Ron Smith)

Like any start-up partnership, optimism billowed their sails, a can-do spirit keeping the craft buoyant. Exhilaration, purpose and passion were the motherlode burning in their furnace. Birthing eco-tourism, marrying science to scenery, strenuous walking for spectacular reward—these were new things. Kate looked forward to the summer when they could run their enterprise together, candidly owning to frustrations on the farm, which they planned to let go once a stream of tourists could support them. In mid-November, Gustav's mare Belle had to be shot after an accident in the stables during the night. 'The poor thing laid in terrible agony with broken bones sticking out through the torn skin and flesh … there was no hope.' Kate wondered if Jolly might be responsible since he wouldn't let anyone near the mare's body, where he had stood sentry all afternoon. 'I am sick of losses … I have such a headache with the upset over the poor horse.'[43] She heaved an emotional sigh. Gustav, phlegmatic as usual, doesn't appear to register any distress at the news of his horse's death: 'Letter from Kate saying Belle died on 13th. Had to be shot on account of broken leg.'[44] Thrown by the death, Kate can't find their insurance papers; the weather was blowing a gale; she had a cold, and the farmhand had jacked up over his share of butter churned from their cow. 'No use talking,' she shrugged, looking forward to harvest time, when 'I wash my hands of the farm and everything if I can. Such a fine little farm too.'[45]

Waldheim welcomed twenty-three guests during the debut 1913/14 season, including five naturalists from Melbourne and two European visitors, Franz and Julius Malcher, veteran Austrian mountain climbers. The Malcher brothers attempted to find their way from Pencil Pine Creek to the chalet at twilight. They'd left their lantern in Sheffield. Both non-smokers, they were lucky to carry a matchbox that had four unused strikes. After losing their way twice, they lit a fire and camped under their mackintoshes on a bed of leaves until morning's light led them to the chalet, where Gustav was cooking breakfast. They were enchanted, their enthusiasm for the venture a fillip to Gustav's faith.[46]

Promoting Waldheim preoccupied the couple. The Malchers put the Weindorfers in touch with Melbourne-based printmaker Oscar Binder, another Austrian immigrant, who designed stationery for them.[47] The letterhead was striking, with Waldheim Accommodation House announced in an elongated art nouveau font beside a woodcut of the snow-clad Cradles rising above Dove Lake's shimmery expanse; the left-hand margin skited of gorges and ravines, lakes, rivers and falls, high places and summer snowdrifts in the heart of the mountains.[48] The couple began advertising their business and forest home in letters to tourist associations, travel agency Thomas Cook & Sons and the railways. Gustav wove his narrative so as to minimise the problem of access by spotlighting the destination.[49] The chalet's creature comforts were even more important if the getting there was rocky. At last the

Oscar Binder's design for Waldheim stationery, 1914

kitchen had a stove, hauled into the valley on a stretcher with the help
of Hubert Overall, a fellow botanist interested in alpine flora, whose
family owned a nursery on the north-west coast.[50] *Manus manim lavat.*
One hand washes the other. Lugging the iron beast took them two days.
Once installed, Gustav set flagstones around its feet. The kitchen was
now roofed in, the walls lined with pine shelves, the back porch and the
pantry finished, the big room ventilated by a second window. Gustav
crafted a washstand for the bedroom, a bread board, small adornments to
cosset weary visitors, seats in the nook, even carved hooks for wet coats.
The forest pushed inside as boughs and branches were sculpted and
carved into the beading on mirrors, picture frames, soap dishes, every
contrivance imaginable. The 'noble' fireplace was nearly complete,
earning its hallowed place as the conversation pit. This generous altar
was the gathering place where frostbitten toes would be warmed, where
animals would come in one by one to sit on the wombat hearth rug
in a cautious truce with the dogs, where men and women would yarn
into the wee hours sharing tales of their journeying, the sights from
the summit, the grandeur of nature in a sanctuary where there was no
time and nothing mattered.

The beauty of the mountains and lakes needed no embellishment.
But the narrow, boggy track from Pencil Pine Creek to the front door
served as a daily reminder of Gustav's reliance on authorities. If he
could metal the road himself, then the thing would be done, but instead
he must grovel. In March the chief engineer of the Department of
Public Works confirmed there was no money for a road that year.[51]

If it takes a village to raise a child, then a dream must be hoist
on the shoulders of scouts and wingers, whispering encouragement,
nurturing confidence, discounting the disappointments then readying
for another tilt. Some of these high-country giants had chosen this
region as home. Men like Wilmot farmer Bob Quaile, whose team
of horses and wagonette would grease the cumbersome business of
getting people to and fro. Quaile discovered Cradle after joining the
search for Bert Hanson and soon afterwards began a cart service to
the mountain from his stock run at Daisy Dell. Others Gustav courted
deliberately: politicians, local newspaper editors, surveyors, community
members with clout.

Then there were the accidental troupers, like solicitor Edward Adams
from the north-coast district town of Westbury, who was rescued by the

Weindorfers while bushwalking in December 1913. Adams was swept away by the charm and beauty of their house in the woods, promising to 'tell all my friends of its beauties and its natural wonders'.[52] Overcome, he writes Gustav a series of wistful letters as he floats back to earth. 'I don't know if the wife has a name for your home but I thought of the Sanskrit or Icelandic "skva" or the place where shadows play, the same word as sky, it seemed to fit the valley and its canopy.'[53] He became an instant convert to the cause, writing immediately to a bevy of ministers and politicians on their behalf. 'I feel sure something will be done to make the road good to your lovely home ... We will keep at it tho' progress is rather slow. I know you have plenty of hope, my stock is alas small.'[54] He fell for the experience of Waldheim's sanctuary, wrapped in its forest shawl. 'I shall not easily forget your hospitable house and its beauty. I was quite done up. It was like heaven getting into that straight, pine bed.'[55] The epiphany narrowed Adams' legal office into a pinched space, mired by the paperwork of petty conflicts. 'I will keep doing all that I can ... as I am amongst all these people without eyes,' he wrote, reciting a verse from Virgil as he recounted news of Foucault's experimental display in London demonstrating to children the motion of the earth. 'We are all children when we look into space.'[56] We are all children when we peer into the wild.

Melbourne naturalists George and Una Coghill were won over after visiting in January, despite incessant rain. 'We both feel that wherever you lead, us or anyone else, could follow.'[57] Botanist Dr Sutton arrived for his third visit to the valley, his first under the shingles of Waldheim, the bond between them reaffirmed. As the year unfolded, Gustav and Kate tasted the sweet rewards of sweat and the weeks of separation. The director of Sydney's Botanic Gardens had been in touch thanking Gustav for herbarium specimens; the German-born Tasmanian geologist Fritz Noetling wanted him to write a paper for the Royal Society on moraines, the glacial boulders that stud the valley, while the Tasmanian government geologist had heard of Gustav's reckoning that Barn Bluff is 200 feet higher than Cradle Mountain when the reverse had stood as gospel until then.[58]

From this distance not even the war smothered their exuberance, though they worried for Gustav's brothers, who were likely to enlist, and for his parents' welfare. 'We in this peaceful island can scarcely realise the horrors of war,' Kate wrote to her parents-in-law on

16 August 1914 on freshly minted Waldheim stationery shortly after Great Britain joined the battle. 'There is never much to record from here except the simple everyday routine and the glorious scenes which greet the eye on every side. Here in the solitude and solemn peace of the majestic mountains it is impossible to realise that war is raging on the other side of the world. Outside the snow lies thickly on the ground but a fine fire of logs burns in the big fireplace and little Flock lies in front on the wombat rug, peacefully asleep, but we feel anxious as to what news tomorrow's mail will bring of the war … Gustav is very busy every day with the building … The house feels quite homely already and when Gustav has put all the finishing touches it will be very comfortable. I pray that God may bless and take care of all the dear ones. With most loving wishes ever your affectionate Kate.'[59] She thanked them for the postcard of a grand Austrian chalet in Villach. 'Perhaps one day we have as fine a house here,' she mused.

Two days after posting this letter, Kate took to her bed nursing a pain in her chest. The sharp discomfort bothered her through the next night and day, snug under cover while Gustav worked outside; he dug a drain and garden beds, skinned a wombat, hunted with the dogs and cut a track to Hounslow Heath.[60] When they returned to Kindred in September, Kate consulted her doctor in Ulverstone, who diagnosed 'acute indigestion'.[61] There were cabbages, peas and turnips to plant, carrots to sow, and for all the gloom of world conflict and her inexplicable ill health, Kate was happier this spring than last since Gustav was there with her, the rhythms of their movement between mountains and farm now in synch. 'We returned from Waldheim last week,' she told his parents. 'The garden is beautiful, wattle and acacias in flower and fruit trees laden with blossom … gay and sweet with spring flowers. It was a great homecoming with all the dogs, poor Bixie was so pleased to see us. Flock had four puppies. Dan has a car. Wish you were here to play lovely duets.'[62]

They spent Christmas and summer in the mountains hosting five guests between January and March, several of them neighbours from Kindred. They fished at Perkin's Creek and on hot days they bathed in Wombat Pool, writing feverishly at night to telegraph Waldheim's opening: Kate to the Tourist branch of the Tasmanian Government Railways, Gustav turning out a newspaper article for the *North West Post*. Another Waldheim whisperer had joined the fray. Evelyn Temple

Emmett, the spirited director of the Tasmanian Government Tourist Bureau, a bushwalker awake to the island's natural amphitheatres, promised to include Cradle Mountain in a forthcoming guidebook, the second of its kind under his stewardship.[63] Canny in the art of persuasion, he shared Gustav's knack for producing advertorials under a pseudonym and was another true believer in the potential of their secluded haunt, consoling them over the poor season, a state-wide slump possibly due to the grim disturbance of the war. Conscious of shifting sentiments even this far from the battlefields of Europe, Gustav reported his status as a former Austrian reservist to the police, though his naturalisation in 1905 technically cancelled any enemy allegiance.

At Easter they found a tenant for Roland Lea, liberating Kate from the obstreperous manager, who bridled at her authority. 'He always seems to me to think that it is your work,' she grumbled of his efforts to shirk jobs and slough her off.[64] But just as she was looking forward to being at Gustav's side, the nagging pain returned, and when next he ducked up the mountain, she stayed behind at Kindred with her dearest sister Laura. In letters to him, her handwriting began to tighten, her neatly formed script smaller, as if to contain the uneasiness unsettling her. When she told him that his fourth letter had arrived safely, she admitted: 'I shall know them all by heart as I get them out and reread them when I am longing for you.' Though the new farmer was in charge, he had 'been asking when you are coming home', wanting advice on paddocks and crops. She placed ads in the paper to sell one of their horses. The fowls were not laying, 'though they are singing and looking red'. She'd burned sulphur in the kennels because Bixie had mange, and whooping cough and diphtheria were menacing the district. Although she felt a little better, the pain worsened whenever she exerted herself. Dr Gollan, who previously suspected indigestion, prescribed two bottles of medicine, though the tonic did little to revive her. For distraction, she read 'a pretty American story called Bambi', glad for the new books they'd been lent by Walter Malcolm Black.[65]

'I often picture the valley at sunset and then with the moonlight shining on the snow making it like day and all the solemn stillness surrounding you. Just a Mo-poke now and then I suppose or per-haps Flock after a tiddle-winks and the fiddle sticks and the little brook murmuring while the snow lines its banks.'[66] She'd adored his description of the circus when Flock had shirtfronted a tiger cat in the

dining room, pleased he was living more in the large room than in the
kitchen. 'I think it is more cheerful to see the big blazing fire and
the kitchen is damp in winter. How I wish I could be with you.' Always
questions about the dogs and Flock's puppies: 'Hope Brown boy is
learning his lessons … and not losing his master's trail again. I do miss
his little brown paws at my bedside in the morning and then sitting up
and asking me to get up. Of course Plilly keeps your feet warm at night
… Does she ever ask where I am or do you think Brumby ever thinks
of me? Laura sends greetings to you and thinks you must be lonely out
there. With heaps and heaps of love.'

Kate's health improved enough for them to visit the valley together
in June, stocking firewood in the porch, preparing for summer guests,
thrilled when they learnt that the Tasmanian government botanist,
Leonard Rodway, the author of the Weindorfers' bible, a definitive
guide to the state's flora, had booked Waldheim from Christmas 1915
into the New Year with a party of eminent scientists. The group
included zoologist Professor Theodore Thomson Flynn, actor Errol
Flynn's father, recently appointed to the inaugural biology chair at
the University of Tasmania, and geologist William Noel Benson, a
lecturer at the University of Sydney fresh from study at Cambridge's
Museum of Earth Sciences. Other luminaries were Lyndhurst Giblin,
the acclaimed Cambridge-educated economist, W. F. Dennis Butler,
a Hobart barrister, and Englishman Arthur Garnett, a horticultural
journalist from a literary family, whose brother Edward corresponded
with D. H. Lawrence, encouraging publication of *Sons and Lovers*.[67]

Lifted by an eddy of good fortune, they saddled up Jolly at Middlesex
station, the cart lighter for the return journey, their hearts lighter still.
They careered over the grassy verge of Bull Plains. At the northern
end, as they crested Lehmans Hill, Kate swung around in her seat as
she always did for a last lingering glimpse of the Cradles before the
mountains dipped from sight.

6

LOSS

Holed up in a plush room at The Towers lodging house in the centre of Launceston, directly opposite the town's museum, Kate endeavoured to comply with doctor's orders: rest up.[1] As her eyes wandered over the botanical brocade papering the walls, she allowed a wan smile at the very idea of Gustav similarly corralled under a throw rug. Sitting still was akin to torture for him. Even with a book in his hands, his legs grew twitchy, and thinking of him like a coiled spring made her smile. Days bled into nights as snatches of afternoon sleep disrupted her circadian rhythms. By the luminous glow of the moon, her mind would pace, making lists, mostly for Cradle, but once in this darkness she'd gone grimly through her few possessions, earmarking the music box for a niece and their stepmother's velvet and rosewood easy chair for her sister Laura. It was Laura who'd treated her to a week of idleness in this two-storeyed hostel distinguished by a slate-tiled turret. Laura had accompanied her on the shuffle from doctors' suites to specialist rooms, boosting her spirits when they sagged, escorting her to the flower show, finding amusement wherever Kate could manage the walk.[2] Kate suspected she'd caught her nasty cold from the Launceston hospital where they'd waited for X-rays in a freezing corridor rife with germs. Gustav always insisted the Cradles were hermetically sealed from the bugs and bacteria at large in city streets. 'I dropped my cold on the way up,' he'd jest.

She was in medical limbo. Her condition had so eluded diagnosis that she'd begun to wonder whether these stabbing chest pains were a figment of her stricken mind. Sick of herself momentarily, she was seized by the desire for company when the dinner bell rang. She smoothed her hair, shook out her skirt and went downstairs to the wood-panelled dining room, taking the chair next to an elderly gentleman with a vast white beard. Recently widowed, he'd moved here from Deloraine, a small settlement not so far from the Cradles, a place so constantly in her thoughts that it was on her lips before they'd exchanged names. At the mention of this wilderness, the man's face beamed and he introduced himself with the enthusiasm befitting discovery of a long-lost friend: 'Dan Griffin.' A former police superintendent, he'd spent weeks prospecting through this country in 1888 and 1897, his intricate knowledge of the terrain earning him a place in the second search party dispatched to retrieve Bert Hanson's body from the mountain's clutches. Soon they were deep in the thickets, the gorges, the rivers and the fog so dense 'a crow could not fly through with any measure of safety unless he carried a glow worm in his beak'.[3] She laughed at his quick wit, amazed by his familiarity with creeks and landmarks and the verse of Adam Lindsay Gordon, a poet as taken with the pedigree of race horses as himself. Like Gustav, he dabbled in print, easy with prose. His regular musings under the byline of 'The Tramp' told of bush rambles, but he was best known for an insider's grasp of the track, where he often served as a handicapper judge. Kate could sense Gustav in him even before he admitted to childhood games of Burke and Wills venturing for the Gulf of Carpentaria.[4]

After dinner they strolled together to the drawing room, where they sat beside the fire. Kate listened to his tales of the Hanson search, of trudging through drifts of snow that had covered all trace of the young trapper and his dog. The loyalty of that kelpie, standing sentry, moved Griffin still. Kate might have told the old man of Ron Smith pocketing the dog's skeleton two summers ago. As the fire dwindled to embers, the smallest of worlds collided in a corner of the island where degrees of separation are measured in fractions. There was yet another connection between them. 'My father bought the mother of my horse from him,' Kate exclaimed excitedly in a letter she dashed off to Gustav the moment she returned to her room. 'He says there ought to be a great future for the Cradles and reckons the accommodation house should do well.'[5]

Confidence beating in her breast, she woke the next morning well enough for an exploratory visit to the Launceston Tourist Bureau. She went incognito, a trick straight from Gustav's playbook, enquiring how one might travel to Cradle Mountain for a holiday. She was told to write to Mr Black of Liena, who guided tourists from Middlesex to the mountain. 'Yes there was an accommodation house there. I did not make myself known. I simply said that motors could go within four miles of the house ... Excuse scribble, am writing on my knee in my room. Heaps of love and kisses from your loving Kate.'[6]

The throttle of motor vehicles was a noise transforming streets and towns. Kate's brother Dan owned a car, as did Stephen and Blanche; everyone who could commandeered steering wheels, their impact on travel and tourism barely yet understood. Dr Bennett, the dentist Kate saw in Devonport, revealed his plans to visit Waldheim 'as soon as peace comes', and was concerned whether his motor car would be able to navigate the soft bogs of Weaning Paddock Creek.[7] His enquiry underscored Gustav's impatience for a road to their door or as near to the valley's entrance as possible. Another doctor on Kate's rounds had hiked in Alsace and hoped to meet Gustav. The couple were attracting attention like a pair of astronauts on the moon since the mountain was a mysterious place.[8] Kate was the guest of honour at four afternoon teas given for her in Devonport. 'If I were vain I would feel quite a "personage",' she advised Gustav wryly. 'Of course I enjoy them immensely.'[9]

Her cheer hid a gnawing fear that she might not recover from whatever plagued her. Local physicians, practised in the commoner complaints of whooping cough, mumps, influenza and diphtheria, had no diagnosis or remedy for her trouble. After suspecting acute indigestion, the doctor at Ulverstone then decided the pain in her chest might be angina. Further examinations detected a small lump, possibly an enlarged muscle, 'hard to say what it might be', warranting the X-rays in Launceston that found nothing sinister.[10] Her attacks persisted, striking randomly, sometimes at night or in the morning. There would be nothing for two days, then a sudden onset, her walking becoming difficult because of having to stop frequently for the pain: 'so distressing to me—and so slow ... I do hope I shall feel better soon.'[11] The refrain became her anthem. *I do hope I shall feel better soon.*

She missed Gustav terribly; but there were several blissful afternoons spent sunbathing on the beach at Devonport with her nieces, Blanche and Stephen's daughters. At night heavy winds rattled her, as did 'the monotonous roar of breakers', jangling nerves already on edge. 'I felt dreadfully homesick yesterday and such a depression came over me in the evening.' She was grateful for the lulls of fortune when she slept well, mercifully pain free, her energy renewed. 'When you come could you bring the Rodway?' she instructed him, referring to their well-thumbed compendium on Tasmanian flora by botanist Leonard Rodway.[12] Both of them were looking forward to Christmas, when the author, whom they knew well, would be among the party of eight scientists staying at the chalet—'it is not often so many intellectual men come together', Kate wrote. Blessed by a whole day rid of illness, she felt a flutter of hope. 'We might have a profitable year at the valley after all. Mr Griffin said he thought it would have a great future.'[13]

Bookings for the 1916 summer season ran back to back, with a revolving door of twenty-four guests expected from Christmas Eve and right through the first months of the New Year, all of them men. Some were neighbours from Kindred, others small business-owners in surrounding towns. The scientists brought gravitas. Energetic tourism tyro Evelyn Temple Emmett would visit in March. Outdoorsy and a wordsmith, Emmett grasped the scenic glitter of Tasmania's high country.

Gustav darted up the valley in December to replenish pantry shelves and gather fuel, freeing himself to guide guests up and down the summit with picnics by the lakes. He was busy in a good way, because sharing their El Dorado was what had lured them all along. He had no idea from this remove that Kate's cold had worsened into pneumonia. When he returned to Kindred in mid-December, he was distressed to find she'd been ferried to Matron Morton's Hospital at Ulverstone, 12 miles away.[14] Desperately tired from his daylong journey, he cycled there immediately, fired by adrenalin, collapsing into bed at Kindred around 2 am. For the next week, he rode to the hospital, sometimes twice in a day. Gradually she regained strength, tapping into his reserves as they walked circuits of the hospital garden. Not yet sprite enough to join him, she'd shown sufficient improvement that her doctor waved Gustav off to the Cradles with his blessing so he could be there to welcome Leonard Rodway's party on Christmas Eve.[15]

Kate arose on Christmas Day in her narrow hospital ward, brightened by a brief visit in the morning from her brothers, Bert and Dan, who brought her a posy of flowers picked from her garden at Roland Lea. Laura, who had been by her side on this medical merry-go-round, was in Devonport with Stephen and Blanche and the children. 'It is lovely not to have that pain in my heart but of course I still have a wheeze in my lungs and shortness of breath at night … I am always thinking of you and how you are getting on,' Kate wrote to Gustav from the hospital in a spidery scrawl on Boxing Day, wondering how the catering had gone since this had been her job in the past.[16] She kicked herself for not arranging for the neighbour, who'd baked him puddings, to make cakes as well. Present at Waldheim even from a distance, she blamed her forgetfulness on the morphine she'd been given. She sent her greetings to the scientists, sad at missing the fun. 'Doctor sends kind remembrances and says go ahead and enjoy yourself up there and do not worry about me.'[17] With no plaintive appeal for her own sake, she exempted him from his duty of care because they were at the cusp of success—she felt it as surely as he did—and she wouldn't dare sabotage this forward march. As if to reassure him, perhaps at Kate's behest, Laura dispatched a separate note to confirm Kate was looking well and cheerful 'although very thin … Hope you and the professors have had a good time.'[18]

The scientists arrived at the chalet frisky with the possibilities for research. Armed with a theodolite and trigonometrical gear, the surveyors focused on settling the dispute over the heights of Barn Bluff and Cradle Mountain, crowning the former as king of the peaks in the paper they later submitted to the Royal Society of Tasmania.[19] Botanist Leonard Rodway, zoologist Theodore Thomson Flynn and geologist William Benson rambled through the lower regions seeking mammals, plants and moraines. Euphoric at the array of flora and fauna during a patch of fine weather, they exhausted themselves. Flynn was studying the embryology of marsupials and was delighted by his observations of wombats and possums. Rodway pored over liverworts and mosses in the myrtle and beech forests behind the chalet. He wrote to Kate on his return to Hobart, 'extremely sorry' at her absence, for not only would she have appreciated the scientific discussions around the fire every night, but the two of them were expert in the plant kingdom's small, exquisitely wrought dwarf family of mosses, lichens and hepatics or liverworts. He promised to send her samples of those

An empty chair beside the hearth, 1929 (Gustav Weindorfer)

he'd collected, including one or two new species. 'I think it was the most glorious time I've ever had,' he cooed. 'The only drawback was shortness of time. I collected vigorously at all available occasions but I only half did the place. It must be done again. I hope next Christmas.' He said he'd like to push north towards Black Bluff and Lake Lea, insisting there were enough prizes in the upper end of the valley to absorb a collector for weeks. 'It was very good of you not allowing us to throw up the trip. Had I known you were so near a dangerous attack as pneumonia I do not think I should have taken the responsibility of taking Mr Weindorfer so far away. I was in considerable fear till your letter came that you may have had a relapse and I should not have forgiven myself for being so selfish.'[20]

She'd have given anything to be at Waldheim with the guests, sharing the delight of Rodway's discoveries, adding to her own herbarium, helping Gustav cater for their comfort, fixing meals, clearing up the living room, walking with the dogs in the valley, gathered around the fireplace at night talking plant taxonomy. Sickness was a curse she suffered with forbearance so long as she sensed the sweet prospect of tomorrow. She reminded Gustav to bring the matting screen around her bunk at Waldheim so that she could shield a space on Roland Lea's veranda where she'd lie 'weak as a kitten' until exertion took less of a toll.[21] Soon she was able to garden, walking a little, gaining confidence and strength for accomplishments she once took for granted. Illness shrank her scope. The garden at Kindred became her universe, where she was busy with the French beans coming on too quickly, a 'horrid little black rabbit' devouring them. One day sitting out in the sun under the cherry trees while Laura picked raspberries, a goanna crept out from the cabbages, followed by a whip snake, smaller than the jet-black fellow spotted by the well.[22] She watched the sky signalling changes of weather, wondering if the storm had reached the mountains yet, forcing them indoors. 'I suppose the Professor will be able to study and dissect the animals.'[23] The recurring pain in her chest and left lung she blamed on fatigue after the journey home. 'Thanks to Laura's unremitting care I have put on a little flesh but my strength comes back very slowly ... There seems nothing fresh to tell you as life is going very quietly and of course I miss you and look forward to your homecoming ... so sick of bed and weakness ... Kind wishes to the Professor. I hope he has found some marsupial mice.'[24]

Always starved for news, she seized upon his letters to her, amused by stories of Flock, Bixie, Kate's dog Fuschs and the puppies, or the wombat stew he'd made, or his search for the Velvet soap, which he'd found eventually in a tin above her bunk, or the guests' euphoria at the view from the summit as clear as the day they'd first climbed it together, six years ago that very month. She skirted burdening him with guilt since she knew he must play host, yet she couldn't help a hint of despair at missing the season's joyful swing: 'Business seems so good out there this year and it does grieve me that I cannot be with you.' When the wait for his return became unbearable, she chided herself: 'I must expect my dear boy when I see him and be patient in the meantime.'[25]

Leonard Rodway forwarded her another batch of mosses that he'd gathered in the valley, apologising for his 'man like' behaviour, putting himself first, preoccupied by his personal obsession with the hepatics or liverworts and neglecting to procure specimens she would fancy in her collection. His admission of 'man like' self-centredness betrayed a precociously modern sensibility, confirming his respect for Kate and his regard for her botanical acumen.[26]

Her spirits were high when she wrote to Gustav on 25 January the moment his letter arrived, finally, after days of silence: 'I cannot say how glad I am to have it. We have been looking and listening for you almost every evening since the middle of last week … I am getting stronger each day and feeling altogether better.' She counted herself lucky, almost, for she'd survived pneumonia while young Miss Cleaver's fiancé went into the same hospital with some trivial complaint and died after catching it. 'Yesterday I played some music for the first time since I came home.' Her ears were cocked for the clip of hooves and the crunch of cart wheels on the driveway; she was missing the dogs, especially her Fuschsie, finding it too quiet without their bark.

When Gustav finally returned to Roland Lea in early February, she didn't rush out to greet him. Laid low, she'd taken to her bed and was so frail that he summoned her physician, Dr Gollan, the next day. Kate's closest female neighbours rallied to nurse her in Laura's absence, but after a sudden debilitating relapse late one evening, Gustav cycled 12 miles to fetch her doctor, who drove them both to Matron Morton's Hospital in Ulverstone. Torn between Kate and their forest dream, Gustav succumbed to fears of losing both. He visited her daily, riding back and forth from the farm while Waldheim sat empty, relieved when she was strong enough to get out of bed. This reprieve lasted a moment. 'Got news of mother's death. Kate not well at all.'

The double whack winded him[27]—a huge loss, for nobody loves a man as unconditionally as his mother, except perhaps the woman now weakening before him. He'd delayed returning to the valley for as long as he possibly could, monitoring Kate's condition, grateful for Laura's arrival to comfort Kate. News in late March that Evelyn Temple Emmett was arriving with two colleagues for a visit that could put Waldheim on the travellers' map forced another separation upon them. Emmett's silvery tongue and modern ideas about tourism's future danced in step with theirs. After a long day leading the group up to the summit, Gustav herded them safely back down before the light died, arriving at Waldheim at 7 pm to find a scribbled note left on the large pine table by William Hitchcock, the mine manager at Moina. He'd received a telephone call from Ulverstone: 'Either Mrs W was no worse or worse I could not distinguish which but you are wanted as soon as possible.'[28] Gustav headed off in haste, travelling through the night to reach Kindred after noon, then onwards to Ulverstone by bicycle, arriving at 6 pm. The sight of Kate so thin and sallow flattened him.

He rode to her bedside every day for four weeks, sometimes sleeping overnight, stroking her hand, telling her stories of the dogs' mischief, drawing a smile to her lips as she pictured them squabbling over the wombat rug in front of the fire at Cradle. In mid-April he dashed back up the valley to retrieve the dogs from Middlesex station where he'd left them in his hurry home. Their oldest kelpie, Bixie, was dead. If he kept this sadness from Kate, he brought her 'some sphaerocephalus', the buttongrass flower she'd requested to remind her of their haven. He also brought lemon boronia to dull the antiseptic whiff in the ward, and a snippet of good news. A telegram from Emmett. He'd inhaled Waldheim, loving the Weindorfers' launch pad to Tasmania's world-beating magnificence. Gustav's sudden departure hadn't sabotaged their trip. One of the party had taken over as cook, while Emmett's publicity arm was already cranking out copy: 'You will see an account of the trip in Saturday's paper. I sent the same account to my daily paper. I also sent a little account of it to the local weekly paper and to *The Age*.' He promised to send Gustav books to while away winter evenings, 'one simply a love story beautifully told'.[29]

With love swings the pendulum of loss, for the harder you fall the worse the parting. Kate was fading, the doctor doubting her recovery before she let go of hope herself. In late March she added a codicil to her will, ensuring profits from the sale of her farm be invested by the trustees, Gustav one of them, to provide him with a steady stream of income.[30] The land at Cradle Mountain, also in Kate's name, would fall to him unconditionally upon her death. His diary entries graphed the daily back and forth on one axis beside Kate's downward spiral: precise, succinct, exhausted physically and emotionally by the vigil he kept until late in April, when they spoke the truth: 'Kate realises the hopelessness of her state.'[31] It was brave of her to name the end, clearing a space for things to be said on the brink of goodbye. He smuggled her little Fuschs in for a visit as she sank 'very, very low', before lapsing into a coma. The next day she took her last breath. 'I have lost my best friend,' he wrote of his wife alongside his signature meteorological observation—'Glorious day'—'man like' in his capacity to compartmentalise these two events, as if climatic fluctuations were equivalent to the seismic disruption of Kate's vanishing.[32] She was fifty-three, a short life even then. Her death certificate records the cause as chronic nephritis and uraemia, but cancer of the breast or lung seems more likely from her symptoms and her rapid decline.

Best friend, lover, wife, botanical associate, fellow mountaineer, 'your true pure helpmate', as Ron Smith's wife Kathleen described Kate in a letter to Gustav, for she assisted him in the back office, occasionally the front office, brought provisions, made mattresses, dried his animal skins for sale, wrapped him in the arms of her extended family, walked with him, kept up with him, fretting over things she could have done for him even as she slipped away. She'd encouraged him to go up the mountain where they both should have been. Perhaps that was where Kate went as she lost consciousness, groggy on opiates, sauntering through the buttongrass heath of Cradle Valley on a glorious day, Gustav by her side, the dogs around them, pausing for a moment to admire the vivid red bells of flowering mountain rocket, before stepping up the grassy slope towards the forest behind their home. He would glimpse her from time to time in the moss-covered trunks, or hear her voice in the wind, reminded of her by the flight of a hawk just like the bird they'd watched circling above Dove Lake, for of course he'd pick up where they'd left off.

He buried his best friend in her family's plot at the Don cemetery near Devonport. The funeral was small. Afterwards Gustav sorted through Kate's belongings with sister Laura, both of them grieving in their different ways. He could smell Kate in the pine dresser as they packed her clothes, pausing to admire the silk slippers from her wedding still in their box, prompting memories they each pocketed as they sorted gifts she'd bestowed on chosen relatives: her music box to a niece, her piano loaded onto a float, her legacy bound to outlive all the things that eventually turn to dust.

Waratah, Tasmanian wildflower series (J. H. Robinson)

7
THE SPY

His German tongue, his European taste for garlic and coffee, a fondness for kissing the hands of women he met, his Tyrolean hat always turned up at the brim, instead of straight as the locals preferred, plus a tourism venture called Waldheim—these were all an advertisement for trouble during the Great War. Australians mourning the deaths of sons, brothers and fathers sought to punish enemy aliens in their midst. Liquored-up mobs hurled stones and bottles at German clubs in Melbourne, Sydney, even Broken Hill, while a quieter, thin-lipped anger simmered in the breasts of patriotic citizens.[1] Gustav and Kate had always been a target for stickybeaks. This was the tithe they paid for being different. Though Gustav had been naturalised as a British subject, the war snatched back every tenuous protection granted in peacetime. Without Kate to insulate him from links to the Kaiser, the barbs of curiosity rasped with nastier intent.

Little Annie Perkins at the foot of Mt Roland heard the accusations peddled at kitchen tables whenever conversation touched on the war. 'They used to say he was a spy,' she recalled as an elderly woman.[2] Gustav knew of the whispering campaign, which escalated in 1916 as the toll of Australians wounded or killed rose. A friend of Kate's wrote to him warning of blowback: 'I think I should tell you what the people are saying. Of course I tell them they are wrong but it will be better for you to know. They say you are a spy and pro-German and that is why you are out on the mountain and a lot more of the same talk. I feel it my duty as a friend to tell you so hope you will not feel hurt but take it as meant for the sake of dear Kate.'[3]

Ill will festered. Doors were slammed in the face of anyone who might harbour enemy affection. Members of the Ulverstone Club, where Gustav was a member, initially tolerated his presence. Alex Crawford, who'd been to Waldheim, wrote, very pucker in August 1914, that 'I would like to see you, old boy, and tell you how sorry I am that England should be at war with Austria … all through that blasted Kaiser. We have spoken of you several times in connection with this war and I assure you our feelings have been warmly in sympathy with you and your land.'[4] In his next letter, he is like a boy with a toy army, cheering the latest military strike: 'Brits sank four German cruisers off Falkland Isles.'[5] Two years later the membership's mood had soured into talk of expulsion. In September 1916, former Kindred schoolteacher William Carnie urged Gustav to resign from the club in a pre-emptive strike.[6]

Well before the war, the Weindorfers had farewelled Carnie with a garden party at Roland Lea, followed by a ceremony at the hall. Gustav had sung a German song, earning an encore, before the floor was cleared for dancing.[7] But anyone who dared perform a German song while Australians were dying at the front risked a lynching. 'Feeling ran high at the mention of your name by me last night,' Carnie revealed to Gustav. 'One who has just lost a near relative at the war constitutes himself a leader to "purge" this club. He gave notice to have you expelled. I suggest that you immediately send one in dated Wednesday or Tuesday last in your politest form. Yours very truly.'[8] Gustav had just paid his annual subscription.

The Ulverstone doctor who had treated Kate was an office-bearer of the club. He accepted Gustav's resignation regretfully, grateful none-theless for his 'wise' course of action. His sentiments came gilded in mealy-mouthed platitudes of friendship and regard.[9] Carnie hid behind the same shield. The snub was a paltry sting for Gustav, but the turning against him for sins of birth, language, culture and an affinity with the enemy made him even more of a fringe dweller in the wake of Kate's death.

His Austrian and German friends in towns and cities fared far worse. German-born scientist Dr Fritz Noetling, a scholar interested in geology and palaeontology, had been acting German consul in

Hobart for a short stint during 1914. An enthusiastic participant in the esteemed Royal Society of Tasmania, he'd served on the council alongside botanist Leonard Rodway, zoologist Professor Theodore Thomson Flynn and economist Lyndhurst Giblin, who was one of two military intelligence officers in the state.[10] Rodway, Flynn and Giblin had been among the party of scientists who'd visited Waldheim. Noetling knew of the valley's significance. He'd asked Gustav to write a paper on the glacial moraines at Cradle for the Royal Society.[11]

The two men had much in common beyond their European heritage and German tongues. Gustav often spoke of the Cradle Cirque as 'Noetling's Glacier' since here was a fellow whose fascination with the geological origins of Cradle Mountain and nearby Barn Bluff matched his own. When the Danish consul published an account of visiting Waldheim in a Danish newspaper, Gustav's sister Rosa sent him a translation. 'That he believes me to be middle sized doesn't harm me very much,' Gustav harrumphed at the consul's unflattering reference to his height, 'but that he describes Barn Bluff as granite is unpardonable.'[12] Noetling would have appreciated Gustav's brain snap. Both men married Tasmanian women and had become British subjects, but they would not be spared the shrapnel of suspicion.

Noetling was set upon at his home in the south-west Tasmanian town of New Norfolk by a gang armed with rocks and taunts. Seven men were charged with disturbing the peace. On the morning of Friday 26 November 1915, they appeared in the local courthouse pleading not guilty. The case was adjourned until the afternoon. When Noetling failed to appear, the matter was set aside *sine die* with no mention of his iron-clad excuse.[13] He'd been arrested under the *War Precautions Act 1914*, aimed at enemy aliens who were reasonably suspected of being in any way dangerous to the safety of the realm. Authorities had intercepted letters written by Noetling in German containing newspaper clippings and tables of troop figures that he'd sent through his sister in Switzerland for delivery to a German general.[14] While these were hardly state secrets, he'd nonetheless been caught on the wrong side of the new law. Reporting suspicious behaviour was a patriotic duty that overrode friendship or favour. Noetling was stripped of every position he held and sent to Holsworthy internment camp south-west of Sydney.

Here one minute, the next disappeared.

Nobody protested the rights of citizens whisked away on the flimsiest of undisclosed grounds. Hobart's German consul, Alfred Dehle, who ran the firm Dehle, Heritage & Co., was interned with his brother, not for what they'd done but because of what they might get up to if they weren't locked up. An intelligence report shrugged off the lack of 'tangible evidence' against them. 'The general consensus of opinion is that they are at heart disloyal and would if the occasion arose do everything in their power to aid Germany.'[15]

Melbourne businessman Franz Wallach, a director of the Australian Metals Company, who was interned at Langwarrin in Victoria, challenged the government's proof of his disaffection. He won a brief reprieve when the Full Court of the Supreme Court of Victoria upheld the principle of evidence in *habeas corpus* and refused to impound the German-born defendant on the basis of a blank charge sheet. Wallach walked free, only to be arrested again half an hour later under a freshly drafted amendment to the Act that enshrined the government's right to intern enemy aliens as it sought fit.[16] The Minister for Defence, Senator George Pearce, boasted of Australia's record of interning more enemy aliens as a proportion of population than any of our allies.[17]

Soldiers marching through Hobart before leaving for the front, 1916

Tasmanian Premier John Earle alerted loyal citizens to wireless telegraph stations that could be communicating with the enemy. Easily constructed using a car engine and a mast 'erected at night in isolated areas near the coast', this prospect sent flighty imaginations into overdrive.[18] The cast-iron range oven that Gustav had installed at Waldheim became, in some paranoid minds, a means for transmitting code, while the coils of copper and brass wire he used for snares, even the clothesline he hung for his washing, were believed to be signalling devices. The scare was reported to police, who were bound to investigate.[19]

Defence authorities had been watching Gustav since December 1914 according to a surveillance report compiled by intelligence officers attached to the 6th Military District.[20] Captain Lyndhurst Franklin Giblin, one of two Tasmanian officers attached to this unit during the war, knew Gustav from his visit to Cradle Valley. Giblin's brother Arthur, a lawyer and botanist, was a Waldheim regular. Perhaps Giblin protected Gustav by dowsing specious rumours—certainly he could have been given a rougher time, since he'd belonged to the German National Party in Austria and served briefly as an Austrian reservist.[21] Police didn't need to produce evidence of disloyalty to intern an enemy alien, simply plausible suspicion. His early biographer, Dr Bergman, believed his carefree attitude was 'very naïve' given the state's heavy-handed patrol.[22]

Gustav's chalet was searched by police in December 1917. His alien record sheet noted that 'Reports concerning him were … conflicting, he being accused of being a spy. His correspondence has been rigidly censored but without result.'[23] So long as the war lingered, there would be scaremongering. When he applied to enlist in the AIF in 1917, he was rejected 'in view of all the circumstances', which may have included his age; at forty-four, he was just a year shy of the army's cut-off. He'd sought to quell apprehension about his loyalty and told Smith that while he couldn't fight against Austrians, he 'wanted to do his share of winning the war for us'.[24] Tasmania was a bellicose state, voting 'Yes' in the conscription referendum. Gustav argued for the draft at a meeting in Kindred.[25] These gestures may have helped dampen antagonism towards a man who ultimately bemused authorities. 'Weindorfer has a hut on Cradle Mountain which provides accommodation in the season for tourists who visit the locality,' his intelligence file declared.

'He himself traps and shoots native game and gives as a reason for his secluded life that he was studying botany.'[26]

Seclusion saved him. His closest former compatriot, Franz Gossler, felt constant anguish in the crush of Melbourne: 'The general hatred against us all makes my life at times unbearable. To be looked upon as a worst type of criminal or outcast is not a pleasant feeling particularly when one feels one has done nothing to deserve it. Quite a large number of my old acquaintances cut me dead now. We go nowhere and only rarely receive a visit. I neither talk nor write merely for fear my expressions might be misinterpreted. One cannot be too careful. It is chiefly for this reason I'm not writing this in our mother tongue.'[27]

Gossler was frozen out of a porcelain company that he'd spent three years growing, losing everything he'd invested. Many businesses refused to employ enemy aliens. German and Austro–Hungarian firms became commercial pariahs. The unfortunately named Frankfurt Sausage Company loudly declared not only British heritage but also a supply line to the Defence Department, since any link to the enemy brought retribution.[28] Gossler told Gustav that their mutual friend Frank Wallner, who owned a garage in Fitzroy, had been raided by police on a hunch he was making bombs. A thorough search revealed nothing apart from a dusty box containing a broken automatic pistol that a friend had given him to repair three years earlier. This was enough to haul him before the court under the Aliens Restriction Order 1915. Though naturalised, his Austrian birth disqualified him from possessing firearms, even an old, dud gun. Gossler dismissed the weapon as 'scrap iron' undeserving of a ten-pound fine or the more prohibitive cost of the negative publicity, which sank the business.[29]

Those with links to enemy nations were watched closely. Gustav used his American and Swiss contacts to help friends like Gossler keep in touch with relatives, potentially breaching the law.[30] Tasmanian authorities pounced on attempts at evading censorship. A young German electrical engineer at Mt Lyell mine in the state's west was interned at Bruny Island because he'd asked a fellow miner of Swiss origin to post a 'harmless' letter home for him from the neutral territory of Switzerland.[31]

Mail in and out of Waldheim was thumbed by the censor. Leonard Hubbard, a subeditor at *The Daily Post* who'd accompanied Professor Theodore Thomson Flynn to Cradle Valley in 1916, informed Gustav that his letter had arrived 'passed' by authorities. 'I felt inclined to write to you in German to amuse the dear man and give him some work to do for a change but I'm afraid it might delay or even stop the letter altogether.'[32] The Coghills told Gustav they weren't bothering to seal envelopes addressed to Waldheim, for the censor's convenience.[33] Another Melbourne friend despaired at the delay of a letter from Gustav: 'It had been opened by the censor then forwarded on to me.'[34]

Letters from Austria took even longer than usual to reach him. Gustav learnt belatedly of the deaths of his brother Lothar, due to surgery complications in September, then his elderly father, Johann, who passed away in October. He amended his diary to record each death many months after the fact, using a blue pencil in larger than normal print.[35] Orphaned and widowed within a twelve-month span, he had lost the most significant people in his life—his mother, his wife and best friend, one of his siblings and his father. Nearest of kin, the givers of unconditional love, wiped out, not through war but through the toppling dominoes of circumstance, cutting a similar swathe to the bullets that felled sons in battle. From this remove he could not participate in rituals of mourning. The thick blue pencil was all the ceremony he had.

Ron Smith's safe return from the trenches of Gallipoli revived their friendship. 'I think it is about time that we both drop the stiff prefix of "Mr",' Gustav suggested as they resumed their correspondence.[36] These two bushmen were entwined through their attachment to the Cradles. As a respected military man, becoming known in the district as 'Major' for his gallantry, Smith got swept up in the 'Spy Scare' circling Gustav once he'd arrived home. 'It was my duty to report on some of these rumours after my return, for every rumour had to be investigated, however impossible or absurd it might be.'[37] His custodial role extended to storing Gustav's possessions as the knocks of life threw them together with a brotherly intimacy.

Several of Gustav's in-laws squirmed at the enemy alien in their nest. Kate's brother Bertie Cowle, a co-executor of her will, flagged legal problems with the transfer of the Cradle property she'd left to him since 'the fact of your nationality must be mentioned'.[38] The War Precautions Act proscribed sale or gift of land to enemy subjects. Neither one of us nor one of them, he occupied a limbo zone. Far from the shoulder-rubbing interaction of city street or country lane, he was sovereign of a mountain where he could at least be alone with his thoughts, his kelpies trailing behind or barking at the scent of prey, in a timeless magnificence. Nature was a safe welcoming place for a stateless person; the birds and animals didn't discriminate between two-legged interlopers, and the weather systems came and went regardless of who was getting wet.

Gossler envied him his sanctuary 'away from this awful turmoil ... People seem to be losing control of themselves. One never knows what the next day will bring. I always had the greatest respect for the calm and deliberate temperament of the Australian but if they continue as they are they will take the cake from our friends the Italians as regards the lack of control of their feelings ... My most ardent wish is to get a thousand miles away from everybody.'[39] The lads who threw stones at German targets in cities and towns faced a long, sobering walk if they wanted to reach Waldheim. Tourists also stayed away. Numbers dwindled to twenty-two guests in 1916, thirty-eight in 1917, twenty-eight in 1918. 'I live now like a bachelor again,' he wrote to sister Rosa in September. 'The farm is leased and most of the time I spend in the mountains. There you do not see or hear anything of the war.'[40] Then came the awful death of Kate's dog Fuschs. Gustav found her in spasms, her limbs rigid. He suspected strychnine poison.[41] The burial of this sweet-natured, affectionate, living, breathing reminder of Kate—the puppy she had fussed over and favoured—hurt. He had no proof of malice, but suspicion begets suspicion. Inside his sanctuary, slights from afar could be tolerated with a punishing work ethic and with eyes and ears that never grew tired of nature's ingenuity.

'Public opinion would have regarded him as a "master spy" ... without thinking that there was very little to spy upon,' his biographer concluded mistakenly.[42] For of course he was spying. From his perch in the landscape, he made fastidious notes of the flora and fauna. He'd sit for hours watching a light-brown, white-spotted native cat play in a hollow log. He studied the scanty nests of the sooty crow-shrike or currawong, stalking the forests and the ridges, Flock and Flick his only company for days on end. Every morning he'd record rainfall, temperatures, humidity, carefully calibrating monthly minimums, maximums and means. He surveyed the geology of the landscape, taking elevations, fathoming lakes, mapping waterways, naming the topography. While Melbourne's *Argus* debated whether German composers should be

The weather station at Waldheim, 1929 (Gustav Weindorfer)

discarded, Gustav played Bach and Beethoven and the Viennese music of Strauss on his wheezy gramophone with the volume drowning out the tinkle of water in the creek beside his home.[43] If the currawongs and bush mice objected to this musical treason, none complained. Wilderness was the kindest buffer, shielding him from the worst of humanity, soothing wounds of loss with a kinship he recognised in the hardy alpine cushion plants on the high plateau or the pines hundreds of years old or the hexagonal thrusts of dolerite exposed before calendars marked the trudge of our existence.

His stoush with authorities over the road he so sorely wanted was surely political as well as budgetary since there would have been discomfort at allocating scarce public money for the benefit of an enemy alien. In 1919 the Kentish council found a small grant to improve a section of road across Middlesex Plains, largely to provide a gang of returned soldiers with employment. Smith, who'd been wounded at Gallipoli, knew several of the men from the 26th Battalion. He wrote to federal senator H. Payne, from Launceston, one of the dreamers in

Gustav's corner, recalling two of the gang working under fire on a steep hillside the day after they'd set foot on the Turkish peninsula. They'd been ordered to make a road for the mule trains out of reach of flooding from the winter rains: 'I remember the first day two men were killed by shrapnel and after that there were casualties every day.'[44] The peacefulness of the Middlesex Plains on Cradle's doorstep must have been paradise for veterans haunted by bloodshed, a healing place of birds and creeks and weather-filled sky.

The Cradles were Gustav's sacred ground, where Kate's presence flickered before him. He was glad to have Smith home safely. He needed stout hearts and wily souls to help him draw attention to nature's finest handiwork so that people everywhere could read from the book and learn the significance of the saga it recounted. 'I can quite understand you being busy,' he wrote to Smith. 'I am going from morning til night.'[45] He threw himself into improving the chalet, designing a bath house that diverted a flow from the creek via a scooped-out log into a cauldron, where a fire lit below could heat the water. He'd carted the cast-iron tub along the track to Waldheim on his shoulders just as he'd done with the stove. He fenced garden beds, which delivered bulging lettuces, cauliflowers, rhubarb and enough cabbage to pickle sauerkraut in an empty beer barrel, also carried home on his back, no doubt triggering loose talk of his intentions as he left the Wilmot store.

He'd also pushed on with scientific research, filling sixty pages of foolscap with firsthand observations patiently wrought over nine years among the wild brethren in his forested neighbourhood: ringtail and brushtail possums, tiger cats, native cats, rufous-bellied wallabies, kangaroos and currawongs, their harsh cry a distinctive refrain of the Tasmanian highlands. He described their quirks, nesting and mating patterns, their pugnacity or sociability, their tricks for getting free from the snares he laid, their language, their tracks, the taste of their flesh and the market price, down to the last pence, fetched for their skins. The Cradle bush was his research laboratory and his larder. 'When the ground is all covered with snow I do build a big fire, open my door, seat myself very, very, quietly in front of the blazing logs, and, presently, one by one in they would come, without their usual fear of man or of one another, and share with me in stillness, the grateful warmth,' he told his Melbourne botanist friend Charles Sutton.[46]

Sometimes he'd sit observing for several hours, as he did one day in May 1918, tracking the migratory return of an endless train of currawongs, concluding they'd flown a distance by the rests they took in the trees. Hunting at night with an acetylene lamp fixed to the rim of his hat by a metal spring band, he'd study an animal's escape from predators and dogs, impressed by the superiority of rufous-bellied wallabies, who did not panic when caught in a 'wire-necker' trap: 'With almost human

Hand-fed wallaby at Waldheim (Fred Smithies)

like intelligence it tries to remove the inconvenient encumbrance with its front paws, leaving sometimes a little tuft of fur attached.'[47]

These copious notes became the basis of a long, authoritative article on Tasmanian wildlife that Gustav co-authored with George Francis, a stockman and trapper from Middlesex station who'd spent a lifetime on the tramp. They were the only two permanent inhabitants of an area that was then primarily unoccupied Crown land, sharing between them a wealth of material picked up 'in an accidental way' on their meanderings. Published in four instalments by the Victorian Field Naturalists journal in 1920, these vivid vignettes were scaffolded by Gustav with scholarly references to Tasmanian Museum director Clive Lord's 1918 paper 'Notes on the Mammals of Tasmania'.[48] His attachment to all creatures, even the wombat, whose 'body has developed rather at the expense of its brains', is clear from the respectful way he inhabits their thinking. The wombat may be stupid, 'so little alive to the approach of danger he has been known not to budge even after a passer-by has gently reminded him by the toe of his boot that he was in the way and has continued unconcernedly grazing in spite of the insult. Yet the beast is as tenacious as the tiger cat, an excellent swimmer, the taste of its meat redolent of young beef.' An admirable pet, loyal to a place or master, it was an everyday occurrence 'in one of our small country towns to see an old lady going to the railway station for her mail followed by a pet wombat' smugly aware of its mistress's dexterity in warding off dogs with her stick.[49]

He deciphers their language; the native cat in flight uttering a noise like 'the cracking of nuts in quick succession'; the possum's laugh heard over great distances, most often on moonlit nights, 'perhaps the outcome of satisfaction and contentment'; the distress call of a currawong who has lost a mate 'answered from all points of the compass' by a hue and cry as others join in the search; the 'whistling cry' of the ringtail warning its family of danger; the postprandial purr of the native cat under his bunk bed after a raid on the Waldheim kitchen.[50]

He and Kate spoke to each other through animals, wild and tame. As farmers and mountaineers, they relied on horses and dogs for transport, hunting, safety, even conversation. Gustav attributed human qualities to every breed. The brushtail possum in shades of grey, umber and black was a roamer and loner, these inquisitive 'sweet toothed' beings often raiding camp sites, the serrated rim of empty jam tins their guillotine. He described flocks of currawongss gathering for days in a 'pre-nesting corroboree' each season. The birds voiced 'political and social views' in an endless ear-piercing chatter until matters were settled and breeding began. But even dispersed, he detects 'a communistic government' in these ranks, with the presence of a leader 'whose voice, distinct from the rest, may be first heard at early dawn in a soft and somewhat melodious sounding "Ghiglia-glag-glag-glag".' On some mornings there would be no answer. Then the reveille would sound again in a renewed and higher tone. From afar the first faint reply would sound, then another from a different direction, 'and in a very short time every bird will have announced the beginning of another day'. The currawongs occupied the forest behind Waldheim, greedy for food at the kitchen door, once snitching handkerchiefs drying on the bleaching ground for a nest.[51]

The ringtail possum he found the 'most respectable' since it married for life, the males sharing with a chosen mate the care of offspring, working as a pair to build a house then rearing their young, often three in a pouch. Here was a peaceful animal not given to pugnacity, even in pursuit of sex. The bachelors 'seem to take their lot philosophically … and live their lives in single blessedness until the fates choose to provide them with partners.'[52] Gustav kept four ringtails for a period in the old fowl yard, fitted with branches 'and a snug little nest. My word you should see them, how they romp about … you hardly feel their little feet upon your hand.'[53] He befriended tamer creatures, fed them, studied them, yet he also snared them on the hunt, selling their skins when the price was good. He cooked and ate them (their flesh in a stew 'bears favourable comparison with chicken'), aware even as he sucked their bones of their endangered future. Yet he wanted to protect them, warning the population was at risk now that hunters used acetylene lamps, as he did, to search out prey.

'In Tasmania few persons have taken the slightest interest in the war of extermination now proceeding between man and the native fauna,' these articles concluded. Demand for leather and furs would only increase and though 'animals were made for the use of man', one side had overstepped a line, 'by his want of foresight or by his greed for gain' seriously reducing their numbers and laying waste to large areas of game country.[54] 'Wherever man begins to subdue the wilderness and to cultivate the soil or to win the precious metal, there a battle royal at once ensues between him and Nature; but why, in a civilised community, the feud should be carried on with the risk of utter extermination is hard to conceive. The State possesses large areas in its interior which … could most effectually be turned into game reserves, where undisturbed by the presence of man, the species could at least preserve themselves.'[55]

At the same time as he worried for the future of native animals in the valley, he was fretting over the fate of the King Billy pine, a sought-after commercial timber for its durable, pliable strength. Located in five groves around the valley, this species preferred rising ground with an easterly aspect and a constant supply of moisture. Just as the ringtail possum mated with a partner for life, the King Billy flourished in the company of deciduous beech trees. Gustav had built the chalet by felling several trees and recycling older logs found in the litter of the forest floor, some of these yielding many hundreds of palings.[56] What alarmed him most was their slow rate of growth, with the young pine averaging 3-inch spurts of height in a favourable year. 'This fine and valuable species would seem to be doomed to a comparatively early extinction,' he wrote in a scholarly study of Tasmanian conifers for a short-lived publication called *The Gum Tree*.[57] Based on meticulous observations of growth rings in felled trunks, combined with the results of experiments he and Smith had conducted measuring and comparing the proliferation of seedlings replanted in different habitats, he concluded the species had already taken a battering, 'represented now by only a fraction of a one-time much richer distribution' because 'its incredibly slow growth … does not permit it to keep pace with the exploitation of the timber trade.' Inaccessibility had kept trees safe from loggers. 'But difficulties of this nature will be overcome sooner or later and the State of Tasmania … will realise only too late that an effective forest policy in the past would have been very much to its advantage.'[58] Nevertheless, he contemplated selling pine from his own land, just as he snared the animals whose future he sought to secure.

On the forge of Waldheim's hearth, he was smelting arguments for a national park, weapons to be used in a gentler campaign that would be waged once the current world conflict subsided. Forced indoors during the winter of 1919 by 4-foot drifts, the heaviest snow storm he'd encountered, he wrote to Smith with a stirring of hope and contentment. 'Just you imagine a well-constructed building covered with four feet of snow … the porches full of firewood, the kitchen equally well supplied with tucker, opposite the fire two dogs, outside the thermometer down to 26 degrees … inside a man writing down his experiences in nine years of bush life, every morning shovelling a track to the snow gauge … and you get my position in a nutshell.'[59] Summer in peacetime would bring fresh legs and brave hearts to advance a cause bigger than all of them.

Snow-bound wombat, 1929 (Gustav Weindorfer)

8
GIANTS

Curled up in the farthest corner of Waldheim's inglenook, a young boy 'bright eyed and quiet as a bush mouse' made himself smaller among the trousered tree trunks of men whose crowns almost touched the timber ceiling as they stood around the fireplace. Shadows were thrown large against the chalet wall by the glow from a hurricane lamp hooked on a rafter. Wafts of tobacco smoke and the aroma of coffee beans spiced the air. Little Ray Tilley listened to the voices talk over each other above the spit and pop of pine logs burning in the grate. They spoke of the movement for a national park, impossible roads, rough tracks and mountain adventures. Getting here had been excitement enough for him. Hoisted up on the front seat of farmer Bob Quaile's wagon, his legs dangling far from the footrest, he'd been awestruck by the immense bulk of the driver, a man who knew every dip and trough along the way. The four horses, jingling and snorting from the strain, would halt or turn on commands belched from beneath an impressive white moustache as the driver deftly flicked the reins, occasionally grabbing the youngster's jacket to save him from being tossed overboard when the slim iron-shod wheels hit a boulder. He'd felt like a king up that high. Whenever the giants knocked at the door of his parents' coffee palace in Wilmot begging a favour from his father, who helped convey travellers bound for the mountain, he'd peek from behind his mother's skirt hoping they'd come in for a cup of tea or a meal. He worshipped them for their bush craft and the magical world he entered in their company.[1]

There was Ron Smith, tall, sincere and quietly spoken, who'd been decorated for bravery in the war. Charles Fenton Monds, son of a wealthy flour mill merchant, who'd taught young Ray the value of a penknife. Carl Stackhouse, a lawyer with Shields, Heritage, Stackhouse & Martin, a firm the giants rebranded as 'Fields, Hermitage, Packhorse & Mountain'. He wore a 10-gallon cowboy hat and leather breeches. Instead of a weapon or a flask, he carried a volume of poetry inside his hip pocket. Fred Smithies, the sinewy daredevil climber always laden with camera gear, allowed the puny tag-along to carry the tripod if he was very, very good. George Perrin was reserved, but kindly. His wife Florence, her bespectacled eyes soft and smiling, was a giantess, a brilliant photographer who seemed in the child's eye to bring these boisterous men to order. Launceston dentist Dr Ray McClinton, an American who'd visited Yosemite, thought Cradle Mountain rivalled that magnificent Californian wilderness. He was the flashy one with a car. Of course there were others, but the delirium of a small boy remembers best the characters who bewitched him, and at the centre of them all was 'Dorfer', sometimes called 'The Fizzle'. Whenever Dorfer kissed the hand of his mother, the boy felt a quiver of alarm, and though Gustav was not very interested in mischievous youngsters, this one was mesmerised by him, his way with animals, his suave charm, the duets sung with his father by the fire. Dorfer was the spark that set the others alight and, as the keeper of a tame bush mouse called 'Yimmy', impossible for a boy to forget.[2]

Fred Smithies and 'Doc' McClinton first arrived at Waldheim in October 1920 just as the business was recovering from the downturn of war. Visitor numbers bounced from twenty-seven the previous season to a record fifty-seven.[3] It was Smithies' third attempt to get here. His first on a motorbike in 1918 took a wrong turn, leading him up Mt Misery on a cold night with no matches. He walked to keep warm, lasting twenty-seven hours without food. A second go with 'Doc' in February aboard a Chevrolet Baby Grand brought them close to Pencil Pine Creek, but their walk in was aborted as night fell. This time, on a motorbike with sidecar, they'd been bogged often and capsized once, leaving the machine battered but not broken outside the valley entrance.[4] They reached Waldheim on foot at 6 pm, greeted with Gustav's home-roasted brew. The 'Doc' drank his black to avoid the pollution of milk. The Launceston pair were captivated by the chalet, their host and the peaks to be climbed. They returned in the Chev months later over the Christmas – New Year period of 1921, with a larger party that included their wives, swept up in the excitement of discovering a seam of such extraordinary country.

They climbed Cradle, Mt Campbell and Barn Bluff, disappointed by swirling mist that hid the view, but Smithies marvelled at the 'grand and awe inspiring spectacle of the gathering storm ... (with) occasional breaks in the wind driven fog and clouds affording brief peeks into the wonderland below'. After marching home in bitter wind and heavy rain, their troubles were 'soon forgotten in the joy of a hot bath and a sumptuous repast awaiting us', since food and warmth are always sweeter after hardship.[5] If Cradle Mountain was an El Dorado for botanists, then consider the spell cast over photographers who found themselves in a sculpture garden of rock and cliff and tree. Here lay the sublime. Windswept plateaus, fathomless gorges, secluded pools, gloomy forests, scenery spread before them in every key and hue and mood. Smithies would become one of Tasmania's greatest wilderness photographers, known for his death-defying vistas from rocky outcrops but also lyrical images of the snow-covered Cradle summit, smooth as the curvaceous hip of a naked woman reclining, a tiny human figure walking along her ridge.[6]

Florence Perrin's diptych, taken after a blizzard on the Cradle plateau, favoured a close-up, tightly framed view of nature. In the foreground, snap-frozen trees bent like hooded pilgrims (shown on page 110).[7] She aimed her camera upward in the forest behind the chalet for a paisley pattern of ice-crusted, leafy boughs, almost abstracting the landscape to reveal the beauty of intricate, random patterns, in stark contrast to the traditional chest-beating grandeur of the wider-angle sweep (shown on page 74).[8] A woman behind the lens brought a different sensibility, just as Australian painters Grace Cossington-Smith and Margaret Preston rendered interiors with hypnotic force. Florence would have appreciated Kate Weindorfer, not simply for providing gender balance but because of their mutual interest in small plants. Whereas Kate's botanical fascination lay with mosses and lichens, Florence became a collector and curator of seaweed. They both tugged at society's leash. Florence shared Kate's love of the craggy heights and became a founding member of the Tasmanian Alpine Club. After climbing Barn Bluff in 1920, she wrote, 'Oh our West coast is a wild and rugged place, how I love it. We spent two hours on top then made our way down and home to camp after a perfect day, the memory of which will always linger with me. The mountains just put their arms around me and hold me and when I am away long they pull and pull till I must go back.'[9] Her words are reminiscent of Kate's sense on Mt Roland of the silent outreach of the soul towards eternal beauty.

Florence's photographs are works of art. Her husband George Perrin, also a camera buff, was welcomed into the North Tasmanian Camera Club while women were not.[10] Florence conducted her own excursions or kept busy with her camera in the giants' company. The introduction of dry-plate technology had quickened exposure times, and the development of emulsions gave photographers more

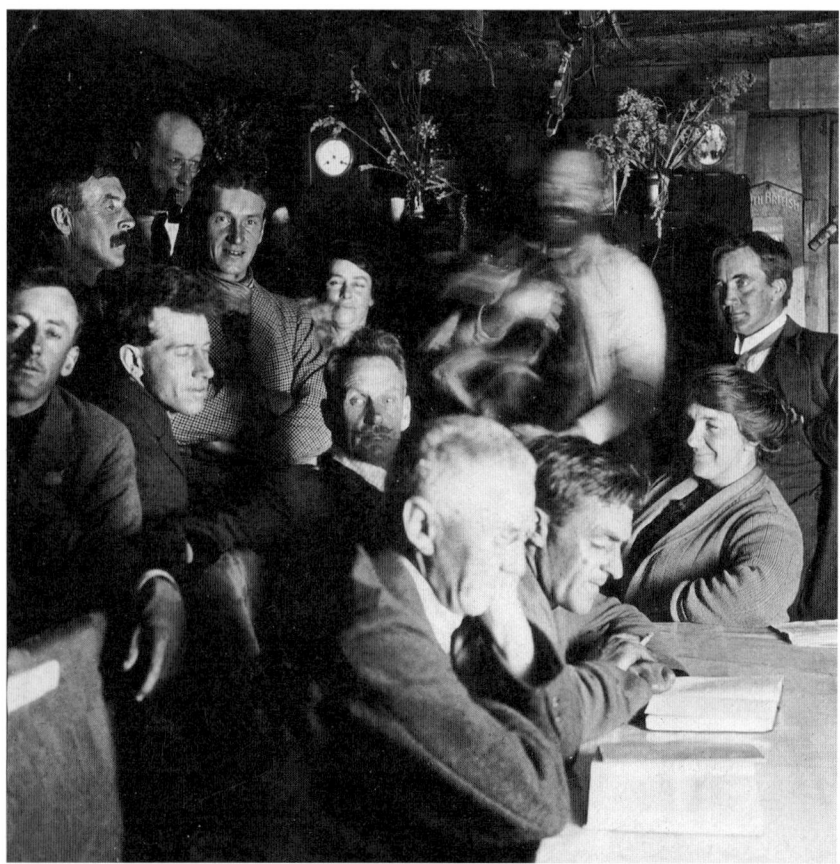

Full house: Weindorfer at the rear with a squirming Flock; Beulah Hills, wife of watercolour artist, Charlie Hills, on his right, January 1922

control to experiment with aesthetics. Amateur shutterbugs purchased Kodak box brownies to capture scenes for their albums. Gustav was prolific, taking hundreds of photographs of plants for the botanical treatise he planned to write. Dr Sutton and Ron Smith sent each other copies of shots they'd taken at Cradle Mountain, comparing techniques and exposures with a childish delight in their new gadgets. Pictures conveyed impressions instantly.[11] Tasmania's photographic studios had an early and keen appreciation of the market for postcard views on an island replete with natural spectacles.

Gustav knew the medium's power because this was how he'd fallen prey to the Cradles spell. Nicholas Caire's images of Mt Buffalo gorge were a deliberate ploy in the campaign for Victoria's first national park. Those who hadn't been to Yosemite knew the Cathedral Dome in black and white. Tasmania's tourism dynamo Evelyn Temple Emmett felt the thrall of scenery. He loved grand vistas and he understood their restorative sway over 'the tired city worker' as cars careened onto streets and boulevards.[12]

Emmett had first visited Waldheim in March 1916 as Kate lay dying. He appreciated the muscle of the media, its ability to massage public opinion and pinch the nerves of politicians. He also understood that money spoke louder than silent majesty, and he quickly mastered the economics of an industry that could exploit the state's most valuable assets at very little cost. He penned an article for *The Examiner* on his return, asking 'who could after a day spent in these surroundings still be unable to understand that magnetic pull "the call of the wild" so strong to some natures as to be almost irresistible'.[13] While he hadn't seen everywhere, he could not seriously quarrel with the claim that Cradle Mountain offered the finest scenery in the country. Back in Hobart he'd moved that the area be reserved at a meeting of the Scenery Preservation Board, and 35,000 acres had been withheld from selection.

But the Cradle proposal slipped off the radar during the war.[14] Gustav's grief over Kate's death distracted him from their commitment to a national park for everyone to share. This vision bore the stretch marks of a decade's wear. With Kate no longer at his shoulder to prosecute their dream and share the running of the chalet, his faith dissipated. Writing to Smith on 5 January 1921, after the departure of Smithies' 'very jolly' party, Gustav sounded strangely flat. 'Since the day before yesterday I am alone again and today being your wedding day naturally my thoughts are very much with you.'[15] Smith had remarried following the death of his first wife, Kathleen, in 1917. Gustav remained single, sometimes accepting it philosophically like the ringtail possum, other times the solitude overwhelming him.

He began moonlighting for pocket money at a small timber mill run by F. H. Haines on Pencil Pine Creek. 'If you could see me you would hardly recognise me,' he told his sister Rosa. 'Covered with the mud of the virgin forest I drive four of the strongest draughthorses, one behind the other, hauling logs with heavy chains. No reins are needed. Words are sufficient … it gives me experience I will soon be able to use in my own pine forest.'[16]

Unthinkable that he might turn the toothed saw on the trees around him. Judicious in his search for King Billy logs to split for palings, he knew the tree was at risk because of its slow growth rate. Yet he entertained the heresy of a commercial assault on the buttresses of his cathedral. Since before Christmas he'd been in talks with Burnie solicitor Wilfred Hodgman, fine-tuning a contract for the sale of timber from his land, with the exception of 4 acres around the chalet, under the strict proviso that trees 'would be removed in a careful manner to preserve natural forest'.[17] This is an inconvenient truth, one of the paradoxes of a man who killed game for skin and flesh then raised the alarm of extinction. Like the husband who covets another's wife, he not only felt the heat of lust; he made plans for their future.

In early February 1921, days before Smith was due at Waldheim with the surveyor general Edward Counsel and the district surveyor Frank Wilks, Smith received a note from Gustav: 'Tell Wilks … to bring his own tucker because I have given up the accommodation business and I am somewhat short in different lines. No people turning up.' His absence as host, cook and guide was a temporary contingency measure to tide him over. 'I am working with Haines the last three weeks. When you come, inquire at the mill about me, though you know where to find the key.'[18] Counsel, who was also chairman of the Scenery Preservation Board, would be a hefty catch.

Fortunately, the bottom fell out of the timber market, saving him from a catastrophic miscalculation. The upside to this economic crunch was that it gave traction to the case for preservation, since the trees weren't worth the cost of cutting them down. Smith, who also considered logging his land during the scarcity following the Great

War, later acknowledged they had both been tempted by a windfall gain, but the prohibitive cost of transport to the coast ultimately made it unprofitable: 'The forest did not contribute to Weindorfer's income to the extent of even one pound.'[19]

Timing is everything. The closure of timber mills around the island coincided with the descent of the giants in the valley. Ten years younger than Gustav, these men, all in their mid-thirties, brought a rush of energy. Effervescent in their superlatives, they could not stay away. A day before the surveying party arrived, Smithies turned up for his third visit in as many months, bringing his wife Ida, her brother, the Launceston architect and alderman Frank Heyward, and Herbert King, a photographer whose family ran a motor business. It was as if they'd stumbled upon a secret door into another world. They called it Liberty Hall. 'To stay in bed as long as one wants, wear what clothes pleases one, to stay up quite late … to bathe in any water in sight … Waldheim is a pleasure in itself. Its charming unexpected nooks, clean, beautiful natural materials, the fanciful yet practical design (fitness to its surroundings), the bath house, the lovely tent room, and the marvellous little garden. The Weindorfer, for there could only be one, to argue with, to joke with, walk with … Scenery … is there anything better in Australia? Why do Tasmanians wander elsewhere when we have the Cradle country and its glories and wonders within easy reach … here surely is a great possession in the shape of a national park, all ready to hand. Perhaps another generation may realise its worth.'[20]

Going home, the party crossed paths with Smith and the team of surveyors, infecting the uninitiated with expectations that were surpassed, Edward Counsel declaring afterwards that the views from Cradle Mountain and the saddle of Barn Bluff were the finest he'd ever beheld.[21]

A whisper caught like a spark in dry grass, whipped along by a can-do crowd with the sensibility to appreciate what Smithies called the 'special spirit' of this place, falling for the landscape and the charismatic man who had settled there.[22] In late February a rave review of Cradle Mountain appeared on the front page of north-western Tasmania's daily paper, *The Advocate*, quoting 'a prominent Launceston resident' who was recently in these parts and was confident they were 'better than the famous Blue Mountains'. But the visitor, 'who has travelled widely', worried at the destruction of native game and damage to trees

Gustav and Flock with a party of guests on the summit, 1922

from fires carelessly lit by 'some irresponsible persons', calling for the state to adopt the protective regime of America's national parks model immediately or face ruin of a place destined for greatness. Yosemite was the template. Since full-time rangers had been stationed in the Californian wilderness sanctuary, Yosemite had become 'even more beautiful than it was 20 years ago'.[23] In the same month as the call for a Yosemite style reserve, photographs that Smithies took of Lake Lilla and Cradle Mountain won first prize in a competition, published in the *Illustrated Weekly Courier*.[24]

Whether a strategy was crafted beside the Waldheim fireplace over rum coffees or unfolded in serendipitous fashion—growing organically, one event triggering another, one warrior recruiting the next—this was the season for success. The collapse of timber gave Emmett an open corridor to pitch tourism's potential as a money-spinner, not just for the state but for every feeder town along the route to Cradle Mountain. He foresaw the incalculable value of Tasmania's natural resources. Interviewed by *The Examiner* on 11 July 1921, he telegraphed a new bid to gazette 35,000 acres of Cradle Mountain, drawing on America's awakening to the beauty of 'their seashores, river banks and mountain tops' and proclaiming parks for posterity. 'Capitalising scenery' was the phrase he coined, pointing to the 40,000 visitors received by Tasmania's Mt Field National Park for a peppercorn investment of 300 pounds a year. In Canada, tourism had become the fourth biggest income earner. Hawaii, an island smaller than theirs, had set aside 76,760 acres of reserve. He was spruiking to the burghers and bureaucrats and bush lovers reading their newspaper at breakfast.[25]

Five days later, *The Examiner* published an interview with Gustav entitled 'Proposed National Park: The Beauties of Cradle Mountain'. He explained Cradle's geological significance, the fifty large and small lakes replete with mountain trout, his chalet now able to sleep twenty, riffing from a script known by heart, even perhaps recited in his sleep, but it's as if he's distilled the arguments for a national park into bullet points, because that's how campaigns are run and won. The boast of bettering America's Yosemite and Yellowstone grabs attention, as does the threat to native animals. Gustav brought startling evidence of the latter. Ten years ago he would rouse thirty kangaroos in a day without the aid of a dog. 'Now one is rarely seen.'[26] He was in Launceston finessing plans for a committee to advance the park under the auspices of the new northern branch of the Royal Society.[27]

He wrote to Smith excitedly: 'Bad weather but I am having a good time. In the paper you will have noticed the movement about the national park is on foot. I am expecting the return of Alderman Heyward and on Monday I think I am going to Hobart. I will let you know when to kill the goose for I am looking forward to a good square feed of the Westwood variety.'[28] His next letter, written on 21 July 1921 on stationery from the Tasmanian government's Tourist and Information Bureau, announced his arrival in Hobart, advising, 'I cannot yet give orders with regards the bird'.[29] Using Emmett's office as campaign headquarters, they planned lantern-slide lectures to rouse public support within the Royal Society and the Field Naturalists Club, where they had friends galore. Gustav stumped up at the Parliament House office of the Liberal minister in charge of scenic reserves, Alec Hean, with a cheer squad of Emmett, botanist Leonard Rodway (a member of the Scenery Preservation Board) and museum director Clive Lord (secretary of the Tasmanian Field Naturalists and an authority on native mammals). Next stop the National Park Board.[30]

Smith cheered him on from his property, Westwood, by the Forth River: 'It really looks as though it will be proclaimed; but if by any chance it isn't it will have been well advertised and a good start made for a try later on ... the goose comes up twice a day for peas so she ought to be fat.'[31] Gustav's reply, still using government letterhead, has the swagger of success in its beat, written between lantern lectures at the Hobart Town Hall and the Mechanics Institute: 'You will see from the papers that I am still going strong ... Tomorrow I leave the city of dust and half naked undersized women' for Launceston, where the recently formed northern branch of the Royal Society had called a public meeting on the proposed Cradle reserve. 'I got enough of city life to last me for five years.'[32] There is yet another wink at when to kill the goose—cheeky, given he's beating the drum for preservation of game.

The giants could be spotted milling near the front of the crowd at the Launceston Mechanics Institute Hall on Friday 29 July. Gustav, Emmett, Smithies, Perrin and McClinton took their seats as Alderman Heyward introduced 'a place of rugged grandeur and singular beauty', talking up Gustav's plan for a national park that would extend from Cradle Mountain at the northern end through to Lake St Clair in the south.[33] Emmett took the floor with a stirring call for activism. He urged Launceston folk to get out of their armchairs and put 'backbone' and shoe leather into a scheme that would bring tourist traffic by their front door. There was spontaneous applause. 'Doc' McClinton worked the slide lantern, screening hand-tinted pictures by two of Tasmania's greatest wilderness photographers, J. W. Beattie and Stephen Spurling, with additional pictures from the albums of Smithies and others, including Mrs Annie Lindon, wife of a Hobart headmaster and an amateur botanist in Cradle's fan club.[34] Seen from the warm interior of a civic hall, these scenes went off like fireworks, each one eliciting rapturous sighs and aahs, for many had never climbed so high or seen such expansive vistas or walked in dense forests of myrtle, beech and pine with the weird spiky pandani tree a startling trespasser in the grassy valley.

The photographs were breathtaking entertainment for an audience as interested in the new technology as in the mountain's glory. Local MP and Labor Opposition leader Joseph Lyons, a future prime minister, suggested Emmett tour the proposal through north-west coast towns.[35] The committee appointed by the society's new northern branch to

Climbing Weindorfer's Tower, 1921 (Stephen Spurling)

champion the park was stacked with giants: Smithies, Perrin, McClinton and Heyward.[36] This was a big stride forward after a frenetic few weeks. 'Kill the goose,' Gustav ordered Smith on paper he'd swiped from the Launceston Tourist Bureau.[37] He wanted Smith to accompany him to the Cradles with Smithies and Spurling the following week. They needed more photographs.[38]

In early August, Gustav announced a road trip to be undertaken by Emmett, armed with 200 slides to be screened in Deloraine, Smithton, Sheffield, Latrobe and Burnie. He also let slip that a party of government ministers would visit Waldheim in the summer.[39] The tour of coastal towns was smart politics. Meetings were well attended despite inclement weather, passing a raft of unanimous motions in favour of the park so that they could hold Minister Hean's nerve steady.

At Penguin, on the coast, Emmett uttered a burst of purple prophesy. 'In days not so very long ago the tourist traffic was looked upon as a fad,' he noted, but the time was approaching when it would become the 'one staple item on the state bill of fare … the prime asset of Tasmania and the more the mainland prospered the bigger the trade would grow.'[40] Attuned to the tyranny of self-interest, he unpacked the proposition in pounds, shillings and pence for the merchants and men wanting work. 'If 100 people came into a district for over one week, they would spend at least one pound a day,' he explained. 'That's 700 pounds and the gains to the place would be substantial indeed.' Forget timber, he told them. 'Cradle Mountain has infinitely more value as a place to be looked at.'[41] The proposed national park would be one of the finest showpieces, with nothing to compare in Australia or New Zealand.

Within a year, Gustav had shifted from the precipice of despair to an ecstatic sense of possibility. Smith's prediction that Waldheim would benefit from the public attention, whatever the outcome of the park, rang true, as a revolving door of guests kept Gustav busy. Visitor numbers doubled from fifty in 1921 to 111 the next year.[42]

In December he and Smith entertained a party of four women, including Keva and Viti Allardyce, daughters of Tasmanian Governor Sir William Allardyce, and a local girl, Frances Cole, from Deloraine. Fine weather and the presence of spirited women in a place that transcends time lifted them into the ether. The Governor's daughters were soon off to Newfoundland with their civil servant father, who had resigned his office in a fit of pique over insufficient remuneration. Smith was quite undone by the girls, corresponding with both sisters for many months afterwards. 'I never enjoyed the mountains more than the three days we had there this week,' he wrote.[43] Gustav appeared similarly tipsy and lovestruck by what had transpired.

A shameless publicity hound with a nose for the cache of a vice-regal imprimatur, he cajoled Viti Allardyce into putting her name on a piece he would write for the paper. 'I do not know how the ladies will like it but it was rather difficult for me to write from a woman's point of view since I know so little about women,' he informed Smith, who was to forward the article so that Viti could alter it as she saw fit: 'Ask her to put her name after the word "By" or if she prefers, a pseudonym.' He supplied a covering letter for the editor of *The Examiner*.[44] But the girls wimped out on returning to Government House, and Gustav barely concealed his annoyance. 'If the girls would have had any sense they would have got it typed under a pseudonym and all would have gone well,' he grumbled to Smith. 'It is stale now … I make a lot of use of the papers and I cannot disgust them by coming along with too much stuff.'[45] To repair the rift, Viti passed on a letter her father had received from Leonard Rodway confirming that the Cradle reserve would be considered at the next meeting of the National Park Board.[46]

The Examiner had been a staunch ally of Gustav's crusade. A senior reporter from the paper, Edward Leeson, joined Clive Lord and Evelyn Temple Emmett for a tour of Cradle's landmarks prior to Christmas, producing a florid burst of advertorial.[47] Gustav took them here, there and everywhere in a three-day express tour. Shouldering packs of 35 pounds each, crammed with blankets, tents and provisions, they set off the first morning in mist to the plateau, lunching on grilled lamb chops washed down with mugs of billy tea. The sun lifted conveniently on cue, the ribbed top of Cradle above them, Barn Bluff nearby, like a bulwark in the clouds, as they made for the summit, and down again after twenty minutes to lay camp in pine scrub below the ridge of the bluff. Lord joked that when he went to blow out his candle that evening, the flame was frozen. Gustav got up throughout the night

Picnicking on the shore of Dove Lake, Gustav third from left

to put logs on the fire. The next morning, climbing up the Bluff, he took them by a cirque, a natural arena formed by the slow rasp of ice in a glacial age. Explaining that it had originally been carpeted with deciduous beech, he showed them where the forest had been burned a year ago by a prospector looking for coal. Halfway down, a member of the group remembered he'd left a camera on top. Gustav beetled back up to retrieve it, a mere stroll for this marathoner.[48]

Crossing the plateau on the way home from Barn Bluff, they heard shouts from above. Herbert King, the photographer and motorcycle enthusiast, had led a party to the Cradle summit and was shouting instructions for those below to hurry home and prepare dinner for the crowd of guests.[49] Two groups of tourists in one day signalled a new phase in the valley's history. The next day the groups merged for a tour of the back of Cradle Mountain. Standing on Rodway Peak, named after the botanist Leonard Rodway, overlooking Flynn's Tarn, a tribute to zoologist Professor Theodore Thomson Flynn, the tourist chief Evelyn Temple Emmett drew Gustav's gaze to a large lake in the bottom of a gorge. Whether or not Gustav's surprise was fabricated, he announced the pool would be known henceforth as Lake Emmett in a gracious salute to his tireless lieutenant. *The Examiner*'s journalist was

Flynn's Tarn (Frank Hurley)

also rewarded with a landmark when he overtook the others cresting a 400-foot bluff on a ridge at the rear of the chalet overlooking the grassy plains of Hounslow Heath. This became Leeson's Lookout.[50] Like a king anointing his favoured courtiers, Gustav never ran short of bluffs or lakes with which to remember the characters deserving of recognition. Women were well represented too, from Truganini Point to Marion's Lookout (named after his sister-in-law, Dan's wife, Marion), Kathleen's Lake (after Ron Smith's first wife, who'd visited Cradle with Kate and Gustav) and Mt Kate, in honour of his wife, while Lindon Tarns curtsied to amateur botanist Annie Lindon. Significantly he left himself off the map.

Leeson's account of Cradle gave the park proposal another forceful nudge. Entitled 'The New Scenic Reserve', his article urged the government to get moving on the scheme, as well as a better track to Waldheim's door. 'Without doubt Cradle Mountain and Barn Bluff are the greatest mountain attractions in the Commonwealth. At one's feet are lakes and mountains uncountable, some of them a deep violet hue … others shining like gold in the brilliant sunshine. The views from either rival anything in the world.'[51] There was no greater advocate for a park than the landscape itself.

Nothing beat sleeping under the stars, listening to the sighs of the wind through the trees or the tinkle of water pooling in creeks, finding a path through impenetrable shady groves, or walking until your calves ached at the end of a trudge to the top of the world, overwhelmed by what lay beyond. Gustav and Emmett knew the best means of convincing politicians of Cradle Mountain's merits was to entice them into the wilderness. To this end, a party of Tasmanian government ministers was scheduled to arrive in early February for an excursion that would clinch the park's future.[52]

The comparisons with Yosemite suggest that participants in the push for the Cradle reserve knew the forward and backward steps of the American campaign. Proclaimed by an act of congress in 1890 after lobbying by naturalist John Muir, the park was controlled initially by the State of California. Its boundary did not corral the area around Yosemite Valley. In 1903, US President Teddy Roosevelt wrote to Muir proposing a camping trip through the Yosemite wilderness, where they could thrash out a policy for America's greatest scenic wonders. 'I do not want anyone with me but you,' Roosevelt wrote to the naturalist, who looked like a prophet with his straggly grey beard and rake-thin streak, swimming in a crumpled jacket and trousers. The President was a ruddy-cheeked man, up for roughing it, in baggy jodhpurs with a Norfolk jacket, leather puttees, a neckerchief and knee-length leather boots.[53]

Accompanied by two mules laden with tent, bedding and food, the two men slept the first night in the Mariposa Big Tree Grove. Roosevelt had a pile of forty woollen blankets to keep him warm. Muir bedded down on a mattress of boughs swaddled in a cloth he carried in his knapsack. 'Lay in the darkening aisles of the great sequoia grove,' Roosevelt wrote in his diary. 'The majestic trunks beautiful in colour and symmetry rose around us like the pillars of a mightier cathedral than was ever conceived even by the fervour of the Middle Ages. Hermit thrushes sang beautifully in the evening and again with a burst of wonderful music at dawn.'[54] They survived a snowstorm at Sentinel Dome on the second night before seeking warmer shelter below on the edge of Bridal Veil Meadow in Yosemite Valley for their last fireside chat.

Three years later Yosemite's parameters were extended to protect the Mariposa Grove and prevent grazing in the valley.[55] California ceded control of the park to the federal government. In 1916 the *National Park Act* was introduced to regulate the management of wilderness areas. 'Our people should see to it that they are preserved for their children and their children's children forever, with their majestic beauty unmarred,' Roosevelt declared.[56] He signed five national parks into existence during his presidency.

Australian Prime Minister Billy Hughes was not such a rugged type. As a young British immigrant, he'd worked for 18 months as a rouseabout travelling outback Queensland and New South Wales, but decades later his support for extending the Commonwealth's powers did not stray into parks and wildlife. He could have been a soft target, given his enthusiasm over the Cradle Mountain lantern slides shown at a civic reception at the Majestic Theatre in Launceston on the evening of Wednesday 8 February 1922. So intrigued was he by the photographs of Smithies, Heyward and McClinton that he asked to be shown them a second time after the formal entertainment had concluded.[57]

Since the reserve was a state matter, though, Gustav was relying instead on the forthcoming visit of three Tasmanian ministers: the Treasurer, Sir Elliott Lewis, a keen walker, who brought along his son Arndell Neil Lewis, a lawyer and passionate geologist; Chester Lord, secretary to the Premier; Attorney-General William Bispham Propsting; and Senator Herbert Hays, who was born in Forth and had become acquainted with Gustav when they were both founding members of the Tasmanian Liberal League in 1909. The powerbrokers stayed at Waldheim for four days, but the weather conspired against them. Several of the party launched for the summit hoping for a break in the clouds, but the view from on top was obscured throughout and heavy rainfall soaked them.[58] The Cradle district is more often wet than not, succouring trees and plants that couldn't thrive anywhere else. One fine day was all the ministers enjoyed for their tour of the highlands, but this was enough to ensure a conversion of sorts. Sir Elliott, on the cusp of retirement, told the press that the Cradle district was 'wild rugged and beautiful', a place geologists and botanists would revel in, while tourists would find everything they desired. Bogged on the way in to Cradle, they left the valley in sheets of rain, drenched to the skin.[59]

A decision on the reserve would be made shortly at a meeting of the Scenery Preservation Board in Hobart. The giants continued to thump the pavement, showing lantern slides of Cradle wherever a hall could be found and filled. Gustav allowed a wave of happiness to course through him. Waldheim was flush with guests. Days of revelry with the Governor's daughters and Miss Cole and then Emmett's merry crew had left him euphoric for the first time since his days with Kate. He wrote to Smith with a helium squeal. 'The last fortnight is behind me like a wild nightmare, fun, pleasure, worry, tiredness, over and under-feeding, laughter, music, whisky, rum, port wine, pork chops, sleeping out under barn Bluff without sleep and hundreds of other things, put them in a churn and you get a picture of my brain.'[60]

He'd employed a cook to help him this season, and was running up and down the mountains with guests so many times that he told sister Rosa he almost couldn't wait for the winter pause. Still afloat after the party of girls, he told her his visitors had been 'in the best mood', playing cards, singing. 'I have never had such a good time in all my 21 years in Australia.'[61] His forgetting of Kate in this flippant remark could be explained perhaps by the spark of flirtation with Francis Cole from

Deloraine and the thrill of a moment in time when everything they had worked towards dangled tantalisingly within reach. Surrounded by the giants, he was for the most part dependent on male acolytes, feeding his sense of achievement so that the woman who had drawn him here dwindled to a footnote. Leonard Rodway once apologised to Kate for a moment of 'man like' self-preoccupation. Gustav was prone to the same affliction.

When the Scenery Preservation Board met in Hobart on 29 March, there was robust debate over the future of mining, pastoral and timber interests. Rodway argued the main objective was to protect native animals from indiscriminate slaughter, and the native flora from destruction by fire. 'It was not proposed to make the area a sanctuary,' he declared.[62] Emmett led members through the history of the campaign, crediting Gustav as the catalyst for its resurgence a year ago. The recent ministerial visit had confirmed concerns about the disappearance of native animals and the risk of fire to the scenery, demonstrating the imperative of protection. Chairman Edward Counsel, the state's surveyor general who had visited Waldheim, supported the motion so long as the area was not locked up exclusively for tourists.[63] Thrilled by the result, Clive Lord dispatched a telegram to the giants in Launceston, most of whom were attending the first annual general meeting of the northern branch of the Royal Society in the Mechanics Institute Hall.[64]

Success has a thousand fathers, while defeat is a lonelier proposition, and so it was that manoeuvring began for the credit. Summing up the branch's achievements, Frank Heyward addressed 'misconceptions' that the Launceston band wished to claim ownership of the reserve when the miracle of its conception lay with Evelyn Temple Emmett in association with Gustav Weindorfer, while the giants had locked in behind them to ensure delivery.[65] The inevitable tussle for a share of the plaudits did not perturb Gustav. 'Are you dead? I am almost,' he informed Smith days after Cradle's fate was secured. 'I have a few days' peace then come five from Launceston for a fortnight.'[66]

The campaign for the park alerted Tasmanians to the drawcard on their doorstep. 'Well over a hundred have been there this summer,' Smith boasted to Joan Stawell, who went to Cradle with the Governor's daughters and wrote to him with follow-up questions about the pencil pine trees and the height of the summit.[67] News of the influx of visitors made her anxious that the solitude and remoteness of this garden might be compromised: 'It will spoil it so frightfully if there are always people there.'[68] She put her finger on a fault line of tension between those who welcomed tourism and those who feared the trample of droves through forests and valleys that had forever been spared the footprints of civilisation. Edward Adams had nursed this qualm when he visited Waldheim in 1913: 'I picture the lovely place and the forest so near and yet so far and feel it will be almost sacrilege to let tourists in but I suppose these gardens are meant for all.'[69] When Smith told Viti Allardyce that in a recent rare dry spell, a motor car was able to navigate its way to within half a mile of the chalet, she winced: 'All the pleasures will have gone getting so near to civilisation. I think we will depart further into the bush.'[70]

Muir dealt with this contradiction in his quest to popularise Yosemite, ultimately convinced by the collective benefits that would flow from thousands of viewers 'getting in touch with the nerves of Mother earth'.[71] The massaging of public opinion was not only a necessary political prod in the fight to preserve tracts of wilderness but also vital for the health of society and the welfare of the planet. 'This is fine and natural and full of promise,' he wrote in 1901 of the conundrum. 'So also is the growing interest in the care and preservation of forests and wild places in general … Even the scenery habit in its most artificial forms, mixed with spectacles, silliness and kodaks; its devotees … frightening the wild game with red umbrellas—even this is encouraging, and may well be regarded as a hopeful sign of the times.'[72]

Red umbrellas had not reached Cradle Mountain, though the shutterbugs were busy. Until a better road was built, visitors would have to trek 6 miles—often through the wet, sometimes with packs on their backs—to reach Waldheim's front door. The people who came here were not the sort to twirl parasols, but they did gawk at the game as well as the plants and the cirques, for many of them were natural scientists, fascinated by all there was to behold in this outdoor laboratory. They carried notebooks, portfolios of blotting paper, aneroid barometers, compasses, carefully folded butter-paper maps that Gustav insisted they trace from his master plan so they wouldn't lose their way, even as they got lost in thought, walking along with their heads down, eyes searching for species of alpine flora or studying the glacial grooving in a quartzite slope below Hanson's Peak, reading between the lines of nature's mystery and unravelling the reasons why.

9

BUSH LABORATORY

Grace Blanchard was six months old when she met Gustav Weindorfer in his natural habitat. She'd already, in her short life, come face to face with extraordinary creatures. Slung over the shoulder of her mother, American plant geneticist Dr Frieda Cobb Blanchard, she'd eyeballed the scaly tuatara, an ancient reptile that thrived 250 million years ago when dinosaurs strolled the earth. This living fossil with a spiky ridged back, not dissimilar from the spine of a stegosaurus, is neither lizard nor crocodile but some kind of mythical beast in between. Grace's father, Assistant Professor Frank Blanchard, was a herpetologist who taught zoology at the University of Michigan, happiest wading in a swamp or tramping through the woods or sailing across the Pacific to a remote, rocky lighthouse reserve off the coast of New Zealand's South Island, where the tuatara still burrowed. Her mother was a pioneering scientist and assistant director of the university's botanical gardens. The couple initially shrugged off misgivings about taking their firstborn with them in June 1927 for a year's sabbatical leave from their posts to study the flora and fauna of temperate mountainous regions in New Zealand and Australia. On board ship, Frieda felt exhilarated by thoughts of what awaited them: 'I truly realised now that I was faring to see wonders.' Then she looked at Grace swaddled in her arms: 'What about her? There was no way of leaving her out of the scramble; she must go where we went. I for my part did not intend to be left out. I will sling her to my shoulder I decided and perhaps she will enjoy it too,' she wrote. 'If you happen to be a biologist and want as we always did to see

some outlandish thing or go to some place that is not an exhibition …
there are many difficulties.'[1]

The second baby to visit Waldheim, little Grace was a seasoned
traveller by the time the Blanchard family found their way to Cradle
Valley for eight days of collecting and observing in the field.[2] A striking
couple, both tall and lanky, they were as adventuresome as Gustav
and Kate, sharing passions, shoulder to shoulder in the laboratory and
the academy. Frieda knew of Gustav. She'd been studying the beech
tree when she wrote in 1912 to the Hobart Agricultural and Stock
Department seeking seedlings and samples of Tasmania's *Nothofagus
gunnii*, the deciduous beech tree that colour bombs Cradle in autumn,
and the *Nothofagus cunninghamii*, or myrtle beech tree, thought to provide the strongest botanical evidence of the supercontinent Gondwana.
Both grew at the rear of Waldheim and on the sheer slopes above Crater
Lake. A departmental official contacted Gustav for his help in obtaining
what she wanted.[3] He obliged, happy to answer the calls of science,
particularly from such esteemed quarters. Frieda was born into science.
Her father, Nathan Cobb, had been an agricultural nematologist,
specialising in microscopic worms and pests. He'd discovered root-knot

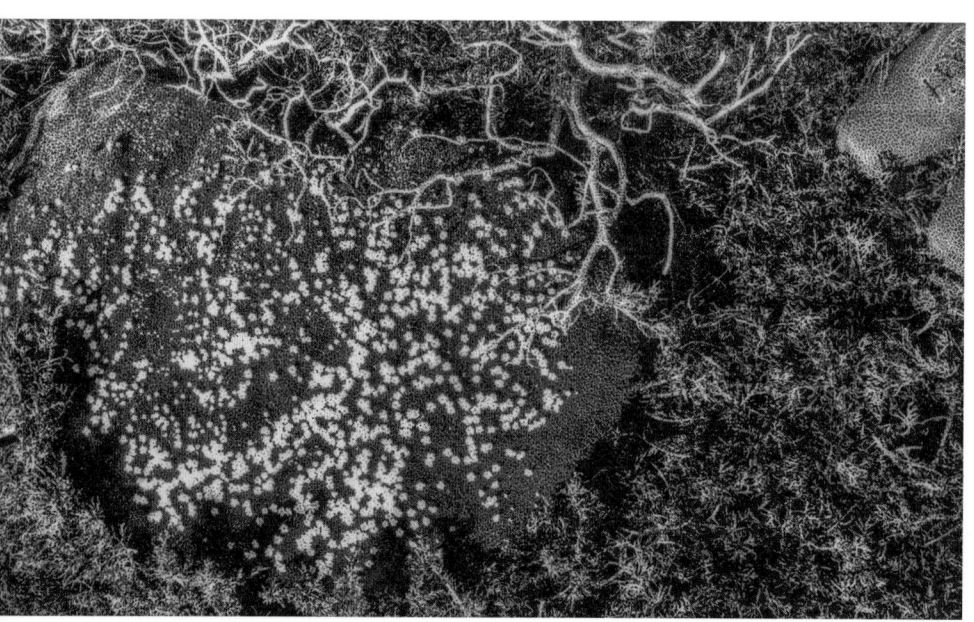

Hard cushion plant (*Dracophyllum minimum*) in summer flower, 1929 (Gustav Weindorfer)
(the toes of his boots have been caught in the top right-hand corner of the frame)

nematodes in 200 cherry trees that Japan had gifted to the United States'
First Lady, Helen Taft, for her 1909 scheme to beautify the Potomac
River in Washington, DC.[4] Frieda's doctorate applied Mendel's laws of
genetic inheritance to certain strains of *Oenothera* or evening primrose.
Gustav must have been one of the few hoteliers in the world so well
versed in botany.

Comfortable handling ringtail possums, he proved an able nursemaid
for the youngest Blanchard in the party. In the evenings he would bathe
Grace so that her mother could admire and sort through the plants
she'd collected on the Cradle plateau.[5] The stranger's waxed moustache,
turned up at the tips, and a trimmed beard must have seemed more of
this world than the wrinkled tuatara. He might have sung an Austrian
song or made her laugh while they splashed, before carrying her to
the warmth of the fireplace inglenook to be dried and dressed for bed.
Sitting at the large table surrounded by leaf and flower and blotting
paper, Frieda could ask him questions or snatch one of the many
leather-bound books on the shelves to clarify a fiddly taxonomical distinction. Gustav's library included English and German compendiums
on flora, thistles, birds, geology, grasses, microbes, ferments and moulds;
a voracious reader, he also subscribed to forestry and scientific papers,
and owned a classical record collection to rival any.[6] Whatever fury was
raging beyond the windows, Waldheim cocooned visiting scientists,
since books and learning were grist for thought in between field trips.

While Frieda explored the flora, her husband Frank spent days
trawling the creeks and waterways of the valley. Challenged by
an American colleague to search for 'a lost frog' known as *Crinia
tasmaniensis*, which had been described from a specimen in the British
Museum but not sighted for fifty years, he found them jumping about
the damp buttongrass moorlands and sedge lands.[7] He was ecstatic.
Frank Blanchard was known as a teacher who, if he arranged for students
to see coupling salamanders on a cloudy night in the wild, always
delivered on his promise since he spent so much time watching and
observing that he knew exactly where to find them and when.[8] The
'lost frog' now rests in Harvard University's Museum of Comparative
Zoology, where records show it was 'wild caught' in Cradle Valley.[9]

Tourists might have taken a while to hear about Cradle Mountain
but the scientific community was drawn from the start. Here was
an environment as remote in its way as Stephens Island, where the

tuatara dwell. A place where zoologists, entomologists, ornithologists, zoologists, could stumble upon specimens rare or new in a vast natural laboratory. Those who couldn't journey there sent requests by mail for samples of flora and fauna to further their research. Waldheim was like a supply station run by a botanist who could shoot, skin, ensnare, press, preserve, package and post anything from the four specimens of *Anaspides tasmaniae* or freshwater shrimp wanted by a Sydney botanist ('if possible two males and two females') to the pieces of *Athrotaxis cupressoides* or pencil pine sought by Professor Joseph Doyle, the newly appointed chair of botany at University College in Dublin who studied embryogeny between conifer species.[10]

Botanists in particular flocked to the gardens of trees and buttongrass and alpine flora. British plant pathologist and mountaineer Mary Dilys Glynne, who was one of a very few women scientists employed in Britain's Rothamsted Experimental Station, visited Waldheim.[11] Potato wart was her thing. Gustav knew his crop blights as a former potato farmer at Kindred. Nowhere else in the world was there anything quite like the moist, damp, ancient hub this host offered to enquiring scientific minds. He had come here for the same reason they couldn't stay away. Generous to a fault in the interests of science, he loved that others cared as much as he did for the pursuit of knowledge and the unpicking of nature's riddles.

Professor Theodore Thomson Flynn, father of the much more famous film actor Errol Flynn, visited the Cradles so often that Gustav named a tarn after him near to Lake Rodway. He would come to replenish his supply of marsupial specimens for research and teaching. A one-man band, he had no assistants to stock his laboratory. 'I am most anxious to get as many porcupines as I can,' he wrote to Gustav in 1929. 'Unfortunately they are not very plentiful at the present time but this is their breeding season and they present a very important field for research. I remember well that they seemed to be fairly plentiful round about the Cradles and I am hoping that with the help of your dogs you might be able to get me 20 or 30 if not more … I am willing to pay 4/- each.' He also asked Gustav when the wombats would begin breeding: 'We have just found out that the wombat possesses a placenta and this is of great interest among marsupials.'[12] Marsupials were no doubt in on the secret. Flynn was fascinated by their reproductive biology. Gustav's 1919 paper on the wildlife of Cradle revealed the wombat does not breed at any particular time of year, 'for at any time—and only one—young, in different stages of development may be found in the pouch. For that reason, it is difficult to say how often a wombat becomes a mother.'[13] That wombats could swim he'd confirmed by throwing several of them into the lake, possibly at Flynn's behest. One weighing about 50 pounds was thrown into 15 feet of water. The performance was repeated twice, each time the wombat re-emerging to the surface with greater alacrity: 'Finally nothing the worse for its first acquaintance with man it relieved its dusky coloured pelt of the adhering water by a vigorous shake, and slowly waddling along left the scene of the experiment.'[14] That the animal could hold out under water was proven in similar fashion when a wombat's brain was required for science. 'Failing a gun it was decided to drown the animal, and it took two men about five minutes to keep the animal under water until its struggles ceased.'[15]

As a young boy, Errol Flynn learnt how to set box traps in the hills of Mt Wellington, where he caught kangaroo rats or bettongs for his father at one shilling a head. 'When school finished I raced home to be at his side to hurry out into the backyard where we had cages of specimens of rare animals.'[16] His father was a single parent since the boy's mother, Lily Flynn, had left Tasmania in 1919. The professor once produced a small marsupial from his pocket at a staff dance.[17] He was known for his flamboyant lecturing style and black bowler hat. His son remembered 'red bushy eyebrows, black hair ... lean, angular, full of charm and good will and a certain professorial quietness'.[18] A colleague's description of a 'very powerful personality full of drive and energy that led him into many adventures' suggests a Weindorfer doppelganger.[19]

In the galaxy of fame, there could be no greater contrast between the oblivion of a scientist and society's swooning over a celluloid star. Medals like the one Flynn collected for his thesis on the reproductive biology of the barred bandicoot, or his spectacular discovery on Tasmania's north coast of a fossil whale 23 million years old, or any number of other specimens he described and recorded for our posterity, for science, for the future of biodiversity, count for nothing beside Hollywood glitter, then, now, forever. Not everybody has a tarn named after them. Although Flynn, with Gustav's assistance, raided wildlife specimens from the Cradle laboratory, they both shared concerns for the future of native fauna.

The newly established Division of Economic Entomology of the Council for Scientific and Industrial Research in Canberra was another keen customer at the Cradle buffet. Its chief, Cambridge educated Dr Robin John Tillyard, recruited fellow dipterist Dr Andre Leon Tonnoir, a world authority on blowflies, who found a new species during field trips to the valley. Small, with bright dancing eyes behind horn-rimmed spectacles, and an impressive beak, Tonnoir signed Waldheim's guestbook 'the restless fly catcher'.[20] After finding a new species in the mix of blowflies he took home from the valley, he asked Gustav to cast the net for more: 'You may not find many about at this time of year [May] yet you should be able to collect dead ones in huts, tents, sheds, which you could send in crumpled tissue paper in a tin.'[21]

If young Ray Tilley felt the hairs on the back of his neck prickle with the excitement of fireplace talk about a national park, then the conversations in the inglenook when the scientists gathered at Waldheim must have crackled with the thrill of their scavenging and their finds and their hopes for research as they took the helm of pioneering institutions and filled university chairs dedicated to new disciplines. Like the Melbourne artists present for the birth of modernism at the Heide home of John and Sunday Reed, the congregating of fine minds and inquisitive souls around Cradle's hearth signified a new confidence and self-belief as the best and the brightest converged here on the cusp of discovering Australia's scientific worth. Amateur ornithologist Stuart Dove was one who revelled in the intellectual joust: 'One meets a good class of people up there, educated men and women with whom it is a pleasure to converse … Mr Weindorfer is well known to the scientists of Melbourne.'[22]

Lepidopterists went crazy for the butterflies. A. Jefferis Turner described clouds of a variety of Nymphalidae with brownish orange wing markings found in abundance in Cradle Valley, 'on the edges of the myrtle forest and never far from it whenever the day was fine. During cold and wet weather, it might be beaten from the myrtle twigs which were covered with a black and white lichen with which its closed wings harmonised so perfectly that it was almost impossible to detect.'[23] His review of 'New and Little Known Tasmanian Lepidoptera' for the Royal Society of Tasmania relied on many species collected in Cradle Valley by Wilfred Bourne Barnard, the son of George Barnard, a famous Queensland naturalist who compiled one of the best collections of bird eggs, butterflies, moths and beetles in the southern hemisphere, and who taught his sons the art of catching and preserving specimens from an early age.[24] George's wife, Maria Barnard, drew or painted whatever was found while the colours were fresh. They lived on a remote, 170–square mile station called Coomooboolaroo, west of Rockhampton, lapping up Aboriginal lore and bush skills from indigenous locals who snatched bugs from the air. In his 1889 book *Among Cannibals*, Norwegian zoologist Carl Lumholtz described the barefoot Barnard boys as the best collectors he'd ever met: 'When they had their tomahawk in hand no tree was too high for them … They cut niches in the bark for the support of their toes … their keen faculty for observation astonished me again and again.'[25]

Australia possessed relatively few entomology collections in the 1920s since insects were of most interest for the damage they caused crops. Charismatic butterflies and beetles were the crowd-pleasers. George Barnard's collection grew so large that he built a private museum on his property before his prestigious hoard was sold to a European institution, and it is now held by the British Museum. His son Wilfred specialised in moths and butterflies collected all over the country, from the northern tip of Cape York through Queensland and New South Wales all the way to Cradle Valley in Tasmania, where he stayed at Waldheim, roaming every day, eyes peeled for a flitter or the blink of closed wings on a lichen-covered bough. The specimens Wilfred preserved were bequeathed to the then Council for Scientific and Industrial Research.

Natural history specimens were procured for study and exhibition at a furious rate. A curator from the South Australian Museum, H. H. Finlayson, begged for supplies of marsupials after learning of Gustav's proficiency, which was duly confirmed when a parcel of specimens 'all beautifully packed and preserved' arrived in Adelaide.[26] Finlayson couldn't resist a visit to this field laboratory. 'I have been well bitten by the high country bug,' he wrote. 'I must see the Cradle again. When the sun came out up there I used to have terrible longings to lie down in the valley by the little brown creek with its fringes of irises and boronias and just gaze up into the dreamy blue and hear the water and the wind. How I could laze. But there was always skinning to do.'[27]

Amateurs were among the keenest foragers. Gustav's great friend and fellow botanist Charles Sutton visited the Cradles on seven

Charles Monds and Fred Smithies with skinned animals at camp

occasions, discovering a new bladderwort in 1922. Stuart Dove was
another regular, offering to identify any birds that were a mystery. All
Gustav needed to do was 'skin the specimen, remove the eyes and brain,
and stuff the skull with some carbolic acid … pepper the skin well'.[28]
Annie Lindon, whose husband was headmaster of the Hutchins School
in Hobart, loved botany, often corresponding with Gustav, who helped
the amateur enthusiast as graciously as he assisted the distinguished
academic. Natural history relied heavily on the initiative and dedica-
tion of individuals and voluntary organisations, even as the disciplines
of botany, zoology and ornithology became increasingly the preserve
of professionals. When Arthur Giblin, brother of economist Lyndhurst
Giblin, led the push for a Tasmanian herbarium under the stewardship
of botanist Leonard Rodway, collection books were distributed to
volunteers, including Gustav, who foraged and preserved specimens
from Cradle Valley.[29]
    Giblin launched the herbarium in 1928, encouraged by Dr Arthur
William Hill, chief botanist and director of the Royal Botanic Gardens

in Kew, London, who'd visited Tasmania, intrigued by the island's 'remarkable flora', which he felt deserved sharper enquiry.[30] Australians' lack of interest in native plants had always bemused Gustav, who relished each member of every tribe. In a public appeal for contributions to the herbarium, Giblin noted the ignorance of Tasmanians who may be familiar with the appearance of the bush yet unable to distinguish its parts: 'The grass tree, musk, dogwood, wax cluster or snow berry, waratah, blue creeper berry, cutting grass, we might manage: and then most of us are done.'[31] He imagined the herbarium as a kind of reference library, where local and botanical names would be indexed, with experimental plots for testing hybridisation. Rodway pleaded for the widest brief, envisaging a collection that would go beyond flowering plants and ferns to encompass the 'lower types' that were often forgotten, including the mosses and fungi that he loved best, taking a particular interest in their impact on vegetation. Species were to be exchanged with Kew Gardens and with the new federal herbarium underway in Canberra.

Giblin, a solicitor by day, was a frequent guest at Waldheim, having first visited the Cradles with Rodway's scientific party in December 1915. Trustee of the Tasmanian Museum and a member of the Royal Society, he corresponded regularly with Gustav, thanking him for a package of dried seeds or the parcel of *Gaultheria*, a plant of particular interest to the esteemed Dr Hill in Kew, 'who is under the impression that some hybridisation is going on between three types'.[32] Rodway disputed the claim, arguing the *Gaultheria antipoda*, a spreading, evergreen shrub with small, white, bell-shaped flowers, grows in dry, open spaces on mountaintops, whereas *Gaultheria lanceolate*, an erect shrub with fleshy red, white or pink fruit, found on the central plateau, occurs around the margins of lakes or valleys, away from its kin. Giblin sought Gustav's opinion. 'I would be glad if you let me have your experience definitely on this point … whether you have ever found them in proximity or close enough for hybridisation to be effected by insects.'[33]

These questions fascinated Gustav. 'How did the alpine flora originate, and where is the cradle of this fairy army?' he asked in an article on the dispersion of pollen by insects and the wind as he wrestled with the great conundrum of how to explain the similarities in forest and flora between Tasmania, New Zealand and South America.[34] The theory of Gondwana, first proposed by German meteorologist Alfred Wegener in 1912, was discredited until the 1960s, but geologists and botanists associated with the Cradle Valley could see traces of a supercontinent in the dolerite caps formed in the Jurassic period 165 million years ago by the cooling magma of volcanic activity as Gondwana broke apart. They saw evidence in the species of myrtle and pine trees found only in Tasmania, Chile, Patagonia and New Zealand. Gustav initially believed the exchange of species between these countries occurred during the Tertiary glacial period. His notion of seeds transported by an eastward ice drift fell short of the truth, but he knew that knowledge constantly evolves and he knew also that the history of our plant life was one of the keys to discovering our geological past. Even an insignificant con- tribution to this debate was worthwhile. 'As long as our knowledge in phyto-palaeontology remains stationary ... so long will we walk in the dark and have to depend on hypotheses which throw only an uncertain light on the wonderful work of nature during past times,' he wrote in his efforts to add another foundation stone to 'the building which our forefathers have begun, which we in turn have inherited, and which our generation ought to be proud to continue and complete.'[35]

His practical experience, scholarly reading, innate curiosity and feverish energy in a pristine wilderness plush with game and botanical feasts made him indispensable to Australian naturalists. He was the go-to man for Tasmanian highland flora and fauna. When the newly appointed Commonwealth Forestry Adviser Charles Lane Poole was setting up the Australian Forestry School in Canberra and wanted Tasmanian beech specimens, the inaugural director of Launceston's Queen Victoria Museum, Herbert Hedley Scott, forwarded the request to Gustav with a covering note: 'I have sent him all I can but when it comes to cutting bits off various trees our dam bursts.'[36] Gustav assisted, for science's sake.

He once sent Scott a bit of fossilised wood that on further investiga- tion proved to be 'from the lost to Tasmania sub-order Cunoniacae ... I polished specimens and did a lot of work upon its histology, with the result that my first idea is confirmed and I have accordingly named it "Pre-Geissois Weindorferii",' Scott wrote excitedly. 'At present it is only a manuscript name as we cannot get papers to press but I thought you would be interested.'[37] The trees at Cradle secreted a compelling narrative. In his paper on deciduous pines for *The Gum Tree*, Gustav took the pulse of King Billy pines in Cradle Valley, calculating their age by counting the rings of a tree felled at the base with a crosscut saw, each ring marking the close of a vegetative period.

Gustav counted over six hundred rings in a King Billy measuring 3 feet in diameter. He had also observed a pine with a diameter of 6 feet at the butt, or double this girth, and assuming it also had double the number of rings, he estimated it at 1200 years old.[38] Such giants are never sound, he wrote, describing their half-dead, hollow trunks, covered below with the agents of disintegration, the mosses, lichens and ferns. Few pines reach this forbidding stature, with most compelled by bushfire or wind to make room for younger generations. He estimated that on account of the humidity and moisture, there hadn't been a substantial wildfire in the valley since some time after the arrival of explorer Abel Tasman in 1642. 'Nature has left us the record of this fire in a most curious and simple way,' he explained. 'In splitting a tree, the surprising discovery was made of some charcoal in the inside of the tree about 200 rings from its periphery.'[39]

Gustav, centre, holds an impromptu bush seminar on calculating the age of a tree through its growth rings

He read the trees for clues to the past, divining a method of climate research only now coming to fruit. Meteorology was a science Gustav treated with utmost respect. In his daily diary, he told the story sparsely with an adjective or two. Overcast, windy, wet, sleet, snow or glorious day. Between these lines he knew rainfall variation to a point, and tracked the slightest degrees of difference in patterns of temperature fluctuation. Every morning at 9 am, he took thirty readings from an array of instruments, some of them contrived with makeshift ingenuity, several supplied by the Commonwealth Bureau of Meteorology, others haggled from fellow scientists.[40] He designed a method of determining evaporation with a rain-measure glass. The hours of sunlight were burned onto a sheet of paper behind a glass ball.[41] Since January 1919 he'd been recording temperature, rainfall, humidity and sunlight. Every five days, he would calculate the mean of these to give him monthly data for dry mean, wet mean, absolute maximum, absolute minimum, mean maximum, mean minimum, grand mean, humidity and rainfall.[42] The front yard at Waldheim resembled an eccentric mix of space-age technology—a wind vane propped like a rocket launch; the thermometer housed in a wooden box painted white with gabled roof; gauges for rain, sunshine and snow—each instrument neatly fenced with palings.[43]

He installed instruments around the valley to widen the net of his sampling, telling Smith in 1924 that the rain gauge he'd recently set on Marion's Lookout on the plateau beneath Cradle Mountain revealed lighter falls than below, a result that astonished him. 'I am now mounting a snow gauge on the hill near Wombat Pool. The study of ecology has brought me into contact with various investigations especially in temperatures, and I am getting more instruments from Launceston.'[44] Chief meteorologist Alan Hunt was impressed by the avalanche of information and experimentation that flowed from Cradle Valley over and above a meticulous accounting of standard meteorological data. He wrote thanking Gustav for the graph he had drawn showing the proportion of time during which different light intensities occurred, as well as notes on the destructive impact of frost on native flora: 'Such firsthand observations are of very great value. I shall have the substance of your report included in the forthcoming volume on the Results of Rainfall Observations in Tasmania.'[45]

Charles Monds dwarfed by a King Billy at Waldheim (Florence Perrin)

There was no glory in the anonymous slog of recording daily weather, but the bigger picture of climate change had long fascinated Gustav, for the shift of glacial ice had brought the landscape of Cradle into being. He had observed weather carefully as a farmer at Kindred, his livelihood depending on its fluctuations; now in the valley guiding tourists through its charms, the wet was both a blessing and a curse, for it dampened excursions and bogged arrivals. Once citing wet, cold feet as the only drawback of his paradise, he lived in a place where the sun rarely shone, while the rain pitter-pattered or pelted without relief, never long absent from the sky or the auditorium of sound. The Roaring Forties sweep across stretches of ocean from South America and around the Cape of Good Hope, colliding with an almost unbroken barrier of mountains on the western coast of Tasmania and then abruptly rising 3000 feet, dropping ten degrees in temperature in the process and unleashing torrents of water on the other side. Guests at Waldheim joked that there must be a Jonah in their midst when rain marooned them by the fire, where they staved off cabin fever with rhymes, argument and games.

Gustav's meteorological instruments, 1929 (Gustav Weindorfer)

January 1923 was like no other. The rain began in late December, delivering 12 inches or 420 points in sixteen days. 'Puck. Lord what fools these mortals are,' writes Arthur Hackett in a long, amusing account of the daily catchment. 'Xmas Monday we start. So does the rain. Reached Rainyheim. Saw Wetterhorn. 91 points of rain. Tuesday. Rain, breakfast, yawns, rain, more yawns. 41 points. Wednesday. More rain. Saw the sun at last. Wild excitement. Jonah arrived in a storm of rain. Felt inclined to do as the whale did only earlier. Rainfall 127 points. Thursday. Sun actually shone for 75 minutes. Dashed up to the plateau. There the rain dashed down. More. Misery. Moisture. Only one more ray of sunshine at 7.30 pm. It had a yellow tinge and was in a tumbler. Rainfall 28 points. Friday. Saw the Crater Lake. The pleasant rumble of raindrops lulled us to sleep. Rainfall 57 points. Saturday. Walked 160 yards. Rainfall 160 points. Sunday. Still raining. Poker. Patience. Pork. Persiflage. Potations. Rainfall not recorded. Rain gauge broke down from overwork.'[46]

Particularly heavy falls in 1923 and 1924 set Gustav thinking in his questing way whether Tasmania had once been wetter. 'Rain, rain, snow, and rain,' he wrote to Ron Smith in November 1923. 'I am sick of looking up the record but I guess I have by now about 120 inches and if it goes on the same way I will be on equal footing with Tierra del Fuego. That is something to be proud of.'[47] Months later he began wondering aloud to Smith about how he might explore climate change in Tasmania through the growth rings of King Billy pines. 'The wet season here caused the flora to look as fine as I ever saw it before, from which one can conclude that Tasmania was once far wetter,' he wrote, outlining his plan to saw off the base of a King Billy pine around 1 foot in diameter to carefully compare the growth of rings during the period he had been keeping meteorological records. 'Perhaps I will be able to draw from them conclusions and theorise about the climate of years before my meteorological data. Anyhow I will try.'[48]

The result of his experiment is not known but his novel idea of tracking climate changes through the growth rings in the trunk of a tree was a hundred years ahead of its time. In 2017 a team of international scientists built a 1700-year King Billy pine chronology to shed light on the environmental history of these years using core samples taken from living and dead trees in the forest behind Waldheim and from the slopes of nearby Mt Kate.[49] Researcher Dr Kathy Allen from the School of

Ecosystem and Forest Sciences at the University of Melbourne explains that growth rings contain so much more information than simply the age of a tree: 'Details like the thickness of a tree or the density of the wood and the morphology of cells can give insights into temperatures, water availability, and major disturbances like bushfires.' Through the technique of cross-dating—where a long series of ring-width patterns are matched across the site and measured under a microscope with a sliding measurement scale attached to a computer, tools not available to Gustav in his primitive laboratory—the team identified pointer rings, very narrow or very wide rings that reflect very severe or very benign conditions such as drought or heavy rainfall. They confirmed Gustav's conviction that the valley had escaped intense fires for the entire 1700-year period, and they found wood from trees that had died around the late 800s BCE, with several having end dates later than that. 'The chronology is one piece of a big jigsaw puzzle that is building a record of past environmental conditions,' Dr Allen argues.[50]

Gustav was an original thinker, a man who examined his world for the insights stored within its folds. Experiments were always underway, ranging from the European alpine plants he grew in dolerite beds at the foot of Cradle Mountain to the glasses he set in Loose Leaf Creek for germinating seeds.[51] During the cold winter months without visitors, he spent the evenings reading botanical texts while carefully attending to the specimens in his personal herbarium, with the intention of fulfilling a long-held ambition to craft an authoritative contribution to Australian plant physiognomy. He sent seeds to Europe, dispersing varieties of tree ferns and eucalypts, just as his hero, Baron von Mueller, had strewn specimens in overseas garden beds to see what grew. His sister Rosa wrote in 1927 that many of the Tasmanian plants he'd sent to the University of Vienna's botanical gardens were sprouting.[52] A year later, in Copenhagen, she reported seeing 'a very nice specimen of Eucalyptus vernicosa which had been cultivated from seeds sent by you'.[53] He was in touch with leading German and Austrian botanists. Vienna's forestry department sent him an address for Dr Adolf Cieslar, a forestry professor who was interested in exotic trees.[54] Gustav sent him eucalyptus seeds. He also posted 100 samples to Professor Wilhelm Detmer, a plant physiologist at the University of Jena. The Austrian botanist Dr Richard Wettstein forwarded a German newspaper report of a lecture by Austrian plant geographer Dr August Ginzberger, which mentioned Gustav's name in relation to Tasmanian alpine flora.[55] These connections with the academic common rooms of Europe lessened his sense of remoteness in the highlands of a small southern island. He never skited of his reach, sharing his activities with sister Rosa, who was his eyes and ears in that part of the world. Botany was his first love. He and Kate had been drawn here by their fascination with the trees and the plants. Since her death, he had had no one with whom to share the hundred and one observations he brought home from wherever he'd been. Holding little Grace Blanchard must have felt strange to him, for all his accommodating dexterity. In his late forties, he could still father a child. But the chances of falling in love again were slim, and the chances of finding a woman who loved the same things he loved slighter still. Once the summer days shortened and the guests cleared out, the days were long and the nights lonely, even when the animals crept inside before the fire, during winters that seemed to last forever.

Bridge near the bath hut at Waldheim (Fred Smithies)

10

SINGLE BLESSEDNESS

Living memory could not recall a fury like the maelstrom that lashed the north-west coast of Tasmania in the first week of April 1929.[1] The oldest residents of Burnie and Launceston bore witness to this once-in-a-century event. Swollen rivers twirled timber and debris dangerously in their churn after the skies dumped 12 inches of rain in thirty-six hours. At the Derby mine, a giant wave burst the dam wall, sucking fourteen people under; a motor truck carrying a family of nine disappeared into the Gawler River, a teenage son the only survivor. Floods in Launceston left 4500 residents homeless. Power and water supplies were cut, bridges washed away, highways blocked; cascading rocks and mud tore roots and foundations from the earth, and wild seas disgorged ocean creatures and tangled kelp onto the shores as if the world had turned inside out. A reporter for the Burnie *Advocate* who ventured forth in the aftermath was humbled by a truth that city dwellers periodically discount: 'One could not help realising to the full how puny man's efforts are when pitted against the force of nature. It was the experience of a lifetime and one never to be forgotten.'[2]

At Cradle Mountain, where the headwaters of the rivers begin their journey seaward, the heavy rainfall had been nothing out of the ordinary. Gustav Weindorfer dutifully recorded 6 inches in two days. His last guest of the season departed as the weather broke, and for weeks there was no mail, a common enough annoyance, so he'd no idea of the havoc wreaked along the coast barely 60 kilometres away.

The absence of a road or telegraph poles or neighbours heightened his isolation. He'd been alone for five weeks when Bob Quaile got through to Waldheim.[3]

His oblivion became a talking point in Devonport. How could anyone living in Tasmania be unaware of the calamity that had drowned twenty-two people, with damage to property and infrastructure estimated at over a million pounds? 'Cradle Mountain Hermit' ran the headline in *The Mercury*'s report on an oddity as curious as the giant octopus, with tentacles 6 feet long, that the broiling ocean had spewed onto Wynyard beach.[4] The hermit handle stuck. It captured neatly his circumstances but completely misconstrued his character.

Gustav was the antithesis of a misanthropic recluse: amiable, loquacious, hospitable, fond of an audience, even flirtatious according to Smithies. Bouts of isolation were thrust upon him by his widowed status in a wilderness that marooned him during heavy rain and snow. Come summer, he couldn't hear himself think for the chatter of guests. That year he'd cooked for twenty at one sitting around two large tables in the living room, carving platters of roast 'pork' culled from the bush, with home grown white turnips and potatoes, followed by steamed plum pudding, stewed prunes and apple. This was the weft and warp of his existence. Social famine or feast.

He curled in on himself during winters. Had Kate not died, he would have had another by his side, sharing the day, helping with chores, her musings lightening the mood. 'I am too often alone and that nobody can bear too long at a time,' he'd confessed to his sister Rosa the year before, still grieving for his kelpie Flock, who had been shot in a terrible accident.[5] The adage acknowledging a dog as man's best friend is insufficient for the death of a bushman's dog, since he may not have another to answer him for days on end or, in Gustav's case, weeks at a time. Yet this was how he garlanded her in his diary after she was struck down in 1927 by a rogue bullet from the gun of a guest. 'I buried one of my best friends in a clearing in a forest,' he wrote in an echo of the expression he'd used to mourn Kate. Flock was his last link to Kate.[6] They'd fussed over her as a puppy, Gustav ever the disciplinarian, since a dog's obedience and loyalty were a lifeline in the wild. She'd shadowed him for eleven years, the length of his marriage, her presence making up for Kate's absence. After Kate's death, Flock slept at his feet on the wombat rug in front of the fire. By day she'd tag behind on trips

Gustav with his best friend Flock on the shore of Lake Lilla, 1922 (Stephen Spurling)

around the valley, or trudges to Middlesex station for provisions and mail, her contented sighs or territorial growls relieving the solitude, which was louder for her absence. Photographer Stephen Spurling III captured them together on the shore of Lake Lilla.[7] Gustav in his hat, shirtsleeves rolled to his elbow, his rifle at the ready in his hands, staring intently at a bird or a fish jumping beyond the frame. Flock stands nearby, her head turned like a pointer following her master's gaze, their still, steady poise perfectly synchronised.

The search for Flock's replacement began immediately with a letter to Smith: 'Do you know of a young English or Irish terrier puppy? Since my dog is dead it is not only awful to be quite alone at times but the tiger cats are getting so bold I'm afraid they are going to eat me. In broad daylight they walk about the place as if they owned it, enter the kitchen at night, goodness knows where, and are smashing

Feast or famine: Gustav (top right) serves Christmas dinner at Waldheim, 1926

up things. Today I heard them fighting in the loft. Well at least one feels one is not quite alone but I would sooner have more congenial company in the shape of a dog.'[8] Flock had kept feral beasts in check. Her wary tolerance of the eastern quolls, then called native cats, and the ringtails who'd steal inside sometimes at night drew a line at the hearth. With Flock gone, the wild reasserted control. Less vicious than the ferocious storm, the quolls' intrusion also testified to a fragile truce between man and the elements. Gustav knew nature's power for he crouched within its grasp. He eventually found another dog.

His quest for a female companion, though, was a private mission that ran hot and cold. Several close friends who'd been widowed found a second partner within the extended fraternity of bushwalkers. After Smithies' first wife Ida died, he married Jean Perrin, the daughter of Florence and George Perrin. These women rode; they climbed; they relished the wild outdoors. They were a rare breed. They came to Waldheim as sisters, daughters, friends of guests or in a group of their own. Smithies recalled his friend 'enjoying the company of all who came to visit him, with, be it said, a lively appreciation of certain members of the opposite sex'.[9]

The communal environment at Waldheim threw guests together. A full house in summer was akin to the breeding seasons of the animals in the forest. These raucous hubbubs were fertile opportunities for matchmaking. 'Somebody made the porridge and somebody else stirred it. A budding young lady—the youngest in the party discovered the coffee grinder and kept up the supply. Others sliced the bacon and cooked it. Others set the table,' as one guest recalled of breakfast when a crowd holidayed in the valley. At day's end, after a vigorous excursion, Gustav retired to the chalet to prepare dinner. 'Among the ladies who returned with him was the "Young Lady of the Coffee Grinder". She prepared the vegetables and was otherwise helpful thereby winning the particular regard of "mine host".'[10]

The hurdle of enticing a woman to keep house in a hermit's lair narrowed the field, but those who proved their worth at Waldheim or striding through the valley were in with a chance. Frances Cole, the eligible daughter of a Deloraine doctor, had been in his thoughts since visiting in 1921 with Governor Allardyce's daughters for a romp through Cradle and Barn Bluff that spun such magic that the experience had sent both Smith and Gustav into a swoon. Gustav kept his cool, but in 1923 the valley was abuzz with his intentions.

'Spring is coming, already the snow is going from the mountains, the birds are singing and so on, but I must not say anymore or you would immediately think I am in love. I only want to tell you the last three days make me feel like I describe it to you,' he burbled to Smith in June.[11] A second chance at love as intoxicating as the heady rush of winter's retreat. He'd confided in his diary, under cover of German, to 'auditioning' two women: Miss Cole, on the one hand; the other a girl called Belle Dunbabin, who had also walked the Cradles as a guest. Weighing up his affections, he decided: 'Frances is and remains my ideal.'[12]

Their suspicions aroused, the bush brethren were as snoopy as the meddlers who left dirty paw marks on Gustav's mail. Quaile told Smith he was 'thoroughly convinced' the Waldheim proprietor was chasing a wife, and Smith passed the news on to Viti Allardyce in a

correspondence that had continued over the years.[13] But there was no
engagement, and there is no explanation in the paper trail as to why
his amorous intentions were not reciprocated. Miss Cole later married
a member of Smithies' Launceston crew, John Savigny. They visited
Waldheim as a couple, Gustav recording the fact in his diary without
envy or regret.

The one female to stake her claim later that year terrified him,
though she seemed to possess the daring necessary to court his affections. Maude van der Reit was a visitor from South Africa who
stayed at Waldheim in September. Alone together for three weeks, the
cohabitation began well enough. His diary records the walks they took
around the valley, with Maude cooking wallaby one evening, everything peaceful until the whisky ran out. 'Maude van der Reit behaves
strangely. She seems to suffer from sadism. Is the woman quite right?' he
wonders. 'She is the strangest woman I have ever met.' When Quaile
arrived as arranged to collect her, she refused to leave. 'Told him
nothing except Maude is cranky.'[14] They arranged for Quaile to return
the following week. 'I wonder if she will go then,' he fretted of this
bold suitor, whose ode to Cradle Mountain in the Waldheim guest
book throbs with sexual tension: 'Throned and crowned/ The aching
cradle/ Props the cloudless sky.'[15] Days after her departure, Ron Smith
and his brother-in-law found Gustav 'in a very nervous state', greatly
relieved to see them: 'He told me he considered his life was in danger
from her.' At night he'd slept in one of the huts rather than share the
house with her. 'We stayed there for some days and then he came
home with us. He was afraid the mad lady might come back again.'[16]
She returned on a horse in December for three days, then was not
seen there again.

———————

Much like the male ringtail possums Gustav had observed during the
late pairing season in Cradle Valley, he accepted his status peacefully
without resenting the contentment of those more fortunate in the
scramble for a wife. 'Such males as fail to secure mates seem to take
their lot philosophically,' he'd written of those possums living their
lives 'in single blessedness until the fates choose to provide them with
partners'. At Cradle the males predominated: 'One hardly ever finds a

solitary Ring-tail female unless, perhaps, its mate has fallen victim to the hunter, to disease, or other circumstances.'[17]

As he waited for the fates to prevail, Smith filled the role of his intimate other. But his friend's trips to Cradle became less frequent as he parented the offspring born to his first wife Kathleen and the children from his second marriage to Ethel, resembling in his devotion the luckier male possums who from the moment they hook a mate 'together build their house and rear their young'. The scenes of domesticity Smith described in letters written from his kitchen table might have stirred Gustav's yearning for a clan: 'Ethel is pulling the stems off cherries for jam. Edgar is playing with cups, bottles etc at the sink with the tap running just a little. Charley is sound asleep in his pram in the den and when he wakes he will roar for his bottle of milk.'[18] Imagining Smith surrounded by the gentle chaos of the home front, nursing children through coughs and colds, perhaps made him cherish his freedom.

With the patience of a spouse, Smith obliged when Gustav instructed him to retrieve his evening suit from the bottom drawer—'I think it is rolled up in newspaper'—for an airing on the clothesline as he readied for his trip to the mainland in 1929.[19] His escape from winter's solitude became a seasonal ritual during the latter part of the decade as he sought companionship and a change of scenery. He would be giving lectures wherever he could arrange a projectionist and an invitation to speak. Photographs he'd taken of Cradle Mountain had been displayed in the windows of the Kodak shop in Melbourne's Block Arcade, prompting enquiries and interest that could be seized upon.[20] One Tasmanian acquaintance was amused by the thought of a hermit taking the podium. 'I hear you intend visiting the mainland again,' she wrote. 'I cannot imagine you so much before the public but I hope it is not an unpleasant experience and that you will be very successful.'[21]

He spoke to the Arts and Crafts Society, the Victorian Ski Club, the Clifton Hill Photography Club, and the Malvern and District Horticultural Society, aided by his artful selection from 200 lantern slides, contrasting vistas in summer and then winter to reveal the landscape's varied moods and hues.[22] Red, pink and white alpine flowers of the grassy valley in bright sun, the same scene almost unrecognisable beneath a blanket of snow. Cradle Mountain's craggy columns, formidable in mist, were friendlier against a clear sky. Lantern slides

Cut off from the world: Waldheim in winter

were still a novelty. Gustav understood their fascination, since the 1922 campaign for a national park had turned on the power of images taken by Spurling and Smithies. His word pictures cast another kind of lure. He led listeners through the King Billy pine forest near Waldheim and up the slopes of Mt Campbell, illuminating botanical marvels like the cushion grass or the deciduous beech, recounting the geological history of the landscape, its shimmering lakes gouged by the slow-moving thaw of grit and ice.[23]

Though well attended, his lectures were ignored by the mainland press except for an interview in the Melbourne *Herald*, reprinted in Tasmania, further fostering impressions of a picturesque 'hermit' in his mountain hideaway.[24] Smithies wrote to him, humoured by this stretch of imagination: 'I saw the extract from the *Herald* about the "hermit" of Cradle Mountain! It was quite good and should help in the publicity.'[25] The hermit's account of his venture deleted the role of his late wife from his life's work. This oversight was possibly the result of journalistic licence rather than a sin of his own omission. *He* saw the photographs of Cradle; *he* secured the land; *he* built the house. Technically this was true enough, yet his story forgot the woman who'd shared the dream, who'd paid for the land where the chalet stood, who'd purchased the farm that subsidised their life in the Cradles, and whose estate eked out the income enabling his publicity tour, since the tourism business ran at a loss.

The romantic portrait of a solitary heroic figure also discounted the contributions of Smithies, Smith, Quaile, Heyward, McClinton, Emmett and the other giants who'd rallied for the park. Too many to mention individually. Legends are made stronger by simplicity. Smithies jest at the hermit puffery showed he didn't care. The future of Cradle mattered more than egotistical point-scoring. Besides, these brothers-in-arms had their wives, their families, their day jobs, their city conveniences, while the mountain and its valley defined Gustav's reason for being.

His trips to Melbourne were frenetic: visits to the Botanic Gardens, the University of Melbourne and its departments of meteorology, agriculture and forestry; catch-ups with Naturalists Club friends and his German-speaking brethren. His dance card was full of dinner dates and theatre outings with single women.[26] He was attractive: learned, musical, creative, athletic in stride, with a scientist's measure. Single-handedly keeping house for whoever came to stay, he was a catch of a man, streaks ahead of his peers in his capacity to pickle sauerkraut or bake brownies—Keva Allardyce was so impressed by his savoury sauce she requested the recipe. The chalet was now a palace compared with the pioneering hardships Kate endured in the early days. His slide show included photographs of the chalet, then and now.[27]

Returning from Melbourne, he tramped the plateau of Mt Roland for the first time since his and Kate's honeymoon. His letter to Smith skipped over thoughts that must have been stirred by the camping spots and creeks he'd not seen for twenty-four years. 'Though the light was hopeless as regards photography I enjoyed the magnificent panorama from the summit, one of the best I have seen in Australia. When will they get enough sense to open it up for the visiting tourist.'[28] Smith might have read between these lines. He had stood with Gustav and Kate on Cradle Mountain's peak in the summer of 1909.

Their friendship had thickened and gnarled through all that had followed that youthful adventure: the death of Kate, then Smith's wife Kathleen; the war; their shoulder-to-shoulder campaign for a national park; sharing intelligence on everything from the growth of their King Billy seedlings to the activities of interlopers after timber or game. Once they had composed fictitious letters to entrap a meddler they suspected of reading their mail, but the ruse fell flat. Mostly they swapped quotidian snippets ranging from the antics of the possums devouring rhubarb in Waldheim's garden to the hiccups in their personal health. Barely a month went by without a volley of exchanges between them. Gustav kept a wary eye on Smith's land in the valley, both of them conspiring in the fortunes of the landscape that had brought them together.

'The season is rotten, in fact the worst since the war and the weather as beautiful as I have ever known it,' he told Smith in 1930. 'I guess I will have to do some hunting in winter ... to straighten my finances.'[29] Kate's sister Laura sent him a pair of knitted socks and cuffs, thinking he must be lonely up there.[30] The remoteness that cut him adrift for five weeks at a time was a curse. He wanted guests in every season, for their own sakes as well as for his, because the wealth he treasured most lay vaulted in the beauty and diversity of this landscape, wet, cold feet and the long interludes between one conversation and the next its only thorn. When a local trapper thought of purchasing acreage in the valley not far from the chalet, Gustav wrote to Smith joking he might soon have a neighbour: 'I had to consult the dictionary for that word.'[31]

Loneliness was inevitable for such a sociable creature, though he was better equipped than most, with his passion and curiosity and energy, for pursuits that kept melancholy and madness at bay. His collection of 150 records by classical composers, from Wagner to Ruggero Leoncavallo, spun on his HMV gramophone.[32] He'd burst into German songs from his childhood.[33] Thoughts absorbed him. At night the fire's crackle in concert with the howling wind would accompany the turn of a page as he studied the physiography of plants for a book he was writing to be entitled *Plant and Geographical Features from Tasmania's West Coast to the Summit of Cradle Mountain*.[34] Otherwise there was the scratch of his pen on paper, often recycled, answering correspondence, and every night a brief note in his diary of the comings and goings around him. The first leaves unfurling on the boughs of a fagus beech tree or the sighting of a frog or a bird that had been absent for months kept him abreast of the seasonal shifts that were his most reliable gauge of the world's slow tilt and turn.

His mail bag staggered the visitor who'd stopped at Wilmot with Bob Quaile to collect a haul that was 'almost as much as one man could lift and I wondered which must be the worse, going without mail or deciding which one to answer first from such a pile'.[35] The visitor was puzzled at how he could endure such a solitary life in an era when motor cars were clogging the roads of towns while telephone poles connected one hamlet with another, but Gustav told him he was never at a loss for something to do. Besides, he could not rest until the road was built. Then they would come from far and wide.

Bogged again along the 'road' to Cradle

11

THE ROAD

The posse of young women who'd gathered in the centre of Devonport on a windy morning held on to their cloaks lest a gust expose their trousers underneath. They'd abandoned ladies' fashion for riding breeches, self-conscious since there were lads on the street staring. A quarter of a century had elapsed since porters at Melbourne's Spencer Street railway station spluttered when the naturalists they'd expected to be men turned up in beribboned hats to take the train to Mt Buffalo. Cultural change occurs at the pace of a glacial melt: one heave forward before subsiding, then years of stasis until another surge. Wearing gaiters and puttees for extra protection, they were pleased there would be nobody to ogle, whisper or whistle in the Cradles, where they'd need a free stride to scale the summit. Though they were relying on men to drive them and guide them, they'd brought none along for company. The motor bus collecting them was a beacon of progress, but once the town's steeples had receded from view and the gravelled road that had clung to the shoulder of the hills had petered out in a slurry of mud, this engine of modernity shuddered to a halt.[1]

Bob Quaile clopped to their rescue with his team of horses, smugly dismissive of automobiles and their limitations. These contraptions could not match the stamina or intelligence of his muscular mares, responsive to a flick of the reins or a shouted command as they dodged a stump or a pitfall to soldier through. 'Is the road better farther on?' one of the women asked hopefully as she gripped the sides of the wagonette that Quaile captained across the Middlesex Plains. 'This is a

Bob Quaile with his team of mountain hardies heading out of the valley, 1929 (Fred Smithies)

carpet so far,' he roared, laughing as the cart wheels pitched and lurched over a rock on one side, squelchy mud on the other.[2] He regaled them with tales of horses sunk so deep into the ooze that they'd stuck until a bevy of men with a bullock had yanked them clear, or of passengers who had shot out of the cart like missiles propelled from a cannon. Not sure whether his promise of worse to come was a trick of psychology, for he seemed a cultivated man despite his callouses, they held tight and gritted their teeth.

Soon the few passages of wood, laid like corduroy across marshy reefs and rocks, disappeared into mire, confirming Quaile's candour. Once he'd ridden through here for 2 miles in darkness so black he couldn't see the leading horse—probably Ginger, for she was his veteran, travelling best in blinkers. He kept his hatchet handy to chop through fallen trees as the track narrowed and tunnelled into the forest towards Cradle Valley. Several of the women hopped out and walked to keep warm, for as the darkness descended, the chill soaked their skin. Their leader remarked that it was a pity Charles Dickens hadn't met Quaile, for here was a character tailored to the Londoner's pen.

Cording the black bog along Middlesex Plains (Fred Smithies)

By the light of the moon, the wagon pitched through the buttongrass, grinding over stony creek beds until finally Quaile announced they had another mile to go before the end of 'the road'—which seemed a grand name for a track such as this. The party set off, floundering across the buttongrass swamp and into the pitch-dark forest, where the moon could not penetrate the branches. Every one of them sank knee-deep in mud. They straggled into Waldheim's front yard at 10.30 pm, 'wet, cold, hungry, scratched, bruised and some even a little cross'.[3] These women could have been forgiven for thinking they'd stepped back a hundred years until their host loomed on the veranda with a lantern held high to guide them up the stairs into his chalet, where the fire and coffee would transform the frazzle of getting here into the butt of hilarity.

Motor cars could get within half a mile of Waldheim after a spell of hot weather had baked the ground, but the peaty soil still retained moisture for weeks, and the more reliable dump of rain or melting snow conspired to create a marshy wetland of creeks and bogs. The 'road' deserved quotation marks, for the thing did not exist except

Pack horses loaded for Waldheim (Fred Smithies)

in the ink of correspondence with authorities or in an invisible path through the pages of the Waldheim guest book, where its absence is lamented by those who've left vehicles bogged in the Middlesex Plains, walking 9 miles or more to arrive. 'Someday a good road will be built. Someday a train will run to this unsurpassable scenery. Someday the Switzerland of Australia will be viewed by the tourist population of the overpeopled cities of the overheated Australia,' pined Hector McFie.[4]

Someday.

Mythical almost, the 'road' shimmered like the biblical Tower of Babel in the imagination of Gustav, who knew precisely its grading and topography, for he had trudged back and forth that many times he could find his way blind, once counting the number of steps he took—17,600—from Middlesex station to his front door.[5]

The Weindorfers had pinned their hopes on a repeat of the Mt Buffalo experience, where 6000 pounds was spent promptly by the Victorian government for a road laid by 200 unemployed men within ten years of the park being declared.[6] Over the seventeen years since Waldheim's beginning, there'd been measly amounts dribbled out: 100 pounds for a narrow bridge over Pencil Pine Creek; an ex-servicemen's grant of several hundred for metalling a short, mean strip across the plains after the war; and in the summer of 1929, another 300 pounds had gone to patching 30 chains (640 metres) of the morass between Pencil Pine Creek and Dove River, where the buttongrass peat squelched even during summer.[7]

Build an accommodation house for tourists beside a national park and the road would follow—that was the logic Gustav had applied, thinking one would surely tip the next. Securing the reserve barely cost the government a penny. Constructing a road out of crushed stones bled bucket loads. He had begged, lobbied and cajoled every municipal council, alderman, politician and editor who might swing the money to improve access, but the promises that were made inevitably fell short. It was as if he was chasing thistledown forever blown from his grasp.

'My greatest disappointment always came when people keenly interested in the beauty of Cradle Mountain came to me for definite information and I had to tell them that the transport arrangements for the last 15 miles are twenty years behind the times,' he despaired in an interview given months after the party of dishevelled women from Devonport had hung their sodden breeches in front of Waldheim's inglenook to dry. 'In Cradle Mountain we have one of the most beautiful and scenic attractions in Australia ... and there should be some definite policy on the part of the Government in regard to the road from Daisy Dell to Cradle ... it is not much use awakening people's interest and enthusiasm, and then having to damp them down again. We don't want a bitumen road, but surely it would be possible to make it at least passable so that people could more easily enter into the enjoyment of what the glorious mountain has to offer. Private enterprise will see to the accommodation of visitors—just as it led me to spend nearly a hundred pounds on a trip to Melbourne to advertise the scenic attractions of this state.'[8]

He vented his frustration to Smith in a letter posted on the mainland: 'I cannot go on in this fashion. Either they do something or bust.'[9] When Smith first accompanied Kate and Gustav to the summit in 1910, his trip home from the valley, a distance of 51 miles, had taken him nine hours on a bicycle. Twenty years later, this journey took five hours by car—*if* the weather co-operated, 'but even then only with care in negotiating boggy places and with no certainty that rain would not make it impossible to return'. Even then the cars needed chains on the wheels, and even then the occupants faced a walk of up to 5 miles to the chalet.[10] Incensed by the government's decision to spend thousands on a road to Lake Fenton in the Mt Field National Park at the southern end of the state, Smith redoubled his efforts to badger those holding the purse strings. Eighteen civic bodies from the north-west, including councils and tourism associations, endorsed his proposal for metalling with crushed rock the 15 miles of treacherous track across the plains to the valley. 'No other tourist resort in Australia has such variety of scenery,' he petitioned. The Blue Mountains in New South Wales have cliffs and waterfalls but no peaks. The Buffalo Mountains in Victoria no lakes or forests to compare. The Cradles towered over both yet drew fewer than 150 people every year, compared with thousands going to Buffalo and the Blue Mountains. 'The reason can be stated shortly,' he wrote. 'Ease of access, good roads.' Visitors to Cradle sloshed along 'a bad one'.[11] Not simply bad: impassable.

Still playing catch-up after the devastating 1929 storm, the Tasmanian government was besieged by requests for funds, each borough more desperate than the next. Residual hostility towards Germans and Austro-Hungarians after the war further discouraged expenditure

The road to Cradle (Florence Perrin)

that would benefit an outsider. But the bigger obstacle was a failure of vision. The bush lawyer Edward Adams identified this syndrome after returning from Waldheim in 1914, forlorn at being surrounded by people 'who have no eyes'.

The vision of a chalet on the rim of a scenic and scientific fascinator was half a century ahead of its time. Adams got it. Emmett, too. Smith, of course, and Quaile, Smithies, all of the giants. The scientists busy solving riddles knew the priceless reservoir of knowledge held within this park, and even individual politicians such as Senator Payne or Devonport warden Hector McFie could picture the future, prowling corridors of power on Gustav's behalf.

In 1930 Smith became secretary of the Cradle Mountain Reserve Board, a poorly resourced advisory body that had been set up when the park's boundary was secured. Gustav wrote a formal letter—'Dear Mr Smith'—clearly concocted between the two of them. Short and sharp, it exposed the lunacy of creating a reserve then conspiring to keep people out: 'Has this reserve been made for the purpose (amongst others) to make it more accessible for the general public or otherwise? Yours faithfully, G. Weindorfer.'[12] Days later, Smith replied informally, telling him the board had passed a resolution, endorsed by the local Kentish Council, requesting that money for the unemployed be spent on the missing links. He'd written a flurry of letters to MPs, 'so if we keep on, something should come of it. If you put in a weekly report to the papers whenever you have visitors and make it sound as grand as possible it would be a big help.'[13]

Someday.

Never one who sat still—if he had, there might be no Cradle Mountain National Park—Gustav hit on a solution that would at least make travel breezier for him. 'The first opportunity I have I will buy a light motor cycle and will improve the old Cradle track,' he told Smith.[14] At fifty-four years old, his beard and hair now grey, he could no longer scamper as hyperactively as he once did, complaining in his diary of cramps in his stomach 'whenever I walk or work' and chest pains.[15] He blamed gout, giving up tea, cutting down coffee and quitting smoking. He'd learnt to navigate the seasonal troughs, hunting a little more to tide him over, his mental equilibrium improved by pet projects: the study of plants, his herbarium, the book on Tasmania's alpine plants a work in progress.[16]

He'd planned to commemorate the centenary of the first ascent of surveyor Henry Hellyer in March 1831 by installing a circular metal plaque on the summit inscribed with arrows pointing out every significant peak in a 360-degree radius, but his proposal fell victim to the miserliness that hijacked the road.[17] Instead Gustav marked this anniversary on 7 March 1931 by castling little stone cairns along the track to the summit to acknowledge a hundred years of white man's footsteps up the mountain.[18]

When his new Indian Scout motorcycle and sidecar arrived in the valley in April, the young scion of a Launceston family who sold motor cars and bikes gave Gustav a lesson, lapping the grassy flats of the valley to whoops and applause.[19] The next day his tutor rode with him to Sheffield. 'We will accompany him out but he must come back alone! And as he says "Why not?".'[20] The bike, christened Mabel, gave him wings. During winter, he escaped to the north-east of Tasmania, roaring off in a blaze of smoke. His great nephew Hugh Hadrill, who at ninety-four was my only source of a firsthand memory of Gustav, recalled his childish excitement whenever this wild buccaneer revved into the driveway of the Devonport home owned by his grandparents, Blanche and Stephen Priest. Much like Ray Tilley in the Waldheim inglenook, he was enchanted by the charisma of this daredevil from the mountain: 'I remember a wild-looking man getting on to this motorbike then careering off in a cloud of smoke.'[21]

Stabled in a motor shed that Gustav built behind the chalet, the bike might have drawn a snort from Quaile, who would have wagered his house on the superiority of his horses. 'Sincerely trust that the road will be improved shortly—failing that it must be arranged for Robert Quaile to live forever' was a sentiment shared widely.[22] Gustav blazed a track 5 feet wide through the forest and down the southern slope over swampland to the river flats below. This path eventually joined the track known as 'the road', which led out of the valley on to the plains.

The Launceston giants came to ski in August, cameras slung around their necks. George and Florence Perrin and Charles Monds lucked upon good snowfalls and perfect conditions for a sport new to Australia. Pairs of wooden skis for skimming across country were tucked above

Gustav astride Mabel in front of her garage

the rafters in Waldheim's living room, expanding the calendar of winter activities in store for guests. This was how he and Kate had imagined it would be. Their early tourism brochure hinted at outdoor pastimes not yet pursued in a land of droughts and plains, where settlers clung to a coastal veranda.

Adventurers like the giants would truck here rain, hail or snow. For some guests, the lack of a decent, safe road was a plus: 'Too many motor touts in Hobart. Three days of it made me sick so I came back to this place where the motor car is not.'[23] Others grew resigned to cold, wet feet, just as Gustav had accepted this discomfort as the singular downside of his paradise. In October 1931, Maurice Weston, chairman of the reserve board, grumbled when his car drifted into the 'black bog' of the Middlesex Plains. He bushwhacked his way to the chalet, arriving after midnight. 'Was this a record?' some wag queried in the guest book.[24]

The Fargo motor truck and Chevrolet car carrying 20,000 fingerling rainbow trout to Waldheim in January 1932 to spawn game in Dove Lake for fish fanciers almost lost their precious cargo. The engine boiled, then rain set in, wheels spinning and slipping in mud. 'It was necessary in several places to push both the car and truck and we nearly had to give up,' read the verdict of escort John Vickery and his helpers from the North Western Fisheries Association. An account in the guest book of their journey from Burnie to the Cradle Valley included a hand-drawn sketch of men lugging canisters of trout up a hill captioned, 'Just another quarter mile! Oh Yeah!'[25] Despite the rough beginning, they fell for Waldheim like everyone else: 'The party can wholeheartedly recommend host Weindorfer's hospitality and coffee but certainly not his "just another quarter of a mile".'

How else could he have coaxed hundreds of guests here without dissembling enough to disguise the difficulties and the distance? *Just another quarter of a mile* was a refrain he must have whispered to himself whenever the wink of hope snuffed out. The pilgrimage of visitors in the summer of 1932 came from an ever-expanding geographical circle: Scots, South Africans, Sydneysiders, folk from all over Victoria, Queensland and every corner of Tasmania. As well as the newcomers were faithful veterans on their second, third, fourth visits, some regulars like Smithies or Smith losing count of their trips to the chalet. The revolving door was the truest measure of Cradle's hypnotic power, for whoever came could not wait to return. Occasionally guests were unable to drag themselves away. A German-born woman from Brisbane arrived for two weeks in January 1932 and stayed for three months. She'd first written to him in July 1929 after reading the Melbourne *Herald*'s romantic account of the gifted 'hermit' of Cradle Mountain: 'As a German I am so proud there are still such people.' Inside the envelope was a piece of the edelweiss she'd collected in the Bavarian Alps in 1907 before sailing for Australia. Her adult daughter later wrote to Gustav, noting that her mother had stayed 'for a very long time'. The woman's explanation, written in German, was succinct. '*Warum?*' or 'Why?' she asked of her extended holiday on a page of the guestbook. Her answer: 'Waldheim'.[26]

In autumn the deciduous beech leaves lit the slopes around Crater Lake in coppery amber hues as the forest prepared for winter's assault. Launceston bushwalker John Savigny, one of the giants who served on the Cradle Mountain Reserve Board, visited in early April of 1932 for a week's rambling. 'See Venice and die, but see Crater and Dove Lake and live—to see it again,' he signed off before departing.[27] Alone once more, Gustav stacked firewood, wrote letters and prepared for his winter trip to the coast, where he'd swap solitude and snow for lively company and dry feet. 'Down country … he seemed to develop an insatiable appetite,' Smithies insisted. 'More than once we have dined in a hotel and dined well. Coming out afterwards he has remarked, "That vos very good. Now let us have a feed." And we have adjourned to a café or restaurant and begun all over again.'[28]

For three days he'd been trying to kickstart the recalcitrant Indian Scout as he prepared for his sojourn. 'At last it went this morning only to stop whenever I put the thing into low gear. Probably magneto trouble and moist air. I hope [she goes] tomorrow and am off down the coast,' he scribbled on 4 May in a letter to South Australia's museum curator, H. H. Finlayson.[29]

Rising early on 5 May, he determined to run the bike down the hill so that the engine would catch enough to ride it up the next steep slope. There he would hold it steady using blocks and rope and in this stop-start fashion, fingers crossed, the bike would rip-snort a great plume of exhaust. He would ride it as far as the start of 'the road' that led out of the valley then return home to read his instruments and grab his coat, his bag and the mail that he'd left on the table. The day broke bright and clear. Initially he'd thought of travelling to Melbourne to see Charles Sutton and his Field Naturalist friends, but he couldn't afford the expense right now. One of his stamped envelopes was addressed to Sutton, informing him of the change in plans and chronicling his battle with the bike: 'I presume one cylinder is not working.'[30]

The sound of the currawong corroboree greeted him as he went to the motor shed behind the house. Now and then the cattle that had been grazing here for several months lowed from the grassy river flats below as they mooched for food. He tried to kickstart the motor, again and again, quickly, forcefully, but the blasted, cantankerous beast kept stalling, just when he thought it might catch. He pushed the bike up the first hill then ran beside it, kicking the starter pedal as he went, but there wasn't a sputter or spark. Once on the flats, he wrestled with the damn pedal, his frustration not yet spent. As he tried yet again, a crippling pain in his chest flung him to the ground, lifeless. Tufts of buttongrass pillowed his fall. The mountains stood sentry over him.

Hours later, wombats grazing in the valley might have sniffed their neighbour's scent as they foraged around his cold carcass. His body lay throughout the night in the valley, fearing no evil for there was none to be had beyond the ragged claws of survival in a wild where he knew every plant, every pine, every gum, every swamp, every sphagnum bed. The tannin-coloured waters of the Dove River sung a dirge to him as tiny creeks funnelled into its banks following the course of least resistance, onwards to the sea.

He could conceivably have spent weeks exposed to the elements, just as he had endured lengths of solitude without hearing another's footfall in winters past. But the next morning, cattleman George Stubbs came through the valley with his son to collect their herd before winter. Whether he was led to the shallow open grave by ravens above or perhaps a recalcitrant cow straying off course, he found Gustav curled on the ground. The heart attack that caused his death was written in the set of his fingers, bent stiffly as if clutching the handlebars of the motorcycle.[31] Late that afternoon, police were dispatched from Sheffield with two guides to retrieve the body. As if to remind them of Gustav's Sisyphean quest for a road, their car became bogged at Middlesex like so many before, and in the darkness of night they squelched along the muddy track for 10 miles towards Waldheim, arriving in the wee hours after clearing a huge trunk fallen across their way. In the morning light, they rolled Gustav up and hoist him onto their shoulders as they retraced their steps, returning to Sheffield at 11 pm. Stephen Priest had come to town to arrange for his brother-in-law's burial beside Kate in her family's plot at the Don cemetery near Devonport.[32] When the Launceston giants got wind of this plan, they sought to intervene, man-like in their insistence that Gustav should be laid to rest within sight of his forest home. Smithies rang the town's chief constable. 'He was most uncompromising. Said it just couldn't be done and that was that. He would not even discuss the matter. I, however, thought that was hardly that.' A phone call to Tasmania's Attorney General, A. G. Ogilvy, who knew Gustav, having visited Waldheim the previous Christmas, reversed the order and the casket stayed put.[33] This tug of war warranted mention by *The Advocate*, which noted that some of Kate's relatives felt that Gustav should be interred near his wife, 'but local opinion prevails in the belief that the district which he opened up should have the honour of claiming his remains'.[34]

Smithies and his crew went ahead to select a grave site in the valley and dig: 'It rained and snowed. We had to nurse the car through bogs and creeks over a rugged trail not better than a cattle track.'[35] They too were forced to abandon their vehicle 8 miles from the chalet, walking in through the mud to reach Waldheim by midnight. The next day brought another burst of filthy weather. The men shovelled in the wet, the mountains behind wreathed in mist. Forty miles below them, the sun rose over Sheffield as if it were in another hemisphere. Gustav's cortege left the Town Hall through a local guard of honour, with only a thin crowd watching as the car disappeared out along the West Kentish Road, where Mt Roland's steel grey hulk stood silently. As the gradient rose towards Wilmot, clouds darkened the sky. Black Bluff was glimpsed in a shawl of snow that had fallen the day before. Another brief flutter of white dusted them in the heights of Daisy Dell. From here Gustav was loaded onto Bob Quaile's four-in-hand, Ginger at the lead, hitting heavy weather with snowdrifts 3 feet deep, while the wind 'sang a rude requiem through the trees'.[36] The procession pushed ahead for 15 miles, Gustav oblivious to every jolt. Towards evening, the gravediggers at Waldheim heard the clink of bridles and the clatter of hooves as Quaile's team halted at the end of 'the road'. The men lashed three poles across the wooden box so they might shoulder their friend's dead weight along the winding, slippery foot track to an elevated knoll east of the chalet with a commanding view of the mountain.

The morning of his funeral broke bright and blue, as it often does in the Cradles after a spell of foul weather. Had Gustav felt his passing warranted a diary entry, he would have stuck to the bare bones. 'Buried G. W. Glorious day.'

He didn't chase posterity. Glory was the gift of the landscape he loved.

12
LEGACY

*Twenty-eight photographic negatives; 29 lantern slides; two
ostrich feathers from Ceylon; two glass inkpots; one walking stick
ivoried at each end; one framed picture of Baron von Mueller; a
hanging kerosene lamp; one black frock or evening coat, slightly
moth eaten; one rucksack; fourteen cases of botanical specimens
dried, pressed and labelled, weighing over 425 kilograms.*[1]

These personal effects flummoxed the public trustee appointed to
dispose of Gustav Weindorfer's estate, for he left no will or list of
benefactors. The giants scoured every corner of Waldheim looking for
directions in a notebook or papers tucked between stacks of periodicals
in case he'd made hay for the hereafter. Smith was sure Gustav had a
secret hiding place in one of his huts. 'We went through everything and
inventoried all that was considered to be of any value—you know there
is such a clutter of stuff that is really worth nothing, much of which will
have to be destroyed,' one of the giants despaired.[2] Meanwhile, Smith
mounted his own search through tin trunks and chests that Gustav had
entrusted to him for safe storage.

The contents of Waldheim—books, jugs, wash basins, crockery,
cutlery, stools, rugs, mirrors, curtains, blankets, a tool shed of chisels,
saws, planes, spades, axes—would be lumped in with the property,
which was purchased for 300 pounds by a syndicate of giants 'just for
the love of the place and our earnest desire to prevent destruction of
any kind'.[3] Everything else would be sold individually at Hancock's

auction mart. Gustav's brother-in-law Stephen Priest bid for an antique chest of drawers that Kate's family had brought 'from the old country', but who'd be willing to fork out for a second-hand, threadbare frock-coat or fourteen boxes of dried plant specimens?

Smith withdrew the frockcoat from sale, unable to part with 'an article of clothing belonging to a friend'.[4] But they dithered over the fourteen pine cases of plant specimens carefully arranged, named and classified. Smith had kept the herbarium collection at his house because it was too bulky to store at Waldheim. The public trustee, who was not a scientist, wrote them off as being 'of very little value', without consulting any expert in the field. 'I think they would be of great value to a museum,' Smith retorted, suggesting an approach to the government botanist or museum curators in Hobart or Launceston, who'd be better equipped to assess their worth.[5]

Gustav's sister Rosa wept. 'It makes me feel very sad that the value of the botanical specimens has been put down as "nil" when this work has such scientific value. My dear brother put his whole life into the work and spent nearly half his life at it. Botany was the child of his heart, perhaps even more than Waldheim. You dear Mr Smith will know this yourself. At all events, if there should be a sale, and however it is done, I beg the botanical specimens and all the writing concerning them be excluded.'[6]

Smith found three notebooks dedicated to nature and weather, but the manuscript for Gustav's book on Tasmanian alpine flora, if it existed, was missing, as were the hundreds of slides he'd made of plants, using Waldheim's bath hut to develop his film. But 400 photographs he took survived. They are strong and sharp; the portraits are close up yet casual, and the images of Cradle and the plateau striking. Some of them are reproduced in these pages: opposite, the punt on Dove Lake, his Tyrolean hat on the seat, his coat near the oar. One of a cushion plant, shown on page 160, includes the toes of his boots as if they too are rooted in the soil. The diaries, letters, books, personal papers were archived, but the trifecta of a mountain home, his sudden death and the absence of a live-in spouse to help keep track of paperwork confounded the straightening of Gustav's affairs.

Rosa's fright at the thought of philistines raffling her brother's plant collection would have resonated with present-day French botanist Mark Jeanson. Director of the world's largest and oldest herbarium,

The pine punt Gustav built for excursions on Dove Lake, his hat and coat on its seat, Cradle beyond

the Muséum national d'Histoire naturelle, he faced a similar heresy in 2017 when Australian biosecurity officials from the Department of Agriculture inadvertently destroyed 105 priceless and irreplaceable historical plant specimens gathered in Australia during the voyage of French explorer La Perouse 200 years ago. These archived treasures had been loaned to a Brisbane botanist researching a flowering plant of the Asteraceae family.[7] Among the specimens incinerated in a bureaucratic bungle that the department has refused to publicly explain were six 'type specimens' that were the first examples of a new species ever recorded. These provide a template for comparison with other specimens to determine whether a subsequent discovery is truly new or not. Their value is incalculable, since they inform the study of taxonomy, agriculture, pharmacy and every science based on plants. As Jeanson told *Le Monde*, they are 'the memory of the planet'.[8]

Gustav preserved his collections meticulously. His specimens are found in over a thousand collections held across Australian herbariums, chronicling a lifetime's work.[9] Melbourne's Botanic Gardens has 897 specimens attributed to him from Victoria and the high country of Tasmania, including one known new species of the native bush pea that had been named *Pultenaea weindorferi* in honour of the botanist astute enough to recognise its singular traits.

The science of collecting specimens and recording the precise geographical location enables botanists to keep track of climate shifts and ecological adaptation. A year after emigrating, Gustav began furnishing Australian herbariums with specimens, one of the first a bladderwort native to Western Australia that he'd plucked from the bayside heathlands in Sandringham.[10] Herbarium databanks bulge with his contributions from Cradle Valley.

A former director of Sydney's Botanic Garden, Joseph Maiden, an expert on eucalypts, held him in high regard. 'I've only just learnt your address,' Maiden exclaimed in 1914 when he forwarded a copy of a scholarly article on Australian plants. 'I am very pleased that you are still interested in Australian botany for which you have done so much.'[11] Melbourne botanist J. H. Willis begged to differ. Decades later, he omitted Gustav from his 1949 list of Victorian botanical pioneers, inviting a 'please explain' from Gustav's earliest biographer, George Bergman. Clearly rattled by this challenge, Willis dashed off a long, snooty letter explaining that while Gustav's plant specimens were 'reasonably comprehensive and of some use', a selection of his naturalist papers—not all of them were cited by him—had a 'practically negligible' impact on knowledge of Victorian flora. Willis sampled 'only' six of the twelve articles Gustav had published in serious journals, ignoring his many lengthy newspaper accounts of Victorian alpine flora aimed at educating a broader audience. Willis conceded that Gustav's two early papers on Cradle Valley flora and fauna—'probably the first account ever published'—qualified as pioneering, but since his list was Victorian, not Tasmanian, bad luck. He counted Gustav as a Victorian botanist but begrudged recognising him as a botanical trailblazer. Gustav collected in Victoria for only five years. As for *Pultenaea weindorferi*, Willis sniffed: 'it often happens that quite obscure and unimportant personages are commemorated in this way, the farmer's boy who guided an authority to some wattle for instance.'[12]

He could not fault Gustav's naturalist credentials or his legacy, noting he 'has left an indelible mark on the history of Tasmania—without his enterprise it is extremely doubtful whether we should have that magnificent Cradle–St Clair National Park at all. I admire him tremendously.' Without his finely tuned botanical antenna, though, Gustav could not have taken the full measure of the landscape's significance. He'd kept a framed portrait of Ferdinand von Mueller at Waldheim because the botanist was his North Star, illuminating the role of the collector, gathering the planet's DNA, sending seeds and specimens around the world. Of the forty tree ferns that Gustav carefully packed in earth balls and forwarded from Melbourne to Austria's Schönbrunn Palace Gardens, only two survived the Second World War.[13]

Just as Gustav sought neither credit nor financial remuneration for his elaborate meteorological records, adding to our historical knowledge of climate in Tasmania's highlands, his prodigious collection of plant specimens was a down payment for our future. How else are we to read nature's book, comparing now with then, unless we scrutinise the past? His prescient idea for measuring growth rings in pines to see whether Tasmania was once wetter now preoccupies the University of Melbourne research team crafting a 1700-year chronology from Cradle

Valley's King Billy pines so that clues from previous vegetative periods can steer us through climate change in the decades ahead. As Scottish foresters wrote of their woodlands, 'To stand in them is to feel the past.'[14]

Cradle Valley continues to serve as a research laboratory because Gustav and Kate first understood the significance of its raiment. They were botanists who transcribed the diversity of the plant life, equally intrigued by the governing force of geology. An early paper Gustav wrote on the flora set forth his belief in jimmying nature's secrets loose in a wilderness 'where every walk appears to be the contents of a book, which stimulates innumerable thoughts and pictures. From the rock whose weather worn surface is covered with mosses and lichens; from the alpine flower gardens, where the gentle kangaroo grazes with its young, up to the gnarled and stunted pines and gum trees and the crystal, glittering snow fields, over which the stately eagle soars, are the leaves of this writing of Nature to be seen. The one will read out of this book more, the other less; but all the art of reading rests in this: to analyse and recognise out of the superabundance of appearances and the individual occurrences the eternal law of the whole and the ingenious arrangement of things.'[15]

Archdeacon Henry Atkinson, who ministered the burial rites at Gustav's graveside, knew him from the Kindred parish where Kate had led the choir and Gustav was churchwarden. He'd never encountered such 'infectious' earnestness and enthusiasm: 'I remember wondering how it came to be. I formed the idea that it was my privilege to be working with one [for] whom the majesty and presence of God were very real things.' On his last visit to Waldheim, he had strolled with Gustav over the creek and into the forest behind the chalet. 'He used to say that the creek sang to him, and verily I believe it did.' The two men stopped beside a fallen tree, a giant of its kind. From its trunk a second pine was growing. Atkinson recalled Gustav removing his hat and raising his hand heavenward. 'He said, "This fallen tree was meeting the breezes of God's heaven before Christ preached his doctrine of love and fellowship to man."' They stood in silence for a moment, Gustav 'humble in the presence of the maker of that tree'. The eulogy wreathed him in the robes of St Francis of Assisi for befriending birds and beasts, possums, bush mice, and two currawongs that he'd fed from his kitchen door.[16]

His writings were not imbued with references to God's handiwork, though such genuflection was common at the time, for otherwise how else to explain the origins of wonders not yet deciphered or understood. Gustav was a scientist and an educator who wrote in the popular press and scholarly journals, closely observing the flora and fauna at our feet and encouraging Australians to embrace native gardens. His writings of a century ago are cited still. The paper he co-authored with George Francis in 1920 on native animals was referenced in a 2014 article published by the CSIRO in its *Australian Journal of Zoology* examining the historical fluctuations in quoll populations.[17] His first-hand observations in the wild from a century past are priceless, much like science's bank of specimens.

From lecturing on the mainland to his encyclopaedic commentary as he guided parties around the Cradles, he strove to bring enlightenment. 'He unlocked the secrets of nature that until then had been a closed book to me,' Smithies recalled of their roaming. 'Botanically I learnt to appreciate the many unique trees shrubs and flowers that are found nowhere else in the world. Geologically he pointed at the visible evidence of the formation of our remarkable dolerite capped mountains … Many terminal and sidereal moraines took our discussions into dim past ages when glaciers tore out huge gorges and altered the

Gustav amidst the dolerite

configuration of the whole country. There was never anything heavy in talks with "Dorfer". Information and love of nature just flowed from him easily and delightfully.'[18]

He had a Pied-Piper personality. 'The news of Dorfer's death was received with disbelief, then shock in our family,' recalled Ray Tilley as an older man. 'It was as though a giant heavy door had shut with a thud on a whole era and blotted out a dream—a vision.'[19]

In his 1924 history of Tasmania, author Charles Whitham made the bizarre claim that Cradle Mountain and Barn Bluff 'were created for man by Mr Weindorfer … This is not blasphemy but the stark truth.'[20] Gustav must have roared at such daft hyperbole. He knew he was a wink in the millennia of its history. That he became a kind of demigod was not entirely his fault. He left himself out of the landscape he'd named after others, until the Malcher brothers insisted the jagged eastern peak of Cradle bear the moniker 'Weindorfer's Tower'.

His canonisation as the spirit of this place was enhanced as a result of the decision to bury him in the valley, separated from the spouse who had led him here. Her grave in a lowland cemetery forgotten, while his candle was kept bright with an annual memorial service in the valley that continued until 2016. Tasmanian historians Simon Cubit and Nic Haygarth argue this ritual bolstered a 'quasi-religious mythology' around Gustav as a conservationist: 'In reality, he was not selfless, but a tourism "booster" who aligned a common good with personal profit.'[21] He's impossible to box, blurring the lines between disciplines and professions, as exotic as the spiky-leafed pandani trees set among the yellow gums. Botanist, booster, bushman, author, catalyst, he plundered game for food and skins and split timber for his house, flirting with the profits from commercial sale of his pine, yet he campaigned vociferously to protect the forest and its fauna as a park. And yes, he also coveted a road that no purist would countenance because both he and Kate wanted to share this place for the benefits to science and soul. Our lungs and our laboratory.

Kate's early death abbreviated her role in a dream that drew on the mettle and foresight of two people who to my mind rival Australia's John and Sunday Reed, the midwives of modernism, who created a sanctuary at Heide, their Melbourne home, where painters like Sidney Nolan found new ways of seeing. It riddles me why the Weindorfers are not better known. Was it his ethnicity or their geographical isolation in

LEGACY   213

a remote corner of a small island, or is it because science and scenery have languished in a country blessed with a surfeit of natural beauty and a preference for the heroism of sport?

Geoff Mosley, who has been researching the history of our national parks for half a century, has struggled with our ignorance, disappointed 'that a community which shows fascination with every aspect of the history of entertainment, art, war, etc. and makes grand use of the National Parks apparently has little interest in their history. Is this perhaps a part of taking them too much for granted?'[22]

Two years after Gustav's fatal collapse on the valley's river flats, 'the road' to Cradle came to pass. Every year the stream of visitors rises like the Dove River after rain. In 1916 there were thirty-eight guests at Waldheim walking these mountain gardens. A century later, in 2017, a record 280,000 crossed the Pencil Pine bridge.[23] If only the mean-fisted and short-sighted could have foreseen the groundswell of this secular pilgrimage from overpopulated cities. But that is often the way of trailblazers. They are long gone by the time we heed their call.

A crescent of sand at Truganini Point on Dove Lake

CODA

Two years after becoming acquainted with Gustav and Kate, I set my sights on climbing the summit. A lot had happened in the interim. My father had died; I'd learnt to live alone—Gustav a sterling example of the adage 'loneliness is cured by solitude'; I'd become a grandmother, blessed by two beautiful beings: a daughter to my eldest son and his wife; a boy to the youngest, the son who had taken me to Cradle Mountain with his fiancée. Months after the birth of their child, they separated, a painful schism for us all. During the fallout, I often felt like I was walking up an escalator going down—nothing by comparison with the grief Kate and Gustav withstood, both of them enduring years when they lost nearest relatives, knocked down like skittles.

As I pressed ahead in their footsteps, the summit offered an escape to a place where there is no time and nothing matters. I couldn't possibly write about these two unless I'd stood in their shoes, beholding their realm from the rooftop.

The girlfriend accompanying me had logged on to TripAdvisor for firsthand reviews of the climb, anxious at a degree of difficulty I'd not contemplated, since my head had been buried in the archives reading Gustav's blithe assurances that the ascent was a doddle, easily accomplished by anyone moderately healthy and fit. Like the daily entries in his diary, he left a lot out.

We set out for the peak on the anniversary of his funeral in the valley eighty-five years ago, a day that dawned as glorious as the clear blue beckoning us. The guide who had taken me to Crater Lake on my very first visit to the park in melancholic weather, with a mood to match, came along. His grandfather was a founding member of the Tasmanian Naturalists. Employing the colloquial names for everything that grows here—snowberry, pepperberry, pineapple grass, mountain rocket—his commentary was richer for incorporating indigenous medicine's use of these plants to remedy toothache and indigestion.

On the plateau, we skirted a string of pools frozen lustrously like pearls threaded across this windswept stretch of barren snowfield. At the mountain's foot, huge boulders sewn with lichen doilies in pale greens, ochre, black and copper. Gustav and Kate regarded lichens as the 'pioneers of soil-building', for their humus, which 'tenaciously evolved during many hundreds of years', fashions a pocket for alpine plants.[1]

We pulled ourselves upwards, my admiration for Kate—flying blind without poles or paths, hindered by her long skirt and leather boots— urging me forward. A young girl ahead of me in shorts and sneakers cursed the absence of chains on the final ascent, her fear a fraction of mine. Once on top, all I could think of was getting down again safely. Kate and Gustav spent three hours up here in January 1910.

When the guide produced from his rucksack a straw boater and a Tyrolean-style hat for a reenactment, I played along, but it was hard to re-create this moment amid the comings and goings of climbers around us. The tourists brandishing red umbrellas who John Muir predicted would flock to national parks have grown into legions of fleece-clad hikers crawling over a landscape millions of years in the making.

Since getting to know Kate and Gustav, I've learnt to tell trees apart, to name native plants, to look for nature wherever I can find it in a city towering like Topsy. While writing this book, I'd often commune with a pair of blackbirds in my small suburban garden. I'd watch them forage for their nest or flit from the branch of the fig tree to drink from the tin guttering on next door's shed. Just as Kate thought the 'Egypt' visiting her at Kindred brought a message from Gustav, these blackbirds gambolling in my bower were their couriers from above.

My tiny backyard is a forest of sorts. The ornamental grape vine hooks its tendrils around the legs of the old wicker chair, as fecund as the nursery-rhyme beanstalk. If I sit here too long, it will envelop me. There are dragonflies, ants, butterflies, even a rat—not as cuddly as Gustav's bush mouse, but he doesn't bother the blackbirds as they nibble on ripe figs. If I have any religion at all, its touchstone is a sense of wonder and humility in the presence of nature's power and an unabashed faith in science as our guide. While some of us read from the scriptures less than others, we are all guardians of an inherited bounty.

Cradle Mountain's custodians are a kaleidoscopic cast of indigenous visitors, explorers, giants, naturalists, high-country hardies and adventurers. I see them in the landscape whenever I visit. I imagine Kate collecting bleached sticks to boil a billy at Kitchen Creek Hut on the plateau below the summit, or Gustav's giraffe-like stride around the shore of Crater Lake, Flock at his heels. I hear Florence Perrin's footfall through a crust of snow as she angles her camera upward into the pine and beech forest. I hear the scrape of Ron Smith's boot shifting small pebbles from around the tiny skull of Bert Hanson's dog before he pockets it as a talisman of the mountain's peril. Above Dove Lake, where the prickly scoparia plant can draw blood, I think of Truganini's bone-weary passage through the valley waist deep in snow. I throw forward to my grandchildren, thankful they will be able to walk here, breathe deeply, and lose themselves in the wild.

NOTES

Beginnings
1   R. Smith, 'Birth of the Northern National Park', *The Examiner*, 7 November 1936, p. 11; R. Smith to Dr G. Bergman, Dr Bergman's correspondence, June 1952 – June 1954, A3801, Mitchell Library, Sydney.
2   Ray Tilley, 'Gustav Weindorfer: An Extraordinary Justice of the Peace', *The Justice of the Peace*, 2nd quarter 1989, pp. 5–10.
3   Sally Schnackenberg, *Kate Weindorfer: The Woman Behind the Man and the Mountain*, Regal Publications, Launceston, Tas., 2007.
4   E. Leeson, 'A 250 sq mile National Park: Barn Bluff and Cradle Mountain: The New Scenic Reserve', *The Examiner*, 3 January 1922, p. 8.
5   Simon Schama, *Landscape and Memory*, HarperCollins, London, 1995, p. 17.
6   Quoted in ibid., p. 9.
7   G. Weindorfer, 'Two Botanists in the Cradle Mountains, Tasmania', *The Victorian Naturalist*, vol. 28, 1912, p. 223.
8   Clare Wright, *The Forgotten Rebels of Eureka*, Text Publishing Company, Melbourne, 2013.
9   Hazel Rowley, *Franklin and Eleanor: An Extraordinary Marriage*, Melbourne University Publishing, Carlton, 2012.
10 Tom Griffiths, *The Art of Time Travel: Historians and Their Craft*, Black Inc., Melbourne, 2016, pp. 55–6.
11 Visitor figures for 2013–14 to 2016–17 found at Parks and Wildlife Service Tasmania, *Visitor Numbers to Selected Reference Sites*, <www.parks.tas.gov.au/file.aspx?id=46923>.

1   Awakenings
1   Kate Cowle, 'Notes of a Visit to Mount Roland', *The Victorian Naturalist*, vol. 20, 1903, pp. 70–2.
2   Alfred Hardy to Dr G. Bergman, 27 July 1953, Dr Bergman's correspondence, June 1952 – June 1954, A3801, Mitchell Library, Sydney.
3   G. Weindorfer, 'On the Fertilisation of Phanerogams: Dispersion of Pollen by the Wind', *The Victorian Naturalist*, vol. 19, 1903, pp. 98–101; G. Weindorfer, 'Dispersion of Pollen by Insects', *The Victorian Naturalist*, vol. 19, 1903, pp. 128–31.

4   R. Smith to Dr G. Bergman, 30 July 1952, NS234/11, Tasmanian Archive and Heritage Office (TAHO), Hobart.
5   Field Naturalists Club of Victoria, *Annual Report 1902–03*, FNCV, Melbourne, 1903.
6   Field Naturalists Club of Victoria, *Annual Report 1903–04*, FNCV, Melbourne, 1904.
7   Schnackenberg, p. 7.
8   FNCV, *Annual Report 1903–04*.
9   Cowle.
10   Ibid.
11   Ibid.
12   *The Victorian Naturalist*, vol. 20, 1903, p. 62.
13   G. Weindorfer, 'Some Comparison of the Alpine Flora of Australia and Europe', *The Victorian Naturalist*, vol. 20, 1903, pp. 64–70.
14   Ibid., p. 64.
15   G. Bergman to R. Smith, 18 April 1953, NS234/11, TAHO, Hobart.
16   G. Weindorfer, 'Nach Australien', *Marburg Zeitung*, 1901, papers of G. Bergman, A3801, Mitchell Library, Sydney.
17   Pauline Weindorfer to Gustav Weindorfer, 28 October 1903, Weindorfer's original letters and papers 1895–1931, A3800, Mitchell Library, Sydney.
18   C. S. Sutton, *The Victorian Naturalist*, vol. 19, 1903, pp. 156–8.
19   Weindorfer, 'Some Comparison of the Alpine Flora of Australia and Europe', p. 66.
20   Ibid.
21   Quoted in Sheila Houghton, 'If It Is Not Against the Rules: Women in the FNCV 1880–1980', *The Victorian Naturalist*, vol. 22, 2005, pp. 290–306.
22   George Coghill, 'The Buffalo Mountain Camp Out', *The Victorian Naturalist*, vol. 20, 1904, pp. 144–8.
23   Dr John Wilkinson, 'The Romance of Mount Buffalo', *Victorian Railways*, 16 February 1929, p. 9.
24   Dan Webb and Bob Adams, *The Mount Buffalo Story, 1898–1998*, Miegunyah Press, Melbourne, 1998, p. 34.
25   John Muir, *Our National Parks*, with a foreword by Richard Fleck, University of Wisconsin Press, Madison, WI, 1981 (1901).
26   Ibid., p. 1.
27   Theodore Roosevelt, speech at the Grand Canyon, 6 May 1903.
28   Ibid.
29   Wilkinson.
30   Ibid.
31   Diary of G. Weindorfer, 6 April 1901, Weindorfer's original letters and papers, 1895–1931, A3800, Mitchell Library, Sydney.
32   Jennie Boddington, 'J. W. Lindt, Photographer (1845–1926)', *Art Bulletin of Victoria*, no. 16, 1975.
33   Wolfgang Siebers, *Nach Australien*, 1895, Mitchell Library, Sydney.
34   Weindorfer, 'Nach Australien'.
35   Coghill, p. 145.
36   Carlisle's visitors' book, Bright Museum.
37   Coghill.
38   G. Weindorfer, 'Botany', *The Victorian Naturalist*, vol. 20, 1904, pp. 152–6.
39   Ibid.

40   A. F. W. McHaffie, 'Ornithology', *The Victorian Naturalist*, vol. 20, 1904, pp. 148–50.

41   O. A. Sayce, 'Pond-life', *The Victorian Naturalist*, vol. 20, 1904, p. 151.

42   Coghill, p. 146.

43   G. Weindorfer, 'Visit to Mt Bogong', *The Victorian Naturalist*, vol. 20, 1904, pp. 156–9.

44   Coghill, p. 147.

45   Ibid.

46   Ibid.

47   Ibid.

48   Weindorfer, 'Visit to Mt Bogong', p. 155.

49   Quoted in Paul D. Sheats, 'John Muir's Glacial Gospel', *The Pacific Historian*, vol. 29, nos 2 & 3, summer/fall, 1985, p. 45.

50   P. J. Ryan, 'John Muir and the Tall Trees of Australia', *The Pacific Historian*, vol. 29, nos 2 & 3, summer/fall, 1985, p. 127.

51   A. D. Hardy, 'Giant Eucalypts of Victoria', *The Gum Tree*, vol. 5, no. 18, June 1921, pp. 15–16.

52   Ryan, p. 132.

53   Ibid., p. 129.

54   Weindorfer, 'Botany', p. 152.

55   Richard F. Fleck, 'John Muir's Homage to Henry David Thoreau', *The Pacific Historian*, vol. 29, nos 2 & 3, summer/fall, 1985, pp. 55–64.

56   'One of the Pioneers', *The Argus*, 22 April 1904, p. 7.

57   Ibid.

58   Pauline Weindorfer to Gustav Weindorfer, 31 May 1904, Weindorfer's original letters and papers, 1895–1931, A3800, Mitchell Library, Sydney.

59   Gustav Weindorfer to Johann and Pauline Weindorfer, 9 September 1902; 23 September 1902; 28 May 1902; 18 June 1902; Pauline Weindorfer to Gustav Weindorfer, 31 October 1900; Weindorfer's original letters and papers, 1895–1931, A3800, Mitchell Library, Sydney.

60   Ibid.

61   Ibid.

62   G. Weindorfer, 'A Botanical Trip to the Grampians', *The Victorian Naturalist*, vol. 22, 1905, pp. 45–50.

63   Ibid.

64   C. S. Sutton, 'A Botanical Trip to Mt Erica, Baw Baw', *The Victorian Naturalist*, vol. 22, no. 4, 1905, pp. 58–61.

65   A. D. Hardy to G. Bergman, 27 July 1953, Dr Bergman's correspondence, June 1952 – June 1954, A3801, Mitchell Library, Sydney.

66   Cited in Schnackenberg, p. 7.

67   E. Thiele, 'A Trip to Lake Karng and Mt Wellington, North Gippsland', *The Victorian Naturalist*, vol. 22, 1905, p. 30.

68   F. Reader, 'Contributions to the Flora of Victoria', *The Victorian Naturalist*, vol. 22, 1905, pp. 51–2.

69   Office of the Government Statist, *Victorian Year Book 1905*, no. 26, Government Printer, Melbourne, 1906, pp. 21–6.

70   Ibid., p. 24.

71   Ibid.

72   J. A. Ewart, *The Victorian Naturalist*, vol. 22, 1906, p. 190.

73   G. Bergman to R. Smith, 18 April 1953, NS234/11, TAHO, Hobart.

74 'Kate will Dich nun bemuttern', in Pauline Weindorfer to Gustav Weindorfer, G. Bergman to R. Smith, 18 April 1953, NS234/11/1, TAHO, Hobart; Pauline Weindorfer to Gustav Weindorfer, 2 January 1906, Weindorfer's original letters and papers, 1895–1931, A3800, Mitchell Library, Sydney.
75 Stephen Spurling III, Waldheim Guest Book, 7 February 1922, Queen Victoria Museum and Art Gallery (QVMAG), Launceston, Tas.
76 *The Victorian Naturalist*, vol. 22, 1905, p. 101.
77 Minutes of meeting, 11 December 1905, FNCV Archive Series 58, p. 269.

2   Mountain High

1   'Weindorfer–Cowle', *The North Western Advocate and the Emu Bay Times*, 3 February 1906, p. 4.
2   'Distressing Scenes at Stowport', *The North Western Advocate and the Emu Bay Times*, 3 February 1906, p. 5.
3   Gustav Weindorfer's diary, 1 February 1906, NS234/27/1, TAHO, Hobart.
4   'Recrudescence at Stowport', *The North Western Advocate and the Emu Bay Times*, 1 February 1906, p. 3.
5   Ibid.
6   'Distressing Scenes at Stowport'.
7   'Weindorfer–Cowle'.
8   Quoted in Schnackenberg, p. 23.
9   Pauline Weindorfer to Gustav Weindorfer, 11 February 1906, Weindorfer's original letters and papers, 1895–1931, A3800, Mitchell Library, Sydney.
10 Gustav's diary entries for this period record the Perkinses' help. The provisions were described by the couple in three published letters—'A Roland Honeymoon', *The North Western Advocate and the Emu Bay Times*, 19 February 1906, p. 4; 6 March 1906, p. 3; 10 March 1906, p. 3.
11 Gustav Weindorfer's diary, 3 March 1906, NS234/27/1, TAHO, Hobart.
12 Four Irishmen visited the honeymooners' camp on 4 March 1906. It has been suggested this was the prompt for the letters they wrote in Irish brogue (see note 14 below), but the first letter was published on 19 February well before the encounter.
13 Gustav Weindorfer's diary, 3 March 1906, NS234/27/1, TAHO, Hobart.
14 'A Roland Honeymoon', *The North Western Advocate and the Emu Bay Times*, 19 February 1906, p. 4.
15 Ibid.
16 Ibid., p. 3.
17 Ibid.
18 Pauline Weindorfer to Gustav Weindorfer, 3 April 1906, Weindorfer's original letters and papers, 1895–1931, A3800, Mitchell Library, Sydney.
19 Mr and Mrs Weindorfer to G. Weindorfer, 14 January 1903, Weindorfer's original letters and papers, 1895–1931, A3800, Mitchell Library, Sydney.
20 Kate Weindorfer to Gustav Weindorfer, 15 August 1913, NS234/12/1/2, TAHO, Hobart.
21 'A Roland Honeymoon', *The North Western Advocate and the Emu Bay Times*, 10 March 1906, p. 3.
22 Gustav Weindorfer's diary, 28 February 1906, NS234/27/1/1, TAHO, Hobart.
23 Gustav Weindorfer's diary, 1 March 1906, NS234/27/1/1, TAHO, Hobart.
24 Stephen Spurling III's entry in the Waldheim guest book (1922) confirms that his photographs, published in 1905, alerted Gustav to Cradle Mountain's beauty; Spurling's *Giant Grass Trees, Cradle Mt, 1905* is reprinted in Nic Haygarth's *The*

Wild Ride: Revolutions that Shaped Tasmanian Black and White Wilderness Photography, National Trust of Australia, Launceston, Tas., 2008, p. 68 (plate 46).

25 'A Roland Honeymoon', *The North Western Advocate and the Emu Bay Times*, 10 March 1906, p. 3.

26 Gustav Weindorfer's diary, 23 February 1906, NS234/27/1/1, TAHO, Hobart.

27 G. Bergman to R. Smith, 18 April 1953, NS234/11, TAHO, Hobart.

28 Nic Haygarth's transcript of an interview with Annie Perkins, conducted by Bill Perkins, Devonport, 13 March 1981.

29 Ibid.

30 'The Tramp' (Dan Griffin), 'In the Cradle Country', *The Mercury*, 8 February 1897, p. 4.

31 'The Tramp' (Dan Griffin), 'A Week Out West', *The Daily Telegraph*, 10 May 1905, p. 4; 'The Tramp' (Dan Griffin), 'The Mountain Mystery', *The Daily Telegraph*, 5 August 1905, p. 6.

32 Gustav Weindorfer's diary, 31 March 1906, NS234/27/1/1, TAHO, Hobart.

33 Ibid., 12 April 1906.

34 Ibid., 15 April 1906.

3 Kindred Spirits

1 'Darwin: Mr O'Malley at Kindred', *The North Western Advocate and the Emu Bay Times*, 8 November 1906, p. 2.

2 Manning Clark, *A History of Australia*, volume 5, *The People Make Laws 1888– 1915*, Melbourne University Press, Melbourne, 1981, p. 198.

3 'Darwin: Mr O'Malley at Kindred'.

4 'Kindred', *The North Western Advocate and the Emu Bay Times*, 15 November 1906, p. 2.

5 'Kindred Telephonic Communications', *The North Western Advocate and the Emu Bay Times*, 17 April 1907, p. 4.

6 'Devonport', *The North Western Advocate and the Emu Bay Times*, 25 May 1908, p. 2; 'Kindred', *The North Western Advocate and the Emu Bay Times*, 25 May 1908, p. 2.

7 Johann and Pauline Weindorfer to Gustav Weindorfer, 20 September 1906, A3800, Mitchell Library, Sydney.

8 Schnackenberg, p. 28; Letters detailing Mrs Weindorfer's role as guarantor of loans from Bank of Australasia 18 October 1910, 11 July 1912, 12 October 1912, 9 October 1913, NS234/12/1/2, TAHO, Hobart.

9 Pauline Weindorfer to Gustav Weindorfer, 9 May 1906, 26 December 1906, A3800, Mitchell Library, Sydney.

10 Pauline Weindorfer to Gustav Weindorfer, 25 February 1907, Johann Weindorfer to Gustav Weindorfer with invoice for an agricultural book purchased in Austria, 2 July 1906, Johann Weindorfer to Gustav Weindorfer on his potato-drying experiments, 5 July 1907, A3800, Mitchell Library, Sydney.

11 'The Rural World: Progress by Production', *The Examiner*, 2 September 1909, p. 3; 'Kindred', *The North Western Advocate and the Emu Bay Times*, 18 November 1910, p. 2.

12 'Kindred', *The North Western Advocate and the Emu Bay Times*, 8 November 1910, p. 2.

13 T. P. Cowle's will, File #29/3476, Probate Office Tasmania, Hobart; G. Bergman to R. Smith, 29 July 1952, NS234/11, TAHO, Hobart; R. Smith to G. Bergman, 9 September 1952, Dr Bergman's correspondence, June 1952 – June 1954, A3801, Mitchell Library, Sydney.

14 'Kindred', *The North Western Advocate and the Emu Bay Times*, 22 July 1910, p. 2.
15 Kate Weindorfer to Gustav Weindorfer, 25 August 1913, NS234/12/1/2, TAHO, Hobart.
16 Gustav Weindorfer's diary, 5 May 1906, 21 October 1906, 28 October 1906, 4 November 1906, NS234/27/1/1, TAHO, Hobart.
17 'Kindred', *The North Western Advocate and the Emu Bay Times*, 11 July 1907, p. 2.
18 'Kindred', ibid., 10 April 1907, p. 2; 'Kindred', ibid., 24 April 1907, p. 4.
19 'Kindred', ibid., 30 May 1907, p. 4.
20 Mr and Mrs Weindorfer to G. Weindorfer, 7 March 1907, G. Weindorfer's original letters and papers, 1895–1931, A3800, Mitchell Library, Sydney.
21 G. Bergman to R. Smith, 20 January 1953, NS234/11, TAHO, Hobart.
22 G. Bergman to R. Smith, 28 February 1953, NS234/11, TAHO, Hobart.
23 Thomas Pakenham, *The Scramble for Africa: The White Man's Conquest of the Dark Continent 1876–1912*, Random House, London, 1991, p. 291.
24 G. Bergman to R. Smith, 13 July 1953, NS234/11, TAHO, Hobart.
25 Edith Weindorfer to G. Weindorfer in 1900, letter not dated, and Johann Weindorfer to G. Weindorfer, 4 April 1907, G. Weindorfer's original letters and papers, 1895–1931, A3800, Mitchell Library, Sydney.
26 Schnackenberg, p. 29.
27 James Bischoff Esq., *Sketch of the History of Van Diemen's Land*, J. Richardson, London, 1832, p. 167.
28 R. E. Smith, 'James Smith', in *Australian Dictionary of Biography*, volume 6, *1851–1890, R–Z*, Melbourne University Press, Melbourne, 1976; Nic Haygarth, 'The Father of Tasmania: Measuring the Legend of James "Philosopher" Smith', PhD thesis, University of Tasmania, Hobart, 2003, p. 2.
29 Haygarth, 'The Father of Tasmania', p. 180.
30 R. Smith to G. Bergman, 6 August 1953, NS234/11, TAHO, Hobart.
31 R. Smith visited the Cradles with Charles Riggs in 1907 and again in 1908 with G. E. and R. S. Adams. R. Smith to G. E. Adams, 15 May 1914, NS234/11, TAHO, Hobart.
32 'Peregrinator' (William Dubrelle Weston), 'Up the Cradle Mountain', *The Examiner*, 28 February 1891, p. 1; 4 March 1891, p. 2; 11 March 1891, p. 1.
33 G. Weindorfer, 'Botanical Research at the Cradle Mountain and Black Bluff', *The Examiner*, 19 August 1909, p. 7.
34 Ibid.
35 Ibid.
36 Ibid.
37 G. Weindorfer, 'At the Cradle Mountain and Black Bluff', *The Examiner*, 20 August 1909, p. 7.
38 Ibid.
39 Ibid.
40 Nic Haygarth, 'The Rain on the Plain Falls Mainly outside the Gauge, or How a Black Sheep Brought Meteorology to Middlesex', author's blog, 10 October 2016; 'Supreme Court', *The Age*, 26 February 1885, p. 6.
41 Haygarth, 'The Rain on the Plain'.
42 Weindorfer, 'At the Cradle Mountain and Black Bluff'.
43 G. Weindorfer, 'Two Botanists in the Cradle Mountains, Tasmania', *The Victorian Naturalist*, vol. 28, 1912, p. 216.
44 L. J. B. (Lionel Brown), 'Middlesex: A Tourist Resort', *The Examiner*, 11 February 1909, p. 3.

45 Muir, p. 13.
46 'Kindred', *The North Western Advocate and the Emu Bay Times*, 1 November 1909, p. 2.
47 'Kindred', *The North Western Advocate and the Emu Bay Times*, 22 July 1910, p. 2.
48 G. Weindorfer to R. E. Smith, 9 October 1909, Cradle Mountain letters and papers, vol. 1, 1909–1928, LMSS150/1/1, Launceston.
49 'A. Gnome' (G. Weindorfer), 'Holidays in the Cradle Mountain', Part 1, *The Weekly Courier*, 22 September 1910, p. 87.
50 Ibid.
51 Ibid.
52 R. Smith's typed notes of the trip, sent to G. Bergman, Dr Bergman's correspondence, June 1952 – June 1954, A3801, Mitchell Library, Sydney.
53 'A. Gnome'.
54 'A. Gnome' (G. Weindorfer), 'Holidays in the Cradle Mountain', Part 3, *The Weekly Courier*, 6 October 1910, p. 89.
55 'A. Gnome' (G. Weindorfer), 'Holidays in the Cradle Mountain', Part 2, *The Weekly Courier*, 29 September 1910; Weindorfer's draft for Waldheim brochure, NS234/12/1/3, TAHO, Hobart; Tilley.
56 'A. Gnome', Part 2.
57 G. Weindorfer, 'Some Considerations of the Origins of Our Alpine Flora', *The Victorian Naturalist*, vol. 21, 1904, p. 6.
58 'A. Gnome', Part 1.
59 R. Smith's typed notes of the trip.
60 R. Smith, 'Birth of the Northern National Park', *The Examiner*, 7 November 1936, p. 11; R. Smith's typed notes of the trip.
61 R. Smith's typed notes of the trip.
62 Ibid.
63 'A. Gnome', Part 2.
64 R. Smith's typed notes of the trip.
65 'A. Gnome', Part 2.
66 R. Smith's typed notes of the trip.
67 'A. Gnome', Part 2.
68 R. Smith's typed notes of the trip.
69 'A. Gnome', Part 3.
70 Quoted in 'A. Gnome', Part 2.

4 Welcome to Country

1 James Bonwick, *The Lost Tasmanian Race*, S. Low, Marston, Searle & Rivington, London, 1884, p. 157.
2 Ibid., p. 227.
3 Nikki Henningham and Leonarda Kovacic, 'Truganini (1812–1876)', *The Australian Women's Register*, Australian Women's Archive Project, Melbourne, 2004; Stan Florek, *Truganini (1812?–1876)*, Australian Museum, Sydney, 2017, accessed at <australianmuseum.net.au/truganini-1812-1876>.
4 Bonwick, p. 238.
5 G. Weindorfer to Charles Whitham, 10 August 1923, NS257, TAHO, Hobart.
6 Ibid.
7 G. Weindorfer, 'The Cradle Mountains Tasmania', *The Victorian Naturalist*, vol. 28, April 1912, p. 219.
8 G. Weindorfer to Charles Whitham, 10 August 1923, NS257, TAHO, Hobart.

9   Bonwick, p. 217.
10   Ibid., p. 221.
11   Quoted in John Mulvaney and Johann Kamminga, *Prehistory of Australia*, Allen & Unwin, Sydney, 1999, p. 343.
12   Quoted in ibid., pp. 188–9.
13   Will Pavia, 'National Geo Admits to "Appalling Racism"', *The Australian*, 15 March 2018, p. 9.
14   Quoted in James Bischoff, *History of Van Diemen's Land*, Royal Exchange, London, 1832, p. 171.
15   Quoted in Bischoff, p. 177.
16   Quoted in Bischoff, pp. 178–81.
17   Copy of a dispatch from Lieutenant Governor Arthur to Viscount Goderich, 1 January 1828, quoted in Bischoff, p. 185.
18   Extract of a dispatch from Lieutenant Governor Arthur to Secretary Huskisson, 17 April 1828, quoted in Bischoff, p. 191.
19   Daniel Bunce, *Australasiatic Reminiscences of Twenty-Three Years' Wanderings in Tasmania and the Australias; including Travels with Dr Leichardt in North or Tropical Australia*, J. T. Hendy, Melbourne, 1857, pp. 49–50.
20   G. Weindorfer to Charles Whitham, 10 August 1923, NS257, TAHO, Hobart.
21   FNCV meeting, 14 September 1903.
22   Florek.
23   R. Smith to G. Bergman, 29 October 1952, 28 February 1953, NS234/11, TAHO, Hobart.
24   R. Smith to G. Bergman, 15 July 1952, NS234/11, TAHO, Hobart.
25   Leonard Hubbard to G. Weindorfer, 11 July 1916, NS234/12/1/3, TAHO, Hobart.

5   Forest Home
1   K. Weindorfer to G. Weindorfer, December 1911, NS234/12/1/2, TAHO, Hobart.
2   Ibid.
3   Ibid.
4   G. Weindorfer, 'Native Plants', *The Australasian*, 12 December 1909, p. 11.
5   'Obituary: Mr L. E. Sadewasser', *The Examiner*, 25 March 1935, p. 6.
6   'Mr Deakin's Tour', *The Daily Telegraph*, 3 March 1909, p. 5; 'Entertained at Strahan', *The Daily Telegraph*, 7 January 1910, p. 5.
7   W. Carnie to G. Weindorfer, 12 January 1912, NS234/12/1/2, TAHO, Hobart; John Osborne (on behalf of Frieda Cobb) to G. Weindorfer, 4 January 1912, NS234/12/1/2, TAHO, Hobart.
8   K. Weindorfer to G. Weindorfer, 30 April 1913, NS234/12/1/2, TAHO, Hobart.
9   K. Weindorfer to G. Weindorfer, 20 March 1912, NS234/12/1/2, TAHO, Hobart.
10   K. Weindorfer to G. Weindorfer, 25 March 1912, NS234/12/1/2, TAHO, Hobart.
11   Evelyn Temple Emmett to G. Weindorfer, 22 September 1916, NS234/12/1/2, TAHO, Hobart; Francis Stephenson, School of Domestic Economy, to G. Weindorfer, 10 September 1916, NS234/12/1/2, TAHO, Hobart.
12   K. Weindorfer to G. Weindorfer, 15 August 1913, NS234/12/1/3, TAHO, Hobart.
13   Walter Malcolm Black to G. Weindorfer, 3 February 1913, NS234/12/1/2, TAHO, Hobart.

14 K. Weindorfer to G. Weindorfer, 30 April 1913, NS234/12/1/2, TAHO, Hobart.
15 R. Smith to G. Bergman, 25 May 1953, NS234/11, TAHO, Hobart.
16 Ibid.
17 J. Osborne, Fruit and Forestry Expert, Agriculture Department, Hobart, to G. Weindorfer, 4 January 1912; H. A. Hunt, Commonwealth Meteorologist, to G. Weindorfer, 8 January 1913; S. Dove to G. Weindorfer, 28 April 1914, NS234/12/2 and 3, TAHO, Hobart.
18 Gustav Weindorfer's diary, 26 May 1913, NS234/27/1/3, TAHO, Hobart.
19 F. Francis, 'Cradle Mountain's Unrivalled Charm', *The Advocate*, 4 May 1929, p. 13.
20 Weindorfer's draft for Waldheim brochure, NS234/12/1/3, TAHO, Hobart.
21 Gustav Weindorfer's diary, 9 June 1913, NS234/27/1/3, TAHO, Hobart.
22 Gustav Weindorfer's diary, June 1913, NS234/27/1/3, TAHO, Hobart.
23 Gustav Weindorfer's diary, 29 June 1913, NS234/27/1/3, TAHO, Hobart.
24 Gustav Weindorfer's diary, 18 July 1913, 20 July 1913, NS234/27/1/3, TAHO, Hobart.
25 Gustav Weindorfer's diary, 30 July 1913, NS234/27/1/3, TAHO, Hobart.
26 'Wild Storm at Burnie', *The Examiner*, 4 August 1913, p. 6.
27 K. Weindorfer to G. Weindorfer, 11 August 1913, NS234/12/1/3, TAHO, Hobart.
28 K. Weindorfer to G. Weindorfer, 5 August 1913, NS234/12/1/3, TAHO, Hobart.
29 K. Weindorfer to G. Weindorfer, August 1913, NS234/12/1/3, TAHO, Hobart.
30 Gustav Weindorfer's diary, 6 August 1913, NS234/27/1/3, TAHO, Hobart.
31 K. Weindorfer to G. Weindorfer, 4 May 1913, 11 August 1913, NS234/12/1/2, TAHO, Hobart.
32 K. Weindorfer to G. Weindorfer, 15 August 1913, NS234/12/1/3, TAHO, Hobart.
33 Gustav Weindorfer's diary, 14 May 1913, NS234/27/1/3, TAHO, Hobart.
34 K. Weindorfer to G. Weindorfer, 25 August 1913, 28 August 1913, NS234/12/1/3, TAHO, Hobart.
35 K. Weindorfer to G. Weindorfer, 19 November 1913, NS234/12/1/3, TAHO, Hobart.
36 Dr C. Sutton to G. Weindorfer, October 1913, NS234/12/1/3, TAHO, Hobart.
37 Stephen Spurling to G. Weindorfer, November 1913, NS234/12/1/3, TAHO, Hobart.
38 Stephen Spurling to G. Weindorfer, 4 November 1913, NS234/12/1/3, TAHO, Hobart.
39 Weindorfer's draft for Waldheim brochure, NS234/12/1/3, TAHO, Hobart.
40 Ibid.
41 Ibid.
42 Ibid.
43 K. Weindorfer to G. Weindorfer, 13 November 1913, NS234/12/1/3, TAHO, Hobart.
44 Gustav Weindorfer's diary, 17 November 1913, NS234/27/1/3, TAHO, Hobart.
45 K. Weindorfer to G. Weindorfer, 19 November 1913, NS234/12/1/3, TAHO, Hobart.
46 Franz Malcher, *The Tasmanian Mountains*, translated by Harry Malcher, History Museum, Ulverstone, Tasmania, no date, pp. 1–18.
47 Oscar Binder to G. Weindorfer, 5 May 1914 and 12 May 1914, NS234/12/1/3, TAHO, Hobart.
48 Copy of original letterhead in author's possession.

49   Thomas Cook Agency to K. Weindorfer, 26 December 1914; Tasmanian Railways
     to K. Weindorfer, 7 April 1913; Tasmanian Tourist Association to G. Weindorfer,
     7 March 1914; Alex Crawford, Ulverstone Tourist Bureau, to G. Weindorfer,
     22 January 1914, NS234/12/1/3, TAHO, Hobart.
50   Anton Lade, *Three Indians and the Caterpillar: Destination Cradle Mountain 1828–
     1935*, Anton Lade, Devonport, Tas., 2010, pp. 102–3.
51   Chief Engineer, Department of Public Works, to G. Weindorfer, 3 March 1914,
     NS234/12/1/3, TAHO, Hobart.
52   E. Adams to G. Weindorfer, 2 January 1914, NS234/12/1/3, TAHO, Hobart.
53   E. Adams to G. Weindorfer, 8 January 1914, NS234/12/1/3, TAHO, Hobart.
54   Ibid.
55   E. Adams to G. Weindorfer, 21 January 1914, NS234/12/1/3, TAHO, Hobart.
56   E. Adams to G. Weindorfer, 1 March 1914, NS234/12/1/3, TAHO, Hobart.
57   G. and U. Coghill to G. and K. Weindorfer, 9 January 1914, NS234/12/1/3,
     TAHO, Hobart.
58   Letter from Sydney Botanic Gardens, 18 July 1914; Letter from Dr Fritz Noetling,
     8 February 1914, NS234/12/1/3, TAHO, Hobart; Tasmanian government
     geologist to G. Weindorfer, 23 March 1914, NS234/12/1/3, TAHO, Hobart.
59   K. Weindorfer to Mr and Mrs Weindorfer, 16 August 1914, NS234/12/1/3,
     TAHO, Hobart.
60   Gustav Weindorfer's diary, 18 August 1914, NS234/27/1/4, TAHO, Hobart.
61   Ibid.
62   K. Weindorfer to Mr and Mrs Weindorfer, 20 August 1914, NS234/12/1/4,
     TAHO, Hobart.
63   E. Emmett to G. Weindorfer, 23 December 1914, NS234/12/1/3, TAHO, Hobart.
64   K. Weindorfer to G. Weindorfer, 19 November 1913, NS234/12/1/3, TAHO,
     Hobart.
65   K. Weindorfer to G. Weindorfer, 1 May 1915, NS234/12/1/3, TAHO, Hobart.
66   Ibid.
67   Waldheim Guest Book, 24 December 1915.

6 Loss
 1   K. Weindorfer to G. Weindorfer, 23 November 1915, NS234/12/1/3, TAHO,
     Hobart.
 2   K. Weindorfer to G. Weindorfer, 26 November 1915, NS234/12/1/3, TAHO,
     Hobart.
 3   'The Tramp' (Dan Griffin), 'Reminiscences of Roughing It', *The Daily Telegraph*,
     14 July 1905, p. 5.
 4   Ibid.
 5   K. Weindorfer to G. Weindorfer, 26 November 1915, NS234/12/1/3, TAHO,
     Hobart.
 6   Ibid.
 7   K. Weindorfer to G. Weindorfer, 8 November 1915, NS234/12/1/3, TAHO,
     Hobart.
 8   Ibid.
 9   K. Weindorfer to G. Weindorfer, 18 November 1915, NS234/12/1/3, TAHO,
     Hobart.
10   Ibid.
11   K. Weindorfer to G. Weindorfer, 8 November 1915, NS234/12/1/3, TAHO,
     Hobart.

12 K. Weindorfer to G. Weindorfer, 18 November 1915, NS234/12/1/3, TAHO, Hobart.

13 K. Weindorfer to G. Weindorfer, 1 December 1915, NS234/12/1/3, TAHO, Hobart.

14 Gustav Weindorfer's diary, 14 December 1915, NS234/27/1/5, TAHO, Hobart.

15 Dr Gollan gives him approval to go on 15 December 1915; see Gustav Weindorfer's diary, entries from 14 December to 18 December 1915, NS234/27/1/5, TAHO, Hobart.

16 K. Weindorfer to G. Weindorfer, 26 December 1915, NS234/12/1/3, TAHO, Hobart.

17 K. Weindorfer to G. Weindorfer, 28 December 1915, NS234/12/1/3, TAHO, Hobart.

18 Laura Cowle to G. Weindorfer, 28 December 1915, NS234/12/1/3, TAHO, Hobart.

19 H. R. Hutchinson, L. F. Giblin and W. F. D. Butler, 'A Determination of the Height of Barn Bluff', *Papers of the Royal Society of Tasmania*, 1917.

20 Leonard Rodway to K. Weindorfer, 11 January 1916, NS234/12/1/3, TAHO, Hobart.

21 K. Weindorfer to G. Weindorfer, 28 December 1915, NS234/12/1/3, TAHO, Hobart.

22 K. Weindorfer to G. Weindorfer, 18 January 1916, NS234/12/1/3, TAHO, Hobart.

23 K. Weindorfer to G. Weindorfer, 12 January 1916, NS234/12/1/3, TAHO, Hobart.

24 K. Weindorfer to G. Weindorfer, 19 January 1916, NS234/12/1/3, TAHO, Hobart.

25 K. Weindorfer to G. Weindorfer, 25 January 1916, NS234/12/1/3, TAHO, Hobart.

26 Leonard Rodway to K. Weindorfer, 2 February 1916, NS234/12/1/3, TAHO, Hobart.

27 Gustav Weindorfer's diary, 14 January 1916, NS234/27/1/6, TAHO, Hobart.

28 William Hitchcock to G. Weindorfer, 22 March 1916, NS234/12/1/3, TAHO, Hobart.

29 E. Emmett to G. Weindorfer, 30 March 1916, NS234/12/1/3, TAHO, Hobart.

30 Will no. 10377, Kate Julia Weindorfer, 25 March 1916, Probate Department, Wills, Hobart.

31 Gustav Weindorfer's diary, 27 April 1916, NS234/12/1/6, TAHO, Hobart.

32 Gustav Weindorfer's diary, 29 April 1916, NS234/12/1/6, TAHO, Hobart.

7 The Spy

1 'Turn Verein Threatened', *The Argus*, 15 May 1915, p. 8; 'Rights of German Club Registrations Deferred till War Ends', *The Argus*, 8 December 1915, p. 10; 'Police Guard German Clubs', *The Age*, 13 May 1915, p. 10; 'Sydney Disturbances', *The Argus*, 29 November 1915, p. 8.

2 Nic Haygarth's transcript of an interview with Annie Perkins, conducted by Bill Perkins, Devonport, 13 March 1981.

3 Theresa K. Thomas to G. Weindorfer, 6 May 1916, NS234/12/1/3, TAHO, Hobart.

4 Alex Crawford to G. Weindorfer, 24 August 1914, NS234/12/1/3, TAHO, Hobart.

5   Alex Crawford to G. Weindorfer, 10 December 1914, NS234/12/1/3, TAHO, Hobart.
6   W. Carnie to G. Weindorfer, 14 September 1916, NS234/12/1/3, TAHO, Hobart.
7   'Kindred', *The North Western Advocate and the Emu Bay Times*, 31 December 1910, p. 2.
8   W. Carnie to G. Weindorfer, 14 September 1916, NS234/12/1/3, TAHO, Hobart.
9   Dr Gollan to G. Weindorfer, 16 September 1916, NS234/12/1/3, TAHO, Hobart.
10 H. J. Somerville, 'The Royal Society of Tasmania, 1843–1943', *Papers and Proceedings of the Royal Society of Tasmania*, 1943, p. 218.
11 F. Noetling to G. Weindorfer, 8 February 1914, NS234/12/1/3, TAHO, Hobart.
12 G. Weindorfer to R. Moritsch, 15 September 1916, Weindorfer's original letters and papers, 1895–1931, A3800, Mitchell Library, Sydney.
13 'Police Courts, New Norfolk', *The Mercury*, 27 November 1915, p. 3.
14 Rex Direen, 'War Precautions or Persecution? The Treatment of Enemy Aliens and Others in Tasmania During the Great War', Coursework Masters thesis, University of Tasmania, Hobart, 1996, p. 37.
15 Ibid., p. 78 (Appendix 2, Record of Aliens Files: Examples from the Commonwealth Record Series A401/1, 1914–1916).
16 'Germans and Internment', *The Examiner*, 14 August 1915, p. 6; 'Habeas Corpus A Matter of Internment', *The Examiner*, 5 August 1915, p. 6.
17 'Alien Enemies, Senator Pearce's Statement', *The Daily Post*, 20 May 1915, p. 4.
18 Premier's Department Files, 2 October 1914, quoted in Direen, p. 32.
19 Record of Aliens, G. Weindorfer, Sheet 712, reproduced in Direen, p. 82 (Appendix 2); R. Smith to G. Bergman, 15 July 1952, NS234/11/1/1, TAHO, Hobart.
20 R. Smith to G. Bergman, 15 July 1952, NS234/11/1/1, TAHO, Hobart.
21 Ibid.
22 G. Bergman to R. Smith, 9 May 1953, NS234/11/1/1, TAHO, Hobart.
23 Record of Aliens, G. Weindorfer.
24 R. Smith to G. Bergman, 15 July 1952, NS234/11/1/1, TAHO, Hobart.
25 Gustav Weindorfer's diary, 25 October 1916, NS234/12/1/6, TAHO, Hobart.
26 Record of Aliens, G. Weindorfer.
27 F. Gossler to G. Weindorfer, 22 May 1916, NS234/12/1/3, TAHO, Hobart.
28 'Sydney Disturbances'.
29 Ibid.
30 F. Gossler to G. Weindorfer, 22 October 1916; Herbert Del Cott to G. Weindorfer, 21 October 1916, NS234/12/1/3, TAHO, Hobart. Ms Greta Gudenns in New York and Emil Neher in Switzerland forwarded mail from G. Weindorfer to Austria.
31 Direen, p. 35.
32 L. Hubbard to G. Weindorfer, 8 July 1916, NS234/12/1/3, TAHO, Hobart.
33 G. Coghill to G. Weindorfer, 18 March 1915, NS234/12/1/3, TAHO, Hobart.
34 J. Gillard to G. Weindorfer, 15 March 1916, NS234/12/1/3, TAHO, Hobart.
35 Gustav Weindorfer's diary, 13 September 1916, 10 October 1916, NS234/27/1/6, TAHO, Hobart.
36 G. Weindorfer to R. Smith, 12 July 1916, Cradle Mountain letters and papers, vol. 1, 1909–1928, Ronald E. Smith, LMSS 150/1–3, LINC, Launceston.
37 R. Smith to G. Bergman, 6 June 1953, NS234/11, TAHO, Hobart.
38 B. Cowle to G. Weindorfer, 19 July 1916, NS234/12/1/3, TAHO, Hobart.

39   F. Gossler to G. Weindorfer, 22 October 1916.

40   G. Weindorfer to R. Moritsch, 15 September 1916, Weindorfer's original letters
      and papers, 1895–1931, A3800, Mitchell Library, Sydney.

41   Gustav Weindorfer's diary, 14 September 1916, NS234/27/1/6, TAHO, Hobart.

42   G. Bergman to R. Smith, 9 May 1953, NS234/11, TAHO, Hobart.

43   'German Composers, Should They Be Discarded?', *The Argus*, 21 July 1916, p. 6.

44   R. Smith to Senator H. Payne, 5 January 1920, LMSS 150/1–3, Cradle Mountain
      letters and papers, vol. 1, 1909–1928, R. Smith, LMSS 150/1–3, LINC,
      Launceston.

45   G. Weindorfer to R. Smith, 19 October 1917, 6 April 1919, LMSS 150/1–3,
      LINC, Launceston.

46   Quoted in C. Sutton, 'Gustav Weindorfer', *The Victorian Naturalist*, vol. 49, June
      1932, p. 37.

47   G. Weindorfer and G. Francis, 'Wild Life in Tasmania', *The Victorian Naturalist*,
      Part 3, vol. 37, May 1920, pp. 5–8.

48   G. Weindorfer and G. Francis, 'Wild Life in Tasmania', *The Victorian Naturalist*,
      Part 1, vol. 37, March 1920, pp. 157–60; Part 2, April 1920, pp. 165–8; Part 3,
      May 1920, pp. 5–8; Part 4, June 1920, pp. 12–22.

49   Ibid., Part 1, p. 159.

50   Ibid., Part 4, p. 19.

51   Ibid., Part 4, pp. 20–1.

52   Ibid.

53   G. Weindorfer to R. Smith, 1 March 1920, LMSS 150/1–3, LINC, Launceston.

54   'Wild Life in Tasmania', Part 4, p. 22.

55   Ibid.

56   R. Smith to G. Bergman, 25 July 1953, Dr Bergman's correspondence, June
      1952 – June 1954, A3801, Mitchell Library, Sydney.

57   G. Weindorfer, 'Some Tasmanian Pines', *The Gum Tree*, vol. 3, no. 12, December
      1919, pp. 14–16; vol. 4, no. 13, March 1920, pp. 17–18.

58   Ibid., pp. 17–18.

59   G. Weindorfer to R. Smith, 29 June 1919, 10 September 1919, LMSS 150/1–3,
      LINC, Launceston.

8   Giants

1   Tilley.

2   Ibid., p. 6; C. Sutton to R. Smith, 13 March 1911, LMSS 150/1–3, LINC,
     Launceston.

3   Waldheim Guest Book, 31 October 1920.

4   Ibid.

5   Waldheim Guest Book, 3 January 1921.

6   F. Smithies, *Summit of Cradle, Winter 1925*, reprinted in Haygarth, *The Wild Ride*,
     p. 115 (plate 89).

7   Florence Perrin, *After the Blizzard on the Plateau of Cradle 1924*, reprinted in
     Haygarth, *The Wild Ride*, p. 114 (plate 88).

8   Nic Haygarth and Deb Malor, *Into the Wild: Wilderness Photography in Tasmania*,
     exhibition catalogue, QVMAG, Launceston, Tas., 2013, p. 62.

9   Quoted in ibid., p. 65.

10   Ibid., p. 62.

11   C. Sutton to R. Smith, 13 March 1911; R. Smith to C. Sutton, 25 May 1911;
      C. Sutton to R. Smith, 6 June 1911, LMSS 150/1–3, LINC, Launceston.

12   E. T. Emmett, 'On the Roof of Tasmania', *The Examiner*, 1 April 1916, p. 9.
13   Ibid.
14   'Matter of Scenery Reserve: Preservation Board Decision', *The Examiner*, 30 March 1922, p. 6.
15   G. Weindorfer to R. Smith, 5 January 1921, LMSS 150/1–3, LINC, Launceston.
16   G. Weindorfer to R. Moritsch, 30 January 1921, Weindorfer's original letters and papers, 1895–1931, A3800, Mitchell Library, Sydney.
17   Draft contract for sale of timber, 14 December 1920, NS234/19/1/1, TAHO, Hobart.
18   G. Weindorfer to R. Smith, 9 February 1921, LMSS 150/1–3, LINC, Launceston.
19   R. Smith to G. Bergman, 25 June 1953, NS234/11, TAHO, Hobart.
20   Waldheim Guest Book, 23 February 1921; Lade, p. 134.
21   Waldheim Guest Book, 23 February 1921, pp. 26–7.
22   Ibid.
23   'Cradle Mountain: "Better Than Blue Mountains"', *The Advocate*, 23 February 1921, p. 1.
24   R. Smith to G. Weindorfer, 1 March 1921, LMSS 150/1–3, LINC, Launceston.
25   'A National Park: Proposal for the North: Cradle Mountain Suggested: Interview with Mr Emmett', *The Examiner*, 12 July 1921, p. 4.
26   'Proposed National Park: The Beauties of Cradle Mountain', *The Examiner*, 16 July 1921, p. 9.
27   Ibid.
28   G. Weindorfer to R. Smith, 14 July 1921, LMSS 150/1–3, LINC, Launceston.
29   G. Weindorfer to R. Smith, 21 July 1921, LMSS 150/1–3, LINC, Launceston.
30   'Northern National Park', *The Examiner*, 21 July 1921, p. 4.
31   R. Smith to G. Weindorfer, 24 July 1921, LMSS 150/1–3, LINC, Launceston.
32   G. Weindorfer to R. Smith, 26 July 1921, LMSS 150/1–3, LINC, Launceston.
33   'Proposed National Reserve: Great Economic Value', *The Examiner*, 30 July 1921, p. 8.
34   Ibid.
35   Ibid.
36   Ibid.
37   G. Weindorfer to R. Smith, 29 July 1921, LMSS 150/1–3, LINC, Launceston.
38   Ibid.
39   'Ulverstone: National Park at Cradle Mountain', *The Examiner*, 8 August 1921, p. 2.
40   Quoted in 'Penguin: Cradle Mountain Park: Rare Scenic Beauty', *The Examiner*, 30 August 1921, p. 2.
41   Ibid.
42   G. Weindorfer's annual tally of guests and their geographical source, QVMAG, Launceston, Tas.
43   R. Smith to V. Allardyce, 27 December 1921, LMSS 150/1–3, LINC, Launceston.
44   G. Weindorfer to R. Smith, 29 December 1921, LMSS 150/1–3, LINC, Launceston.
45   G. Weindorfer to R. Smith, 24 January 1922, LMSS 150/1–3, LINC, Launceston.
46   V. Allardyce to R. Smith, 27 January 1922, LMSS 150/1–3, LINC, Launceston.
47   E. Leeson, 'A 250 sq mile National Park: Barn Bluff and Cradle Mountain: The New Scenic Reserve', *The Examiner*, 3 January 1922, p. 8.
48   Ibid.
49   Ibid.

50 Ibid.

51 Ibid.

52 Gustav Weindorfer's diary, 17 February 1922 – 21 February 1922, NS234/27/1/8, TAHO, Hobart; 'Cradle Mountain', *The Examiner*, 27 February 1922, p. 4; 'Sir Elliott Lewis', *The Examiner*, 18 February 1922, p. 6.

53 H. Johnson, 'A Camping Trip with Roosevelt and Muir', *A Journal for Members of the Yosemite Association*, vol. 56, no. 3, summer 1994, pp. 2–4.

54 Sierra Club, 'In Yosemite with John Muir', excerpted from *Theodore Roosevelt: An Autobiography*, The Macmillan Co., New York, 1913, chapter 9, 'Outdoors and Indoors'.

55 Sierra Club, 'A Brief History of Yosemite National Park', sierraclub.org.

56 Theodore Roosevelt, speech at the Grand Canyon, 6 May 1903.

57 'Right Hon. W. M. Hughes: Arrival at Launceston', *The Examiner*, 9 February 1922, p. 4.

58 'Cradle Mountain'.

59 'Ministerial Visit to Cradle Mountain', *The Mercury*, 27 February 1922, p. 4.

60 G. Weindorfer to R. Smith, 2 January 1922, LMSS 150/1–3, LINC, Launceston.

61 G. Weindorfer to R. Moritsch, 31 December 1921, Weindorfer's original letters and papers, 1895–1931, A3800, Mitchell Library, Sydney.

62 'Matter of Scenery Reserve', *The Examiner*, 30 March 1922, p. 6.

63 Ibid.

64 'Royal Society of Northern Branch', *The Mercury*, 31 March 1922, p. 3; 'Royal Society: The Northern Branch: First Annual Meeting', *The Examiner*, 30 March 1922, p. 8.

65 Ibid., *The Examiner*.

66 G. Weindorfer to R. Smith, 10 March 1922, LMSS 150/1–3, LINC, Launceston.

67 R. Smith to J. Stawell, 23 March 1922, LMSS 150/1–3, LINC, Launceston.

68 J. Stawell to R. Smith, 30 March 1922, LMSS 150/1–3, LINC, Launceston.

69 E. Adams to G. Weindorfer, 2 January 1914, NS234/12/1/3, TAHO, Hobart.

70 V. Allardyce to R. Smith, July 1923, LMSS 150/1–3, LINC, Launceston.

71 Muir, p. 2.

72 Ibid., p. 2.

9 Bush Laboratory

1 Frieda Cobb Blanchard, *National Geographic*, vol. 67, no. 5, May 1935, pp. 649–62.

2 Waldheim Guest Book, 8–16 March 1928, p. 113.

3 J. Osborne to G. Weindorfer, 4 January 1912, NS234/12/1/2, TAHO, Hobart.

4 R. N. Huettel and A. M. Golden, 'Nathan Augustus Cobb: The Father of Nematology in the US', *Annual Reviews Phytopathology*, vol. 29, 1991, p. 21.

5 C. Sutton, 'Gustav Weindorfer Obituary', *The Victorian Naturalist*, vol. 49, June 1932, pp. 34–8; M. Sutton to G. Weindorfer, 2 April 1929, NS234/12/1/4, TAHO, Hobart.

6 G. Weindorfer's collection of rare books, QVMAG, Launceston, Tas.

7 Howard K. Gloyd, 'Frank Nelson Blanchard, Scholar and Teacher', *Herpetologia*, Chicago Academy of Sciences, vol. 1, no. 8, 22 March 1940, pp. 197–208.

8 Ibid., p. 206.

9 '*Ranidella tasmaniensis*, Cradle Valley, 15 March 1928', *MCZBASE: The Database of the Zoological Collections*, Herpetology A-19243, Museum of Comparative Zoology, Harvard University, Cambridge, Mass.

10 M. Mette to G. Weindorfer, 9 April 1930, NS234/12/1/4, TAHO, Hobart.

11   Waldheim Guest Book, 17 January 1929, p. 120.
12   T. Flynn to G. Weindorfer, 2 July 1929, NS234/12/1/4, TAHO, Hobart.
13   G. Weindorfer and G. Francis, 'Wildlife in Tasmania', *The Victorian Naturalist*, vol. 37, Part 2, April 1920, p. 166.
14   Ibid.
15   Ibid.
16   As quoted in *Flynn and Flynn: The Professor and the Tasmanian Devil: A Celebration of the Centenaries of Biology at the University of Tasmania, its First Professor T. T. Flynn, and the Birth of His Son Errol, 1909–2009*, online exhibition, University of Tasmania Library, Hobart, 2013, <www.utas.edu.au/library/exhibitions/flynn_and_flynn/ttFlynn.html>.
17   Eric Guiler, 'School of Zoology', *The Sunday Tasmanian*, 8 July 1990.
18   Quoted in ibid.
19   Quoted in ibid.
20   Libby Robin, 'Collections and the Nation: Science, History and the National Museum of Australia', *Historical Records of Australian Science*, vol. 14, no. 3, June 2003, pp. 251–89; 'Obituary: Andre Leon Tonnoir, Entymologist', *Transactions and Proceedings of the Royal Society of New Zealand*, 1 January 1940, p. 55; Waldheim Guest Book, 30 January 1923, p. 57.
21   A. Tonnoir to G. Weindorfer, 14 May 1930, NS234/12/1/4, TAHO, Hobart.
22   H. Stuart Dove, 'New Year at Cradle Mountain', *The Advocate*, 9 January 1929, p. 6.
23   A. Jefferis Turner, 'New and Little Known Tasmanian Lepidoptera: Part II', *Papers and Proceedings of the Royal Society of Tasmania*, 1926, pp. 81–117.
24   Waldheim Guest Book, January 1925, p. 74.
25   Quoted in Glen Ingram, 'George Barnard', *Australian Dictionary of Biography*, volume 13, *1940–1980, A–De*, Melbourne University Press, Melbourne, 1993.
26   H. H. Finlayson to G. Weindorfer, December 1929, NS234/12/1/4, TAHO, Hobart.
27   H. H. Finlayson to G. Weindorfer, 21 April 1931, NS234/12/1/4, TAHO, Hobart.
28   H. Stuart Dove to G. Weindorfer, 28 April 1913, NS234/12/1/2, TAHO, Hobart.
29   A. V. Giblin to G. Weindorfer, 12 November 1928, NS234/12/1/4, TAHO, Hobart.
30   'Royal Society Botanical Section', *The Mercury*, 11 September 1928, p. 2.
31   'Tasmania's Flora: Making a Complete Survey: New Royal Society Section', *The Mercury*, 27 November 1928, p. 6.
32   A. V. Giblin to G. Weindorfer, 21 March 1929, NS234/12/1/4, TAHO, Hobart.
33   Ibid.
34   G. Weindorfer, 'Some Considerations of the Origins of Our Alpine Flora', *The Victorian Naturalist*, vol. 21, 1904, pp. 6–9.
35   Ibid., p. 9.
36   H. Scott to G. Weindorfer, 6 May 1930, NS234/12/1/4, TAHO, Hobart.
37   H. Scott to G. Weindorfer, 14 January 1932, NS234/12/1/4, TAHO, Hobart.
38   G. Weindorfer, 'Some Tasmanian Pines', pp. 14–16.
39   Ibid., p. 16.
40   G. Weindorfer to R. Smith, 19 October 1917, 27 February 1919, LMSS 150/1–3, LINC, Launceston.
41   Tilley, p. 9; G. Weindorfer to R. Smith, 28 June 1925, LMSS 150/1–3, LINC, Launceston.

42 William Smith Watt, *Results of Rainfall Observations Made in Tasmania: Including All Available Annual Rainfall Totals from 356 Stations for All Years of Record up to 1934*, Bureau of Meteorology, Melbourne, 1936; Sutton, 'Gustav Weindorfer Obituary'.
43 Gustav Weindorfer's diary, 4 November 1925, 2 December 1926, QVMAG, Launceston, Tas.
44 G. Weindorfer to R. Smith, 2 October 1924, LMSS 150/1–3, LINC, Launceston.
45 A. H. Hunt to G. Weindorfer, 4 March 1930, 20 November 1929, NS234/12/1/4, TAHO, Hobart.
46 A. Hackett, Waldheim Guest Book, 1 January 1923, p. 55.
47 G. Weindorfer to R. Smith, 16 November 1923, LMSS 150/1–3, LINC, Launceston.
48 G. Weindorfer to R. Smith, 21 February 1924, LMSS 150/1–3, LINC, Launceston.
49 E. Gupta, 'Written in King Billy's Tree Rings: 1700 Years of Climate History', *Science Matters*, 2 October 2017, <pursuit.unimelb.edu.au/articles/written-in-king-billy-s-tree-rings-1700-years-of-climate-history>.
50 Quoted in ibid.
51 Gustav Weindorfer's diary, 4 November 1925, QVMAG, Launceston, Tas.
52 R. Moritsch to G. Weindorfer, 29 March 1927, Weindorfer's original letters and papers, 1895–1931, A3800, Mitchell Library, Sydney.
53 R. Moritsch to G. Weindorfer, 18 November 1928, Weindorfer's original letters and papers, 1895–1931, A3800, Mitchell Library, Sydney.
54 R. Moritsch to G. Weindorfer, 30 September 1925, Weindorfer's original letters and papers, 1895–1931, A3800, Mitchell Library, Sydney.
55 Dr Bergman's correspondence, June 1952 – June 1954, A3801, Mitchell Library, Sydney.

10   Single Blessedness
1 'Phenomenal Storms Leave Death, Desolation and Ruin in their Wake', *The Advocate*, 6 April 1929, p. 4; 'Wynyard's Plight: Beaches Strewn with Debris', *The Advocate*, 8 April 1929, p. 5.
2 'Enormous Damage', *The Advocate*, 8 April 1929, p. 4.
3 'Devonport', *The Advocate*, 16 May 1929, p. 4.
4 'Cradle Mountain Hermit', *The Mercury*, 17 May 1929, p. 7.
5 G. Weindorfer to R. Moritsch, 23 January 1928, Weindorfer's original letters and papers, 1895–1931, A3800, Mitchell Library, Sydney.
6 Gustav Weindorfer's diary, 4 January 1927, QVMAG, Launceston, Tas.
7 Stephen Spurling III, *Lake Lilla 1922* and *The Wild Ride*, in Haygarth, *The Wild Ride*, p. 107 (plate 82).
8 G. Weindorfer to R. Smith, 10 February 1927, LMSS 150/1–3, LINC, Launceston.
9 F. Smithies, interview with Dorothy Barrett, NS573/1, TAHO, Hobart.
10 F. Francis, 'Cradle Mountain's Unrivalled Charm', *The Advocate*, 4 May 1929, p. 13.
11 G. Weindorfer to R. Smith, 14 June 1923, LMSS 150/1–3, LINC, Launceston.
12 Gustav Weindorfer's diary, 18–23 April 1923, QVMAG, Launceston, Tas.
13 R. Smith to V. Allardyce, 29 August 1923, LMSS 150/1–3, LINC, Launceston.
14 Gustav Weindorfer's diary, 15 September – 5 October 1923, QVMAG, Launceston, Tas.
15 Waldheim Guest Book, 5 October 1923, p. 65.
16 R. Smith to G. Bergman, 25 June 1953, NS234/11, TAHO, Hobart.

17   G. Weindorfer and G. Francis, 'Wildlife in Tasmania', *The Victorian Naturalist*, vol. 37, Part 2, April 1920, p. 166.
18   R. Smith to G. Weindorfer, 5 January 1924, LMSS 150/1–3, LINC, Launceston.
19   G. Weindorfer to R. Smith, 17 June 1929, LMSS 150/1–3, LINC, Launceston.
20   Manager of Kodak, Block Arcade, to G. Weindorfer, 18 October 1928, NS234/12/1/4, TAHO, Hobart.
21   'Cradle Mountain Illustrated Address', *The Examiner*, 19 August 1929, p. 10.
22   Arts and Crafts Society to G. Weindorfer, 14 August 1929; Victorian Ski Club to G. Weindorfer, 17 July 1929, NS234/12/1/4, TAHO, Hobart.
23   'Hermit of Cradle Mountain', *The Herald* (Melbourne), 10 July 1929, p. 18.
24   Ibid.
25   F. Smithies to G. Weindorfer, 22 July 1929, NS234/12/1/4, TAHO, Hobart.
26   Gustav Weindorfer's diary, 7 July 1926, 12 July 1926, 2 September 1926, 25 September 1926, QVMAG, Launceston, Tas.
27   'Cradle Mountain Illustrated Address'.
28   G. Weindorfer to R. Smith, 20 October 1929, LMSS 150/1–3, TAHO, Hobart.
29   G. Weindorfer to R. Smith, 18 February 1930, LMSS 150/1–3, TAHO, Hobart.
30   L. Cowle to G. Weindorfer, 1 June 1930, NS234/12/1/4, TAHO, Hobart.
31   G. Weindorfer to R. Smith, 19 March 1930, LMSS 150/1–3, TAHO, Hobart.
32   C. H. Burgess, 'The Spurling Legacy and the Emergence of Wilderness Photography in Tasmania', PhD thesis, University of Tasmania, Hobart, November 2010, p. 310.
33   R. Smith to G. Bergman, 24 July 1953, NS234/11, TAHO, Hobart.
34   'Ulverstone', *The Advocate*, 19 June 1928, p. 4.
35   E. Leeson, 'Cradle Valley: What a Hurried Trip Revealed', *The Advocate*, 25 March 1931, p. 12.

11 The Road
1   F. Francis, 'Cradle Mountain's Unrivalled Charm', *The Advocate*, 4 May 1929, p. 13.
2   Ibid.
3   Ibid.
4   Waldheim Guest Book, 24 January 1921, p. 24.
5   Gustav Weindorfer's diary, 21 July 1913, NS234/27/1/3, TAHO, Hobart.
6   Webb and Adams, p. 48.
7   F. Smithies, Notes on the Cradle Road, NS573/1, TAHO, Hobart.
8   'Hermit of Cradle Mountain', *The Herald* (Melbourne), 10 July 1929, p. 18.
9   G. Weindorfer to R. Smith, 4 August 1929, LMSS 150/1–3, LINC, Launceston.
10   R. Smith, 'Road to Cradle Mountain', submission to Kentish Council, NS234/19, TAHO, Hobart; 'Cradle Mountain National Park: Tourist Asset: Motor Road Needed', *The Advocate*, 11 July 1929, p. 11.
11   R. Smith, 'Road to Cradle Mountain', submission to Kentish Council, NS234/19, TAHO, Hobart.
12   G. Weindorfer to R. Smith, 2 August 1930, LMSS 150/1–3, LINC, Launceston.
13   R. Smith to G. Weindorfer, 7 August 1930, LMSS 150/1–3, LINC, Launceston.
14   G. Weindorfer to R. Smith, 21 May 1930, LMSS 150/1–3, LINC, Launceston.
15   Gustav Weindorfer's diary, 3 December 1927, QVMAG, Launceston, Tas.
16   'Ulverstone', *The Advocate*, 19 June 1928, p. 4.
17   G. Weindorfer to R. Smith, 18 February 1930, LMSS 150/1–3, LINC, Launceston.
18   Waldheim Guest Book, 19 January 1929, p. 122.

19   Lade, p. 216.
20   Cecil King, Waldheim Guest Book, 20 April 1931, p. 141.
21   Author's interview with Hugh Hadrill, Hobart, 9 August 2017.
22   Waldheim Guest Book, 1 January 1923, p. 53.
23   Ibid., 11 November 1931, p 122.
24   Ibid., M. Weston, 31 October – 2 November 1931, p. 143.
25   Ibid., 31 January 1932, pp. 147–9.
26   R. Fichter to G. Weindorfer, 24 July 1929, NS234/12/1/4, TAHO, Hobart;
      Waldheim Guest Book, p. 150; Letter from daughter to G. Weindorfer, March
      1932, NS234/12/1/4, TAHO, Hobart.
27   Waldheim Guest Book, 5 April 1932, p. 152.
28   F. Smithies, interview with D. Barrett, NS573/1, TAHO, Hobart.
29   Quoted in Lade, p. 228.
30   Sutton, 'Gustav Weindorfer Obituary', p. 38.
31   F. Smithies' personal account of G. Weindorfer's death, NS573/1, TAHO, Hobart.
32   'Late Mr Weindorfer', *The Mercury*, 9 May 1932, p. 5.
33   F. Smithies' personal account of G. Weindorfer's death.
34   'The Hunter Home from the Hill', *The Advocate*, 10 May 1932, p. 2.
35   F. Smithies' personal account of G. Weindorfer's death.
36   'The Hunter Home from the Hill'.

12   Legacy
1   R. Smith to Public Trustee, E. Kemp, 22 June 1932, LMSS 150/1–3, LINC,
      Launceston.
2   C. Monds to R. Smith, 11 June 1932, LMSS 150/1–3, LINC, Launceston.
3   C. Monds to R. Smith, 7 December 1932, LMSS 150/1–3, LINC, Launceston.
4   R. Smith to E. Kemp, 4 July 1932, LMSS 150/1–3, LINC, Launceston.
5   Ibid.
6   R. Moritsch to R. Smith, 8 September 1932, LMSS 150/1–3, LINC, Launceston.
7   Nick O'Malley, 'Lost Species', *Good Weekend*, 24 February 2018, pp. 13–15.
8   Ibid.
9   David Cantrill, email to author, 20 March 2017; Details of 962 plants sent to
      Hofmuseum in Vienna, G. Bergman to R. Smith, 9 May 1953, NS234/11,
      TAHO, Hobart.
10   Specimen Record List, 683054, Royal Botanic Garden, Sydney.
11   H. Maiden to G. Weindorfer, 19 June 1914, NS234/12/1/3, TAHO, Hobart.
12   J. H. Willis to G. Bergman, 11 June 1954, Dr Bergman's correspondence, June
      1952 – June 1954, A3801, Mitchell Library, Sydney.
13   Herr Hofrat Matschkal to G. Bergman, 21 May 1953, Dr Bergman's correspond-
      ence, June 1952 – June 1954, A3801, Mitchell Library, Sydney.
14   Quoted in Derek Niemann, *A Tale of Trees: The Battle to Save Britain's Ancient
      Woodland*, Short Books, London, 2016, p. 160.
15   G. Weindorfer, 'Two Botanists in the Cradle Mountains, Tasmania', *The Victorian
      Naturalist*, vol. 28, April 1912, p. 223.
16   'The Hunter Home from the Hill', *The Advocate*, 10 May 1932, p. 2.
17   David Peacock and Ian Abbott, 'When the Native Cat Would "Plague": Histori-
      cal Hyperabundance in the Quoll', *Australian Journal of Zoology*, vol. 62, no. 4,
      2014, pp. 294–344.
18   F. Smithies, interview with D. Barrett, NS573/1, TAHO, Hobart.
19   Tilley.

20   Charles Whitham, *Western Tasmania: A Land of Riches and Beauty*, Davies Brothers Ltd, Hobart, 1949, p. 5.

21   Simon Cubit and Nic Haygarth, *Mountain Men: Stories from the Tasmanian High Country*, Forty South Publishing, Hobart, 2015, p. 57.

22   G. Mosley, 'Celebrating National Parks—Nineteenth Century Origins', in A. McConnell (ed.), *With Every Step: Reflections on the Place and Meaning of Tasmania's National Parks and Reserves*, proceedings of NPWAC Public Seminar, Hobart, 5 October 2001, NPWAC, Hobart, 2002.

23   Visitor figures for 2017 found at Parks and Wildlife Service Tasmania, *Visitor Numbers to Selected Reference Sites*, <www.parks.tas.gov.au/file.aspx?id=46923>.

Coda

1   G. Weindorfer, 'Two Botanists in the Cradle Mountains, Tasmania', *The Victorian Naturalist*, vol. 28, 1912, p. 220.

ACKNOWLEDGEMENTS

Books grow as slowly as King Billy Pines. The seed for *Kindred* was planted by Joan Masterman, who introduced me to Tasmania's wilderness twenty years ago. Jenni Stafford nominated Cradle Mountain as her cherished destination, encouraging my visit in 2015. I fell for Kate and Gustav Weindorfer the first time I met them, but it wasn't until MUP's executive publisher Sally Heath lit up with enthusiasm that I committed to writing their story, blessed by her insight and guidance. Christine Middap, editor of *The Weekend Australian Magazine*, who spent her childhood in the shadow of Mt Roland, gave me leave and encouragement. Sally Schnackenberg, author of *Kate Weindorfer: The Woman Behind the Man and the Mountain*, was generous with her time and insights. Gary Presland, archivist at the Field Naturalists Club of Victoria, delved into source material. Ross Smith at Launceston's Queen Victoria Museum and Art Gallery, was a prodigious scout. Staff at the Hobart Library history room were unwaveringly patient, particularly conservator, Stephanie Macdonald, and Rebecca Taylor. High-country historian Dr Nic Haygarth made corrections to the draft manuscript. Botanist Linden Rae Gillbank gave valuable assistance. Tim and Diana Williams fed and sheltered me in Hobart. Cradle Mountain guide John Elliott accompanied me on rambles through the reserve. Amanda Buckley came with me to the summit. Penny Viney walked with me up Mt Roland. The editorial team at MUP watered and fertilised the manuscript, with special thanks to the fine judgement of Lucy Davison and Cathryn Smith. Catherine Morrow was my IT help desk. My family sustained their interest in the project that swallowed me: Greg Hywood read the manuscript; Jack and Jane Hywood who applied the acronym WWWD (What would the Weindorfers do?) to family dilemmas; Tom Hywood and Elizabeth Anile arranged my first excursion to Cradle Mountain–Lake St Clair National Park. Once grandchildren Ollie and Margot are old enough for a decent tramp I will show them nature's ingenious handiwork. Thanks lastly to English teacher, Nicky Capriolo, for carolling with magpies and for sharing his forest shack up north.

Captions for full images

viii The forest at Waldheim's door, 1920s (Florence Perrin)
36 All the footwear a girl needs (Alice Manfield)
47 Cradle Mountain from Hanson's Peak, where trapper Bert Hanson perished, 1929 (Gustav Weindorfer)
74 Looking up through snow covered branches, Waldheim forest, 1924 (Florence Perrin)
84 King Billy Pines in Waldheim forest, 1929 (Gustav Weindorfer)
110 Snow-covered trees after a blizzard on the Cradle plateau, 1924 (Florence Perrin)
122 Gustav overlooking Lake Rodway (J. G. Branagan)
138 Gustav leads Charles Monds on a wintry ascent, 1925 (J. G. Branagan)
158 Pencil Pine Falls, 1929 (Gustav Weindorfer)
176 A white wonderland through Waldheim's kitchen window (Fred Smithies)
204 Gustav's desk, a framed portrait of Kate beside the lamp, 1929 (Gustav Weindorfer)
214 View of Cradle from Twisted Lakes, 1929 (Gustav Weindorfer)
218 Gustav in a rare moment of repose (Fred Smithies)

Sources

Dates and photographers are supplied in the captions when known.

Abbreviations

NGV   National Gallery Victoria
QVM   Queen Victoria Museum and Art Gallery
SLV   State Library Victoria
TAHO   Tasmanian Archives and Heritage Office

ii TAHO NS703/1; **vi** QVM 1988.P.0148; **7** Penny Viney; **8** SLV H2007.64/9; **10 (left)** Gustav Weindorfer photo album, Sheffield Museum; **10 (right)** QVM Cowle Family Photographs, Peter Sims Collection, Launceston; **12** QVM 1995.P.0120; **14** QVM, Cowle Family Photographs, Peter Sim's Collection; **15** SLV H89.266/21; **17** NSW Art Gallery, 40.1982; **19** SLV H2007.64/7; **21** Field Naturalists Club of Victoria's Archives, Melbourne; **23** NGV PH72-1975; **25 (left)** SLV H2003.95/130; **25 (right)** SLV H2003.97/117; **26,** SLV H2003.95/27; **32** NGV PH20-1984; **36** SLV H2003.95/5; **43** QVM 1993.P.1636; **47** TAHO NS703/1/35; **48** copy lent by Sally Schnackenberg, Devonport; **51** QVM, Cowle Family Photographs, Peter Sims Collection; **57** TAHO NS703/1/366; **58** TAHO NS703/1/297; **63** QVM 1998.P.1769; **64** QVM 1993.P.1605; **65** QVM 1998.P.0278; **67** Tasmanian Tourism Bureau, TAHO AA 375/1/82; **69** QVM 1988.P.1777; **71** QVM 1998.P.1768; **74** QVM 1988.P.0145; **81** TAHO NS703/1/34; **82** QVM 1995.P.0405; **84** TAHO NS703/1/183; **86** QVM 1993.P.0501; **89** TAHO NS573.4.10.1.1; **91** TAHO NS703/1/11; **94,** QVM 1993.P.2296; **96** QVM 1986.P.0304; **99** QVM 1993.P.1620; **101** QVM 1988.P.0170; **103** QVM 1988.P.0155; **104** author's copy; **110** QVM 1988.P.0153; **116** TAHO NS703/1/266; **121** QVM 1977.P.5649; **122** QVM 1992.P.0145; **126** QVM 1987.P.0387; **131** TAHO NS703/1/48; **133** QVM 1988.P.0077; **137** TAHO NS703/1/258; **138** QVM 1985.P.0103; **142** QVM 1988.P.0194; **146** QVM 1998.P.1755; **149** QVM 1993.P.1596; **151** QVM 1988.P.1764; **152** TAHO AA 375/54; **158** TAHO NS703/1/50; **160** TAHO NS703/1/20; **166** QVM 1986.P.0328; **169** QVM 1983.P.2602; **171** QVM 1988.P.0206; **172** TAHO NS703/1/257; **175** QVM 1986.P.0490; **176** QVM 1988.P.0147; **179** QVM 1993.P.1640; **180** TAHO NS573/4/10/1/20; **184** QVM 1988.P.0233; **188** QVM 1988.P.0133; **190** TAHO NS573/4/10/1/9; **191** QVM 1988.P.0469; **192** TAHO NS573/4/10/1/9; **195** QVM 1986/P/0229; **198** TAHO NS703/1/393; **204** TAHO NS703/1/267; **207** TAHO NS703/1/140; **211** QVM 2000.P.0136; **213** TAHO NS703/1/34; **214** TAHO NS703/1/242; **218** TAHO NS573/4/10/1.

INDEX

THE MIEGUNYAH PRESS

This book was designed by Patrick Cannon
The text was typeset by Patrick Cannon
The text was set in 11½ point Bembo with 14¼ points of leading
The text is printed on 100 gsm Woodfree
This book was edited by Lucy Davison